WILDCAT
FOOTBALL

WILDCAT
FOOTBALL

THREE CHEERS FOR THE
PURPLE AND WHITE

LANCE FLEMING

Abilene Christian University Press

WILDCAT FOOTBALL
Three Cheers for the Purple and White

Copyright © 2018 by Lance Fleming

ISBN 978-0-89112-431-3
LCCN 2018022200

Printed in Canada

Photographs provided by Abilene Christian University in collaboration with ACU University Marketing and Milliken Special Collections and Archives. Specific photographers are indicated where known.

LIBRARY OF CONGRESS CATALOGING-IN-PUBLICATION DATA
Names: Fleming, Lance, 1969- author.
Title: Wildcat football : three cheers for the purple and white / Lance Fleming.
Description: Abilene, Texas : Abilene Christian University Press, [2018]
Identifiers: LCCN 2018022200 | ISBN 9780891124313
Subjects: LCSH: Abilene Christian Wildcats (Football team—History. |
Abilene Christian University—Football—History.
Classification: LCC GV958.A24 F54 2018 | DDC 796.332/63097647--dc23
LC record available at https://lccn.loc.gov/2018022200

Jacket and cover design by Bruce Gore | Gore Studio Inc.
Interior text design by Sandy Armstrong, Strong Design

For information contact:
Abilene Christian University Press
ACU Box 29138
Abilene, Texas 79699

1-877-816-4455
www.acupressbooks.com

18 19 20 21 22 23 / 7 6 5 4 3 2 1

To God, for giving me breath every day
For my wife, Jill, who still takes my breath away
To Ashley and Ryan, the lights of our lives
For my son, Rex, who went to heaven much too soon

CONTENTS

ACKNOWLEDGMENTS

This book is, obviously, about ACU football. But instead of a book detailing the program's humble beginnings in 1919 through the 2018 season—including the opening of an on-campus stadium in 2017—think of this as more like ten or twelve feature stories pieced together to tell you the real story of ACU football. As you'll read later from the great Wally Bullington, it's about more than just wins and losses; it's about taking eighteen-year-old boys and turning them into men who then go on to become great husbands, loving fathers, and community pillars.

It's about a gunslinger from Sweeny, Texas, who lit up scoreboards across the Southwest and made girls swoon when they got a glimpse of the blond mop of hair atop his head. It's about a shy kid from Greenville, Mississippi, leaving Jackson State at the altar, making the six-hundred-mile drive to Abilene to play for Abilene Christian, and ending up in the College Football Hall of Fame. It's about a no-name transfer student from Sweden who set the world of football on its ear one afternoon in 1976 with a world-record 69-yard field goal, a mark that still stands. It's about a sea of great players who left their marks all over the program, the campus, and the university in their days as Wildcats. It's about championships won, games played, coaches who taught more than football, friendships forged, lifetime bonds sealed, and men and women who came alongside the program to provide the resources necessary to attain greatness. It's about a group of quarterbacks who have played the position since the 1950s at a level that separates ACU quarterbacks from those at other schools, all coached by two of the great offensive minds of their eras.

And it's also about a player-turned-head coach who came back to ACU and turned it into a winning program, leading the university and the athletics program on a journey no one could have imagined just a scant twenty years ago. And it's about leadership at the top of both the university and the Athletics Department with the vision and focus to move the department and the football program boldly into the future with a move to NCAA Division I athletics and into an on-campus football stadium.

I would be remiss if I didn't thank the numerous former coaches, players, and athletics staff members whom I interviewed for this book. Getting their recollections of their days in the Purple and White wasn't even the best part of the interview process. The best part was getting to know better these men whom I've read and heard about most of my life. As an Abilenian who grew up following the Wildcats, the chance to talk for two hours with Wilbert Montgomery one late night in February 2017 was a thrill. The chance to reminisce with lifelong friends Jack Kiser, Jerry Wilson, Jim Reese, and others was a trip back to the days of our youth. Jerry passed on a few months after our interview and several months before this book was published. But he didn't need to read it; he's part of the history of ACU football and knew it better than most. Rest in peace, Wolfie.

Thanks to my predecessors in the sports information director role—Dr. Charlie Marler, James Norman, and Garner Roberts—for keeping such great records and for setting the bar so high for this job at this university. Thank you to others who contributed to this book: Dr. Marler,

Garner, Ron Hadfield, and Grant Boone, all of whom love ACU, Wildcat athletics, and the football programs as I do. Thank you to my former boss, Lee De León, who recommended me to write this book, for his understanding and patience in allowing me to work on this project over the past few years. Thank you to the guys in the media relations office whom I'm privileged to work with each day—Chris Macaluso and Seth Wilson—for picking up the slack when I took time away for interviews or writing. Thank you to Jason Fikes, director of ACU Press, for his confidence in letting me write this book, and for his patience in getting chapters to him as I slogged my way through the book and an athletics season. And if you're holding a copy of this book and reading it, thank you!

Thank you to Wally Bullington and his wife, Valrie, for giving up their time for a few lengthy interviews. No story of ACU athletics in general, or ACU football in particular, can be written without the thoughts, recollections, and opinions of one of the greatest figures in ACU history. It's been my privilege to know him for most of my life, and it's my great honor to write a book that is a testament to what he helped build and still loves. And thank you to my wife, Jill Fleming, and our children, Ashley and Ryan, for their patience while I added yet another project to my plate that took time away from home. My wife has long been my biggest fan, but I'm not now, nor will I ever be, half the parent she is to our children. She is the hero of our family.

FOREWORD

by Ron Hadfield

Hopefully, reading this book will feel something like sitting around the Wildcats' proverbial kitchen table, listening to some of the most veteran storytellers in Abilene Christian University history take turns recounting the lore and legend of one of their alma mater's most intriguing athletics programs.

As the 2018 season unfolds this fall, ACU football will be experiencing an exciting but tense renaissance: year two in an on-campus stadium for the first time in half a century, a still-new head coach working hard to rebuild a storied small-college football program and replicate record-setting seasons that made him one of the nation's best at a rival university, perpetual adjustments to academic and athletics realities in NCAA Division I, and expectations of those eager for the winning ways of yesteryear.

Ironically, football at all competitive levels is under the microscope as it was in the sport's early days in Texas in the early 1900s, with a concerned eye on the safety and long-term health of its participants. As you'll read in these pages, it took ACU administrators the better part of a decade to initially commit to the sport on campus. The game has evolved in many ways since then—including its equipment, rules, and management oversight—and will surely continue to change in the days ahead.

Wildcats and their fans are learning that life in FCS (Football Championship Subdivision) is not for the faint of heart. Some 124 colleges and universities in two dozen mid-major conferences like the Southland have a daunting task, especially those in the back yard of Power Five Conferences like the Big 12 and SEC, where an arms race of several sorts is being waged, threatening to further change the landscape of college athletics.

ACU made the move in 2013 to Division I to better align its athletic and academic expectations of students. Recruiting is challenging when competing as a small private university against much larger public institutions, something the Wildcats knew well from their time in Division II. There is still a disparity of scholarships in Division I—sixty-three in FCS and eighty-five in FBS (Football Bowl Subdivision)—yet ACU football schedules in coming years include such formidable foes as Mississippi State, Texas A&M, North Texas, Texas Tech, SMU, and Kansas State, along with FCS rivals across the South and Southwest.

As a Christian institution of higher learning, ACU is familiar with the David and Goliath story. That scene plays out every month in one Wildcat sport or another, yet even today, any young upstart can surprise a larger foe. It makes for plenty of anticipation, a good share of excitement, and occasionally some impressive results. Such is the lot of intercollegiate athletics today, however, and ACU fans are urged to keep the faith, so to speak. Division I is the university's new normal.

The five contributing writers, led by Lance Fleming, represent a collective two hundred or so years invested in following and reporting on Wildcat football. We might have forgotten a detail or two, but we certainly have seen our share of history. On any given Saturday afternoon or evening this fall, you can find us on the top level of Chuck Sitton Tower, in the Working Press or radio booth rooms, preparing to document and describe another game taking place below on Anthony Field. We are all dear friends, with the bonus of representing a unique legacy in sports journalism at our alma mater:

- Dr. Charlie Marler is professor emeritus of journalism and mass communication at ACU, and was Abilene Christian's first sports information director in the halcyon 1950s, when world-record-setting Wildcat track and field teams put the university on the map, and the football teams weren't too shabby, either. His photograph fittingly overlooks the press crew operations at each ACU home game.

- Garner Roberts was ACU's longest-tenured director of sports information. He jokes that between the two of them, he and Wilbert Montgomery scored 36 touchdowns in 1973. That season was the first in which a Wildcat football team won a national championship. In 1977, the program won its second—both with Roberts as sports information director during an esteemed career that eventually saw him inducted into two Halls of Fame. His name also is synonymous with U.S. Olympic track and field media relations.

- Fleming adeptly followed in Garner's footsteps and has been associate director of athletics for media relations for more than two decades of award-winning work while ACU built a small-college powerhouse in NCAA Division II and remodels a new one for Division I.
- When he's not describing college and professional sports events on a CBS Sports broadcast, Grant Boone is the radio and TV voice of the Wildcats, a walking encyclopedia of international athletics history, and a pro's pro in his field.
- I'm editor of *ACU Today* magazine and assistant vice president for university communications, a role I've filled on the Hill for more than thirty years.

We've been blessed to have this unique view of this sport at ACU, which has produced some remarkable people and accomplishments during its first football century.

Wildcat Stadium has invigorated the football program and the university as a whole, bringing with it all the attributes ACU investors and fans imagined in an on-campus place to build community and school spirit, create memories to last a lifetime, and make every game feel like another Homecoming.

Signage on the east side of Wildcat Stadium reminds fans that this gleaming sports venue, sized especially for ACU, is built on the footprint of some other dynamic athletics lore. Old Elmer Gray Stadium once served as the site of the 1960 U.S. Women's Olympic Track and Field Trials and the home of an intercollegiate program that produced dozens of world record-setting athletes and national champions. Wilma Rudolph competed there, as did ACU Olympians Bobby Morrow, Earl Young, Billy Olson, Tim Bright, Delloreen Ennis, and others too numerous to recount on the pages of a book focused on football.

So in many ways, each autumn weekend, the layers of excellence and memories continue to stack atop each other here on Ambler Avenue, near the northwest corner of our *Dear Christian College*, albeit in a different sport, with fans cheering their purple-and-white-clad heroes as loudly as those who competed there decades before.

That sounds sappy, I know. But Texans take their football seriously, the sport that still reigns supreme when leaves turn color and blue northers streak down from the Panhandle.

Discover with us again how rare it is for "little Abilene Christian," as ABC's Howard Cosell once described it for a national TV audience, to make such a mark on the sport in the collegiate, professional, and coaching ranks. Be amazed, as we still are, how Wildcat fortunes turned on an influx of talented players and coaches from places like Greenville, Mississippi, Vernon, Texas, and ACU's hometown of Abilene. It's been quite a ride.

Forgive any repetition in our tales; an aggregate body of work is sure to have some duplication. Excuse any errors; we'll fix them in the second printing. Pull a chair up around the kitchen table, a grab cup of coffee or glass of sweet tea, and relive with us the memories of a collegiate football program with a storied past far beyond others many times its size, and Lord willing, a future as bright as the stars shining above on another clear, crisp football Saturday night in West Texas.

INTRODUCTION

by Garner Roberts

It was a frightful day in September 1939 for seventeen-year-old freshman Rex Kyker as he walked across the Cedar Creek Bridge on College Drive and started up the hill toward the campus of Abilene Christian College. Twenty-eight years later, during his distinguished career as a professor at Abilene Christian, Kyker remembered, "Some huge fellow stopped and said, 'Son, do you need a lift?'" That huge fellow was Tonto Coleman, who was in his second year as the Wildcats' head coach for track and field and assistant coach for football. "I knew he had to be the Wildcat football coach," Kyker said. "But looking at him, I thought we needed him worse as a player— like maybe tackle-coach." Kyker, who died in Abilene in 1996 at the age of seventy-five, and Coleman, who experienced an unmatched career among former Wildcat football players and coaches, remained friends until Coleman's death at his home in Abilene in 1973. Kyker was the featured speaker February 20, 1967, when Coleman was honored as Abilene Christian's outstanding alumnus for 1966. "I think Tonto found a great ministry in athletics," Kyker said. And he recalled that chance meeting with Coleman in 1939. "It bespeaks so well the theme of Tonto's life—giving a fellow a lift."

———

Who better to introduce us to Wildcat football than Arthur Marvin "Tonto" Coleman? No one loved Wildcat football more than Tonto. "The Will Rogers of West Texas" graduated from ACC in 1928 with a degree in English after playing football, basketball, and baseball for the Wildcats. He served as head coach in both football and track and field, later coached at the University of Florida and Georgia Tech, and performed admirably for six years as commissioner of the Southeastern

Conference after his unanimous election and as a member of the NCAA Executive Committee.

He loved life and he loved people, and no one doubted either. Coleman was that rare person to whom the clichés "a man without an enemy" and "a man who never met a stranger" really do apply. He was an immensely popular speaker for civic groups, booster clubs, and national organizations such as the Football Writers of America and the American Football Coaches Association. He spoke at virtually every major coaching clinic in America, including his beloved Texas High School Coaches Association, where he was the only honorary member. Coleman's message often consisted of his three basic points for a good coach: love boys, love football, love to teach. Once, after Coleman's speech at a football banquet, the school's superintendent said, "There are some mighty good preachers in this town, but in my three years here that was the best 'sermon' I've heard. And I know it did more good." A photograph of him at the White House with President Lyndon B. Johnson and fellow football coaches Darrell Royal and Paul "Bear" Bryant hung on a wall in his Lincoln Drive home when he died October 18, 1973. On the photograph, Royal had written, "Tonto, I owe you so much. We both know how I made it to Texas."

Coleman pioneered the 5–4 defense, and the list of invitations for jobs that he declined is equally impressive. Those reportedly include Texas, Alabama, Baylor, and Notre Dame. Coleman called himself "the oratorical equivalent of a blocked punt." The stories this sentimentalist and self-made philosopher told are legendary. Of his popular sayings and stories, he told *Sports Illustrated* in 1966, "That sounds too good for me to have made up. I must have stolen that."

Here's one of his many stories. Coleman was born July 9, 1907, in Phil Campbell, Alabama, and moved with his family when he was twelve to a farm in the West Texas cotton patch near the community of Wastella. He recalled a football game matching his team, Roscoe High School, and nearby Snyder. "They stopped us cold on every play," Coleman remembered. "No matter what we tried, those Snyder boys seemed to know just where the play was heading. We took a bad beating, and after the game I asked one of the Snyder players how they did it. This boy said, 'Oh, we just happened to notice that whoever came out of the huddle wearing the helmet usually carried the ball.'"

One of Coleman's speeches, which was reprinted in newspapers and magazines across the nation and retold on CBS Radio, was titled, "What It Is . . . Is Football." Here's how Coleman described football:

> It is the boy from "across the tracks" playing alongside the boy from "the silk stocking district." It is a series of experiences which will result in the building of good

character and a good life. It is discipline, it is work, it is sacrifice, it is success, it is disappointment, it is perseverance, it is sorrow, and it is joy. It is learning to lose grudgingly, but gracefully. It is learning to win by humility. It is learning to play and live by "the rules."

It is the generator of that intoxicating fervor known as college spirit which permeates the college campuses of America, that intangible "something" that integrates the history-making, action-packed present with the glorious pages of the past, that which brings, binds and blends those who are a part of these two eras into a common bond of friendship and fellowship and gives lustre, personality and individuality to their institution. It is the pulsating force that keeps the old grad close to the bosom of his alma mater.

Indeed, football kept Coleman's alma mater close to his heart. In March 1950, when Coleman resigned to coach at Florida, sportswriter A. C. Greene wrote in the *Abilene Reporter-News*, "There were tears in his eyes when he turned around to the squad. Tonto Coleman is a strong man, but this was like taking his bare hands and tearing his own heart out by the roots."

"I don't know whether I can go through with this or not," Coleman said. "A lot of people can't understand why I should hesitate, why I feel this way going to a big university. They don't know this school. You can't work at a college like this for eleven years and not get deep-rooted. These have been the happiest years of my life. It was a rough decision I had to make, and I tell you I shed a lot of tears to leave fellows I love like you." Greene wrote that Coleman told his players, "I've never asked a team to score for me, but I hope next fall when you're down there close you'll try a little harder to make it. I hope from me you've gotten something to help you hurdle some obstacle in life." Coleman's inspiration wasn't soon forgotten by his players. That fall, the Wildcats he had recruited and coached, now under the direction of head coach Garvin Beauchamp, turned in a perfect 11–0 season—the only undefeated, untied college football team in the nation in 1950.

Coleman's influence in the Southeastern Conference was equally powerful. Boyd McWhorter, who followed Coleman as SEC commissioner when he retired in 1972, came to Abilene to present a check for $10,000 for a scholarship fund honoring Coleman—$1,000 from each of the ten SEC members. "The size of the gift is insignificant," McWhorter said in chapel December 12, 1973, "but it is given with the hope and confidence that this institution will continue to send forth Tonto Colemans to fulfill the noblest purpose of higher education."

—

What it is, is football. Actually, this is Wildcat football. For dozens and dozens of coaches such as Coleman, Wildcat football was their ministry. For hundreds and hundreds of players in the past ninety-six seasons, Wildcat football developed character and taught them to play and to live by the rules. So as this new era has begun, here's an introduction to the coaches and players, wins and losses, championships and memorable games, touchdowns and tackles.

This is Wildcat football.

Three cheers for the Purple and White.

A NOTE FROM THE COACH

by Wally Bullington

It was a long trip from Athens, Alabama, to Abilene, Texas, in the fall of 1949. The 1928 Ford Coupe that I was driving was not very fast, which meant that—despite driving straight through without stopping to spend the night—I arrived one week late to my first fall football camp at Abilene Christian College.

I had played in the Alabama high school all-star game and that was the reason I reported late. That and the fact that I was driving a not-so-fast Ford Coupe. Looking back, though, it was the best trip I've ever taken because it started me on a career at Abilene Christian and in Abilene that is still going almost seventy years later. I met my wife, Val, at ACC, we raised our children in Abilene, and we've been part of the university and this wonderful city since 1949. I was very fortunate to be a two-time all-state selection in Alabama as a high school junior and senior

and received scholarship offers from universities in the Southeastern Conference and other schools in the South, including Alabama, Auburn, LSU, and Vanderbilt. But my father, Clifford Bullington, had attended ACC in 1911 and wanted me, the youngest of his four sons, to attend a Christian school to play college football.

As I look back on my time at ACC and remember the men who were my coaches—men like A. M. "Tonto" Coleman, Garvin Beauchamp, Oliver Jackson, and Bill McClure—I am reminded again that there is much more to the sport of football than just winning games. I was very fortunate to have a successful career on the field (earning all-conference honors three times and first-team All-American honors as a senior), but looking back, the most important things that came out of my time as a college football player are the lifelong friendships that continue today with my teammates from those years.

The 1950 undefeated season was one of the best in the history of ACU football, and it's something those of us who were part of it still reflect on fondly. We won eleven games that season and went on to win the Refrigerator Bowl in Evansville, Indiana, at the end of the season. I enjoyed playing football at Abilene Christian, but an even greater thrill came about in 1968 when I was hired to become the head football coach of the ACC Wildcats. One of the greatest blessings to come out of my nine years as the head coach was the coaching staff we were able to put together in the 1960s and 1970s. Men like Ted Sitton, Don Smith, K. Y. Owens, James Lyda, and Jerry Wilson were not only great coaches but were also Christian men—the kind any parent would want to entrust their son to for four years. Those coaches not only knew the techniques of the game and how to teach them, they also knew how to build men who would be successful in the game of life.

We coached so many great players during that era and were all blessed to be part of two NAIA Division I national championship teams, the first in 1973 and the second in 1977. I was the head football coach and director of athletics in 1973, but passed the coaching baton on to Dewitt Jones for the 1977 championship run. It has been a pleasure to serve under presidents Don H. Morris, John C. Stevens, William J. Teague, Royce Money, and Phil Schubert,

knowing that ACU athletics had the support of the university administration.

Abilene Christian has sent more than seventy-five players to all levels of professional football over the years, which illustrates the great talent we've been able to bring to the campus over the last seventy-plus years. ACU has been very fortunate to have great leaders serve over the years as directors of athletics for the program, and I'm grateful for those men: A. B. Morris, Don Drennan, Cecil Eager, Stan Lambert, Shanon Hays, Jared Mosley, and Lee De León. ACU has also been fortunate to have sports information directors who have helped put ACU athletics on the college sports map. It got started with Dr. Charlie Marler and then extended to James Norman before Garner Roberts went on to a hall of fame career from 1973 to 1998. Garner was succeeded in August 1998 by Lance Fleming, who has been in the SID role for twenty years doing what his predecessors did by promoting Wildcats around the world.

The 2017 season marked the beginning of a new era of ACU football, and I was so thrilled to see it happen. The on-campus stadium that is now available to our student-athletes is state of the art and a reminder of the great generosity of our donors throughout the years. Mark and April Anthony, David and Kathryn Halbert, and many others who gave to the stadium project—no matter the size of the gift— are to be thanked for their desire to give our student-athletes the best experience possible. The ACU football program is one of seventeen sports on campus now, and all adhere to the ACU athletics mission, which is "To honor Christ through excellence in academics and athletics," and vision, which is "To win at the highest level by providing the most Christ-centered student-athlete experience in collegiate athletics."

As I look out at the stadium from my office in the Teague Center each day, I can still see my old coaches and teammates from the 1950s and players I coached in the 1960s and 1970s running through drills and getting ready to go play on a fall Saturday afternoon. When I see them and think about them, I remember the great times, the tough practices, the wins and the losses, friendships made and lives changed. I also remember that those men had the same mission and vision even then, and it's part of what makes us all so proud to be called ACU Wildcats.

THE LEATHERHEADS

by Dr. Charles Marler

Football could have died in West Texas before World War I except that the fit, tough young men who came from the farms, ranches, and small towns wanted to play the game. They wanted the rugby-inspired, competitive, contact game. Nationally, deaths related to football injuries reached fifty deaths per year. In 1905, President Teddy Roosevelt called the presidents of the Ivy League universities together and urged them to dampen the violence of the game through better coaching tactics, game techniques, and gear, which could be purchased for less than per player in the day. Roosevelt also understood that young football players were in need of more protection. Atop the head of the typical early twentieth-century football player was a helmet made from the heaviest bullhide available. The wearer was challenged to enhance his cranium protection with additions inside his leather armor; his ingenuity in enhancing his protective head cushion was a factor in his survival. Colleges began to listen to the president, but the injury rate had fanned an antifootball movement everywhere. Even so, Baylor, Texas Christian, Southern Methodist, Simmons, Howard Payne, and Daniel Baker Colleges were early adopters in Texas.

Since 1906, Childers Classical Institute, now Abilene Christian University, had stood opposed to football, although some intramural and high school level competition was allowed. McMurry University and Texas Technical University did not exist until the 1920s. Simmons University, now Hardin-Simmons University, played full schedules against the top teams playing the sport. Momentum changed in 1909 when the Simmons Cowboys incredibly scheduled two games in Brownwood in one weekend. They were to play Daniel

Baker on Saturday night after facing Howard Payne on Friday night. A tragic injury at the midway point of the Howard Payne game changed everything. Senior Simmons quarterback John Airhart, a quick and steady leader, was carried from the game just before halftime with what newspapers reported was "a fractured skull" after his head hit the turf. Airhart didn't play in the Daniel Baker game, but he did lead Simmons in part of its next two games against Merkel High School and Baylor University. The *Abilene Daily Reporter* dutifully kept its readers current, sometimes in graphic detail, with Airhart's condition until he died March 16, 1910, after further complications from the injury against Howard Payne. Shaken, the trustees of Howard Payne suspended football

Under Sewell's presidency in 1919, Abilene Christian College officially became a four-year liberal arts college.

for a year; but in Abilene, the loss of the popular Airhart cast a sadness so profound over Simmons University and the city that Simmons' president, J. D. Sandefer, suspended football for five years.

Feisty Jesse P. Sewell, another antifootball president, and his wife, Daisy, came to Abilene in 1912 to own and operate Abilene Christian College for its trustees. The thirty-six-year-old Sewell was born, educated, and experienced for the job. Articulate, analytical, and a good teacher, preacher, and businessman, he was a natural leader. The young couple's partnership abilities turned the school into a real college. Jesse and Daisy supported athletics, and the boys were permitted to engage in a little bit of intramural and high school football competition. The pressure that the Sewells faced for intercollegiate football at the junior college level didn't rise to a change of policy until 1919. First, the couple still had strong feelings about the violence of the game. Second, the impact of John Airhart's death was still strong; Simmons didn't play football again until 1915. And, third, World War I lowered the number of young men in college. When the Sewells came to their decision after the war, they most probably discerned they had no choice. The financial health of the college was their burden; they needed all the veterans and a new crop of young men from farms, ranches, and small towns who wanted to play intercollegiate football. Simmons was back in the game and had been since 1915. Abilene

Club, played center in basketball and first base in baseball, was editor of *The Optimist,* and was a charter member and the first president of the Alumni Association. He then became coach of physical activities, a teacher of public speaking and government, and an upperclassman at Simmons to finish his bachelor's degree. At Simmons, McCasland played basketball on an outstanding Cowboys team and wrote for the student newspaper, *The Brand.* He is the only double alum at Abilene Christian and Simmons to work on both student newspapers, coach football at one and play it at the other, play basketball at both, and serve actively in each university's Alumni Association. He was unique. He would leave for Chicago in 1920 to do doctoral work with $7,500 in his pocket from the sale of his Abilene house, probably enough to pay for a doctorate in those days. That decision would lead him to appointment as dean of the School of Religion at the University of Virginia, the presidency of the American Academy of Religion, and authorship of *By the Finger of God* and other works.

Christian had lost one promising football player during the war—not in combat but by the scourge of the Spanish influenza pandemic of 1918. Noll Childress of Hope, New Mexico, a sheep rancher's boy who had been in school in 1915–1916, died in a stateside training camp October 20, 1918. Nicknamed "Bigun," Noll weighed 190 pounds, and the 1916 *Prickly Pear* declared his "hard passes were always right to the mark."

The Sewells' top candidate for coach, the one Jesse and Daisy trusted to handle their first Wildcat football team in the right way, was Vernon McCasland. According to the 1916 yearbook, he was "a stout, robust country boy" from Winters. On his way to earning his associate's degree in 1916, he debated, was a charter member of the A

Missing Noll Childers, McCasland looked at his collection of about one dozen or more prospects who would carry Abilene Christian College into a football experience that is now just short of one hundred years old. Like McCasland himself, they were from farms, ranches, or small towns. None of them carried extra pounds. None of them shirked hard work. Well, maybe one of them, certainly some

of them in future years. Coach McCasland had the audacity to tap Bernard Boone from West, Texas, a young man who had never seen a football game, to lead the 1919 Wildcats. Eyewitness Wendell Bedichek called Boone "the best clown athlete ACC ever had." The *Prickly Pear* immortalized one of his adages, "If you can't ride that mule without spurs, stay off." In addition to quarterbacking the football team, he was captain of the basketball team and was wooing Vera Ray, first president of the Girls' Aid to Athletics, now referred to as GATA, a women's social club. Boone would leave Abilene after one year because

of the death of his father. He transferred to Texas A&M but had to leave there because of an injury. Vera and Bernard married during the Christmas holidays in 1923 in Los Angeles and worked there and in San Francisco where they helped churches before moving back to Texas to deal in milk (Borden Company) and money (Hillsboro Federal Savings and Loan Association).

Ogle Jones, a preacher's son from Roswell, New Mexico, was a possible running back. In 1934, Bedichek named Ogle as the quarterback on the all-time ACC eleven. Ogle would stay two years before transferring to New Mexico, where he was

All-Southwest quarterback. According to sportswriter Wilbur Bentley, Ogle was the greatest player who ever performed for the University of New Mexico. He then moved on to Vanderbilt where he played for two years, then became an East Tennessee doctor. In World War II, he served in a field hospital on Utah Beach during the D-Day invasion at Normandy. His career exemplifies how eligibility was determined by what the presidents and coaches could tolerate.

Over at right end and left guard, "one of the hardest fighting guards ever to play for ACC" was Herbert Love at 160 pounds from Norsworthy. He was the joke editor of *The Optimist*, and, therefore, one of the comedians of the football team. Words attached to Love were, an *Optimist* writer reported, "Sugar Foot" and "Honey Bunch." Herbert went on to become a preacher and the father of Mike Love, high school All-American tailback from Odessa Permian High School. At ACC, Mike was one of the best running backs in the country, according to *Optimist* writer Riley Dunn. Mike was drafted in the fifteenth round by the Pittsburgh Steelers but never played in the NFL.

McCasland's choice for tackle was Weldon Russell, a local boy who also turned out to be the team cook. His English cottage revival home at 302 Graham—just one block from Daisy Hall and with access to Catclaw Creek two blocks away—was often the place for football parties. Weldon's parents, T. A. and Olive, were married in a buggy and lived in a small log cabin near San Saba. After they arrived in Abilene on Christmas Day 1908, T. A. built one hundred houses in one year and the grand home at 302 Graham to provide for his wife, three children, and four children of relatives who had died. They needed this 3,500-square-foot, four-bathroom house to rear seven children, all of whom graduated from ACC, and to accommodate Weldon's teammate visitors. T. A. became a member of the board of trustees and a decade later would second the motion to move the college to its present location. A history major, Weldon later married Ogle's sister, Ethel, and went into the real estate business in Abilene and Midland with his father. The 302 Graham house is now on the Abilene Register of Historic Places.

Ogle's brother, Sewell, could punt 50 to 60 yards consistently and could rival his younger brother running with the ball. Each, according to a Roswell sportswriter, was difficult to tackle because they ran "with their knees high." Sewell and Ogle were also the brothers of Mrs. J. C. Reese, the mother of Leon Reese, an outstanding basketball player at ACC in the 1940s, and grandmother of Jim Reese, the Wildcats' standout quarterback of the 1970s. Sewell transferred to New Mexico State when Ogle went to New Mexico in 1921, and he became the minister for the San Gabriel Church of Christ in Los Angeles after its 1952 founding.

Coach McCasland also mustered Otis Vaden from Temple, an interesting combination of a violin player in the school's orchestra and tackle on the football team. Odis and Bernard Boone were roommates in a little wooden shack near the center of the campus. The roommates named their residence the "BVD," which they claimed meant "Boone and Vaden Domicile," not the brand of underwear. Vaden later returned to his hometown and became a leader in real estate and insurance, including ownership of the six-story professional building in downtown Temple.

Carl L. Etter, a quiet and reserved boy from Kirkland, was at the other tackle and sang second tenor in the Glee Club. He wanted to play the game and achieve some other high ambitions as a historian and missionary. Carl and his wife, Gracye, moved to Japan in 1928 to help plant a church, and he taught English at the Imperial University in Hokkaido. After returning to the U.S. in 1933, he became an outspoken advocate for the destruction of the War Party in Japan. His career turned to education, and he became supervisor of student rehabilitation and vocational training of the Los Angeles school system and author of *Ainu Folklore: Traditions and Culture of the Vanishing Aborigines of Japan* and *Happiness through Positive Action*.

Abilene contributed another native to McCasland's squad, James Thornton Arledge, son of J. S. Arledge, who was chair of the board of trustees during the pioneer years of the Abilene Christian football program. Thornton's strong suit was baseball. When he stepped onto the football field in 1919, he had never played a down of the game, but according to the *Prickly Pear,* he was a "good fullback" blocking for the Jones boys from Roswell. Thornton, nicknamed "Bottles," was the "most popular boy in school," according to the yearbook, and he later became one of the most successful businessmen in West Texas.

Potosi, the smallest and most mispronounced town in Taylor County, sent Lee Coffman to Abilene to earn a bachelor's degree in education in 1921. The son of Potosi pioneers, he also wanted to pioneer the game of football, and he played left guard. He later settled in Abilene, became a principal at Stith and Butman schools, which were eventually consolidated into Merkel ISD, a superintendent at Denton Valley School, and a teacher at Abilene's Travis Elementary School.

Left end Harry Wright breezed into Abilene from the Germanic town of Goltry in northern Oklahoma, the longest trip for a member of this new football team. He also was a critic teacher in the grammar school and an *Optimist* reporter. Marvin Huddleston was equipped to play right end and was favored highly enough by the young women of GATA to be invited to the February 4, 1920, birthday party for two of the club's members, Rubye Pratt and Vera Ray, Bernard Boone's girlfriend.

W. R. Smith brought a big frame to the team when he came to town from Wheeler. Smith made an impact wherever he aimed his body during games in 1919 and 1920. He earned a master's degree from the University of Texas before founding Lee Junior College in Baytown and later serving as superintendent of schools in Baytown, Plainview, and Bradwell. He served on the ACC Board of Trustees from 1933 to 1940, becoming the first former football player to serve the university in that capacity. He was later appointed vice president of ACC, the first former football player to serve in the administration. His students in his Christian Home course famously teased him about running a marriage factory because of the weddings that came out of this class. His son J. E. Smith was a top-rated basketball Wildcat in the 1940s, and his great-granddaughter, Savannah Smith, played basketball for the Wildcats from 2010 to 2014.

Another set of brothers, the Shepards—Sanger "Big Shep" and Emerson "Little Shep"—came from Killeen. Big Shep played center and Little Shep served in spot roles. Big Shep was given a "famous people" role by *The Optimist* because of his quote: "I'd rather have less up here [his head] and more down here [his heart]." After the 1919 season, he wrote to *The Optimist* from Tampico, Mexico, asking for copies of the newspaper "should auld acquaintance be forgot and never brought to mind." Sanger finally settled in Casper, Wyoming, where he died in 1965. Emerson stayed closer to home, becoming a real estate and insurance agent in Lubbock and serving on ACC's Alumni Association Board into the late 1940s.

Tom Wilkerson was one of the two-sport guys, football and basketball, but

Coach Vernon McCasland (top left) with the 1919 charter team.

after an illness before the 1919–1920 basketball season, he left school to teach at a school in Eddy near Waco. Playing end and guard, Floyd Coffee from Loraine wasn't new to Abilene Christian. His relative, Jesse James (not the gang character), matriculated at Childers Classical Institute in 1908. Coffees have been around the university ever since. Floyd became a civic leader in Loraine, where he died at the age of ninety-four.

The 1920 *Prickly Pear* staff teased Alfred Conway with this observation: "Alfred might have accomplished more in school if it had not been for one little 'Speck.'" This feminine Speck happened to be the daughter of Henry Eli Speck, dean of the college from 1914 to 1924. His daughter, Huttie, later married Conway, and they served churches as gospel minister and wife.

Charlie Walker—"a real sure-nuff football player," according to *The Optimist*—came out of New Mexico via the University of Oklahoma and Decatur Baptist College, one of the Texas junior colleges without football. Walker played one year with the Wildcats, the all-important inaugural one. Then, after the loss to Wesley College, he left the little college on the railroad tracks at Christmas to tend to "his oil interests" in Encino, New Mexico.

There they are, eighteen daring men in their funny leather headgear fearing no man, certainly not anyone in football togs. On the football field, they were like X's and O's made from great slabs of Leuders limestone, the foundation for the Wildcat football programs of the next year, the next decades, and into the twenty-first century. McCasland, who turned twenty-three years old in September 1919, was barely

Wildcats from the 1927 Abilene Christian team practice an offensive formation.

older than his young bucks from Texas, New Mexico, and Oklahoma, but he could perchance guide them through a successful season of four games against three faith-based junior colleges. His assistant coach was one of his Roswell players, Sewell Jones. Two of the games were in towns along the T&P Railway, which helped because little Abilene Christian sat on a site no more than seventy-five yards from the railway. They could board the rails for their first game against Midland Christian College with little trouble. Midland had opened as a coeducational college in 1910 and was playing a full athletics program. Neither of these two new opponents in 1919 knew much about the other. Little ink was spent in creating a word picture about what happened in this game. But deduction leads the researcher to believe this game was the setting for one of the brilliant trick plays of 1919, as told by one of quarterback Bernard Boone's sons, Ken.

Boone had Ogle and Sewell Jones as his halfbacks and Thornton Arledge as fullback. The ruse after Boone took the ball from center was for all four backs to converge on a designated spot in a huddle of sorts, then head in four different directions with fakes that looked like each had the ball. Ten seconds later, Boone was 10 yards down the field, yelling "Yoo Hoo!" to frustrated Midland defenders. The only other paragraph of information known about this game is one in a 1925 *Optimist*: "Harry Wright and Charlie Walker were regular ends. Among the linemen were Silas Howell, Herbert Love, Lee Coffman, Marvin Huddleston, Sanger Shepherd and others." The very first football game played by Abilene Christian College was a shutout: Wildcats 46, Midland 0. This opponent closed its doors in 1921, moved to Cisco where it became Cisco Christian College, and evolved into Randolph College, which closed in 1937.

Sports editors' bosses buy ink by the barrels, but the *Abilene Daily Reporter* spent almost no ink money on reporting the first two games of this young football program. The 1–0 Wildcats faced Daniel Baker College in Brownwood on October 25 and came out on the short end, 13–6. The two inches of copy in the *Reporter* read in part: "Reports from Brownwood were meager but indicated that a fast game was played, and the Abilene men showed up well." The next weekend, the two teams met again in Abilene. The *Reporter* headline read: "Christian College players in splendid form and had easy victory. New Mexico lads star." Plenty of ink was laid out this time, including the starting lineups for both teams. For Abilene, it was fullback Arledge, halfbacks Jones and Jones, quarterback Boone, center Shepard, guards Etter and Coffman, tackles Love and Howell, and ends Walker and Wright. The score was 21–7. Daniel Baker scored first in the initial quarter, but Ogle Jones tied the game with a 40-yard run around left end. His brother kicked the extra point to knot the score. The 7–7 halftime tie was quickly broken by Ogle and Sewell, this time for 10 yards around left end. Ogle Jones crossed the goal his third time from the 20-yard line, and brother Sewell again added the one-point kick. So the score really was Jones Brothers 21, Daniel Baker 7.

The season finale was another road game via the rails to Greenville to play Wesley College. The 2–1 Wildcats were optimistic. Wesley College opened in 1912 in Greenville as a Methodist school and closed in 1938. The problem with playing Wesley was Grady "Big Hig" Higginbotham, who would go on to star at Texas A&M and to be head coach at Texas Tech. Bedichek described the formidability of Wesley: "That was when junior colleges and lots of senior institutions did not allow eligibility rules to interfere with the football game. At Wesley, there was an awe-inspiring aggregation of season gridsters, including 'Big Hig' Higginbotham of Texas A&M fame and several other Aggies, who were equipped to whip most any team in Texas." The loss thrown at the Wildcats was Wesley 68, ACC 3. Wildcat tackle Herbert Love described the game in his humorous style, "Wesley College just scattered love all over their football field."

Eight of the 1919 charter team came back for the 1920 season. Coach McCasland was gone to the University of Chicago to become a scholar, and Sewell Jones took his place as coach. Quarterback Boone had gone home to play at Texas A&M so he could help his widowed mother, and Ogle Jones took his place at the signal-caller slot. The other returnees were W. R.

Smith, Weldon and Lee Coffman, Odis Vaden, and Herbert Love.

In that uncertain rules era, the senior college Simmons Cowboys were loaded. But when they went to play the University of Texas in Austin, the core of its team was declared ineligible. However, they could present eligibility at junior college Abilene Christian, and that is what happened. The inheritance included the headline-maker "Fats" Cranfill; Vic Payne, who became the 1920 captain and head coach for two seasons; and "Buck" Bailey, who played two years at Bethany College and transferred to Texas A&M after the 1920 season. Bailey also became head baseball coach and assistant football coach at Washington State University and is in the Collegiate Baseball Hall of Fame. Another addition was the return of George Klingman Jr. from the U.S. Navy. He was the son of Dr. George Klingman of the ACC Bible Department and the most scholarly of the church's preachers of that time. This enriched Wildcat team outscored all opponents 135–10, with a record of four victories and one tie: ACC 29, Clarendon 7; ACC 0, Tarleton 0; ACC 7, Howard Payne 3; ACC 13, Tarleton 0; and ACC 81, Daniel Baker 0. An undefeated (with a tie) second season strengthened the foundation built by the charter team. Another Wildcat team would not go undefeated for thirty years.

Between 1921 and 1924, when they ran out of money, Jesse and Daisy became even more endeared to the football teams because they presented to the players the first white sweaters emblazoned with the "C." The Wildcat teams from 1919 to 1923 were coached by four different men: McCasland, Sewell, Russell Lewis, and Payne, each with moderate success. Apparently, the future of football was a sharp issue on campus as the athletics program was under the magnifying glass. In 1921, senior footballer W. R. Smith, who became a trustee and later a vice president, wrote a letter to the editor of *The Optimist* that probably reveals the gist of the discussion. Smith wrote, "We are looking forward to the time when the colleges will adopt a plan whereby athletics will be conducted with the one chief aim of development of the greatest number [of students] and not victory at any price."

The most durable statistical achievement of the new football program was a 1921 punt return against Meridian College, which the Wildcats defeated, 37–0. The "feature play" of the game, according to Bedichek, was a 95-yard return by quarterback Esker "Eck" Curtis from Vernon. At 135 pounds, Curtis was one of the Wildcats' early series of "flashy, speedy, heady" skitter-bug type runners. Once he brought the Meridian punt under control, he worked toward both sidelines, followed blocking, and broke a couple of tackles for the touchdown. That 95-yard scoring play stood as the Wildcat record for forty-two years until Dennis Hagaman scored on a 98-yard run from scrimmage against UT Arlington in 1963. The longest punt return record of 95 yards stood for fifty-four years until Little All-American Wilbert Montgomery returned a punt 99 yards against Sam Houston State. Eck later coached West Texas high school football teams at Anson, Ranger, Electra, and Breckenridge, then Highland Park High School in Dallas, after which he went to the University of Texas where he was given the credit for introducing the T-formation to Longhorn football. He is in the Texas Sports Hall of Fame.

With a veteran-laden team, the Wildcats defeated Meridian College 35–0 in the 1923 season opener.

In 1923, founding ACC football coach Vernon McCasland penned a letter to *The Optimist* from the University of Chicago, where he was working on his doctorate. McCasland wrote, "The colleges should understand that the matter of health is fundamental to all mental and spiritual achievement. . . . I do not mean to underestimate the value of the mental and spiritual; I simply want to make provision for the complete development and expression of these phases of personality by caring for the body in which they dwell." This profound and still-current dialogue would certainly help drive the next president's decisions.

One of the quirkiest games played in the history of Wildcat football took place on October 21, 1922, in Abilene under Coach Vic Payne's watch against the West Texas State Normal College Buffaloes. With about four minutes to go, the Buffaloes led 7–6. Wildcat safety Matt

Dillingham, formerly a star at Abilene High School and Simmons College, intercepted a Buffalo pass at midfield and with a faultless convoy of Wildcats scored to put his team ahead 12–7. West Texas protested, claiming that Dillingham had interfered with its receiver and tempers rose. Referee Gerald A. Cresswell, an Abilene rancher and cattleman, ruled against the interference claim and tensions escalated. At that point, the Buffalo captain called his team off the field and refused to return. The officials told West Texas Coach Sam Burton he had two choices: return his players to the field or forfeit the game. The Canyon bunch took the latter option, and the official score became ACC 1, West Texas 0. The extra point was never attempted.

But the on-field actions and decisions didn't end the matter. Next came a squabble between the two student newspapers, *The Prairie* and *The Optimist*. The two sets of journalists saw the game through different pairs of spectacles. *The Prairie* took the first shot, including, "Rather than to take the unjust decision of the officials the Buffaloes forfeited the game to the Wildcats." *The Optimist* argued that West Texas players should have returned to the field and determined the outcome on the field with four minutes of play in which they would have had the next possession. *Optimist* editor Bedichek, who also happened to be the Wildcat team manager, used sharp words like "jerk-water" and "football outlaws," defining the latter as "the football players who find fault with the football officials." The journalistic side of the 1923 duel seemed to end at that point, although the heated rivalry between the two schools would last until their final meeting in 2012 when West Texas A&M beat ACU, 36–0, in the Wildcats' final season as members of NCAA Division II and the Lone Star Conference. West Texas A&M Head Coach Don Carthel—whose son, Colby, had served as an assistant coach at ACU under head coaches Gary Gaines and Chris Thomsen and was the WT defensive coordinator for his father in that game—said after the game that the Wildcats "will always remember the last time they played the Buffaloes." ACU coaches, players, and fans probably prefer to remember that the Wildcats were 5–4 against their archnemesis—including the ridiculous 93–68 NCAA Division II playoff win in Abilene in 2008—during the stretch from 2006 to 2012 when both programs were regularly the two best teams in the LSC.

Jesse and Daisy Sewell, the 1919 team's president and first lady, lie at rest in the Cedar Hill Cemetery only one mile from the new stadium where Wildcat young men still want to play the game but in better protective gear. Two of their football-sons also lie at rest near them in Cedar Hill—William Roy Smith, better known as W. R., and Weldon LaFayette Russell Jr., whose murder in 1931 in Midland where he worked as his father's partner was a tragic loss to the team. Buck Jones, a Hollywood lease agent who was looking for land to use for a movie set, pulled a pistol on Weldon and shot him. Weldon told his dad, trustee T. A. Russell, before he died that Jones had told him, "This is the way we do it in California." But the Midland jury in effect told Jones when he was sentenced to twenty years for murder, "This is the way we do it in Texas." Weldon's brother-in-law and teammate Ogle Jones, his quarterback Bernard Boone, his fullback Thornton Arledge, and one of his linemen, W. R. Smith, represented the 1919 band of football brothers at Weldon's funeral at his beloved 302 Graham home.

In 1924, ACC trustees took over the management of the college from the Sewells and named a new president, Batsell Baxter, who was also a football fan. When he and the trustees began searching for a new coach and athletics director, they looked at applications from a dozen potential candidates, but a famous athlete one year out of Texas A&M University was The Man.

Batsell Baxter in 1924, shortly before he became president of Abilene Christian College.

BUGS AND TONTO

by Dr. Charles Marler

"Abie is the smartest football player I have ever seen."
—Coach Dana X. Bible (Texas A&M University 1917, 1919–1928,
and University of Texas 1937–1946)

The Man was a quiet man. He was born Asbury Bratten Morris in Wheatland. Along the way, the name Asbury Bratten morphed naturally like three short hopscotch steps into "A. B." to "Abie" to "Bugs." He was tagged with the final version by his older brother, Charles. But in his prime years, he was "Coach" to everyone, as if his mother had assigned it as his given name. His pedigree in 1924 at age twenty-four included athletics at Wheatland, a degree in agriculture from Texas A&M University, four varsity letters in football and three in baseball, president of the T Club, and leader of Aggie Southwest Conference championship teams in football and baseball.

He also quarterbacked the Aggie team that beat the undefeated Centre College Colonels of Danville, Kentucky, 22–14, on January 2, 1922, in the Dixie Classic, the forerunner of the Cotton Bowl. The Colonels were rated No. 1 in the country and had three All-American players. In this game, E. King Gill, who had quit the Aggie team midseason, left the stands after injuries weakened the Texas A&M team, including an injury to Morris, who had been knocked out. Gill joined the team on the sideline, signaling Coach Dana X. Bible his readiness to enter the game should he be needed. Thus the 12th Man Tradition was born. In Morris's final baseball season, he was named all-Southwest Conference shortstop, and his first job as a head coach was at Greenville High School where the Lions had a 4–3 mark in 1923.

Morris's job description at ACC was as awesome as his pedigree: athletics director, head football coach, head basketball coach (on an outdoor court until he helped raise the money for a new Wildcat gymnasium finished in 1926), head baseball coach, physical education director, teacher

Coach and Director of Athletics A. B. Morris in the 1930 *Prickly Pear*.

Coach A. B. Morris (top left) with the 1927 football team.

of a full load of classes for the entire student body, and all the other little and big items that no one mentioned. The ACC administration also expected Morris to take the Wildcats into conference athletics, which he did. The Texas Intercollegiate Athletic Association was founded in 1909, and in 1924 it consisted of Sul Ross State, West Texas State, East Texas State, North Texas State, Sam Houston State, Stephen F. Austin State, Southwest Texas State, Abilene Christian, Daniel Baker, Texas A&I, and McMurry.

Bugs also regularly officiated high school and college football games and played in the local baseball leagues in the summers. His sense of the longevity of this commitment probably whizzed over

his head in 1924, but he would become the dean of all active coaches when he retired from the basketball assignment in 1956 and the athletics directorship in 1969.

Four relationships developed early in Abilene. He met Rebecca McKay, one of the college beauties, a theatre major and a strong-willed young woman from Ferris, soon after he arrived on campus, and they were married in 1926. She became the director of theatre, and they built their lifetime home at 1417 Washington Boulevard, a block from the campus, when the college moved to the Hill. There they reared their son, Charles, and his friends like Dee Nutt and Dub Orr in the upstairs area.

The second relationship started in 1924 when Morris was offered a right-hand man as assistant coach and he chose Guy A. Scruggs, one of his high school opponents from the DeSoto area. As a Thorp Spring College athlete, Scruggs's baseball arm beat TCU and SMU, and he was good enough to play semi-pro baseball. Like Morris, he was assistant coach or head coach to almost every Wildcat sport. Athletes and students came to love the Morris-Scruggs team.

The third relationship was actually an old one. His cousin Don H. Morris from down the road at DeSoto, whom he had played against in high school, graduated from Abilene Christian as a football player in 1924 before Bugs arrived. Don soon became a speech and debate coach at Abilene High School, but in 1928 he was hired as a speech and debate teacher at ACC. In 1932, he became chair of the Speech Department and vice president of the college. Don was named president of the college in 1940 and served the longest presidential tenure in the history of the university, serving until 1969. The cousin tie and their parallel lifetime commitments to Abilene Christian College made the pair unbreakable confidants. Bugs was the president's coach, and Don was the coach's president.

The fourth relationship was different. Arthur Marvin Coleman matriculated at the college from Roscoe, about fifty miles west of Abilene, in 1924, the first year of Bugs's new career. The big guard, an example of "strapping manhood," was imposing, which was a contrast to little guys like Eck Curtis, who graduated in 1924. Coleman

was born in Phil Campbell, Alabama, the son of a rural mail carrier who moved his family to Roscoe when Arthur was about twelve. Coleman's nickname, as far as can be determined in newspaper records, was slow in coming. He once told Bill Clark of the *Orlando Sentinel* in the 1960s, "I had a friend who wasn't too bright in his bookwork and we named him 'Tonto,' which means dumb. But the buddy flunked out of school and I got the nickname."

Tonto put that story in perspective in a 1928 *Optimist* joke entry, the first time the nickname appeared in the school paper. A classmate, Roy Bullock, was supposed to have asked, "What makes you think you're not a fool?" Coleman's answer was,

Tonto Coleman became the fourth commissioner of the Southeastern Conference (SEC) in 1966, serving until 1972.

"Because I wasn't born every minute." The first time "Tonto" appeared in the *Abilene Reporter-News* came August 23, 1931, in a story about a Roscoe team in a city league baseball game in which Tonto was an outfielder. The nickname pops up the first time in the yearbook in 1939 in his first year as assistant football coach to Bugs.

With the backup team of Rebecca McKay, Guy Scruggs, Don H. Morris, and Tonto Coleman, Bugs Morris was ready to handle West Texas grit in his craw and bullheads on the practice and playing field, and any other obstacle that stood in his way. Sportswriters, coaches, players, and fans through the years scrabbled to find the precise words to describe Coach Morris; their words and those of others would fill more than one large equipment bag:

- "truly a builder of men" by Wally Bullington;
- "strategist" by a headline writer;
- "old-timer" by an *Abilene Reporter-News* writer after Bugs's first twelve years as head coach;
- "optimist" because he scheduled tough opponents;
- "amiable," said another *Abilene Reporter-News* scribe;
- "shrewd teacher" was the descriptor cast by another writer;
- Tonto Coleman's "scout" in 1942 papers;
- "Dana X. Bible disciple";
- "Aggie star," "Abie," and "Bugs" by Aggie fans, according to *The Optimist;*

- "All-Southwest infielder" by Texas sportswriters;
- "president of the T Association" as a College Station senior;
- "handsome" as supported by the photo of him in his Aggie letter sweater in the May 1, 1924, *Optimist;*
- "tactical innovator," according to the October 26, 1933, *Optimist*, reporting "abandonment of their customary huddle . . . [for] calling of the signals in the open";
- Bobby Jones "look-alike" by *Optimist* "Cat" column writer;
- "Trojan sponsor" in the December 7, 1933, *Optimist*; and
- "champion of the little man" by ACU trustee and former player Chesley McDonald.

Morris also was funny in a certain way, as this quote demonstrates: "We are going to beat Howard Payne, but I shall try to hold the score down to keep my men from getting cocky." Habitually, he always assured himself that he had a sawed-off baseball bat on the sidelines "to roll out players' charley horses and get them back in the game." During playing season, he imposed a tighter curfew than McMurry and Hardin-Simmons: 9:00 P.M. for the Wildcats.

Without any reservation, Bugs named one of his earliest players the best athlete he ever coached. Theo Powell, a four-sport letterman from Ralls, was not related to the Wildcats' other Powells. He came in with Bugs in 1924, and he had a nickname too—"Trent." However, "Trent" was reserved as an inside name for use by teammates only, not for headlines. The sportswriters of *The Optimist* left a trail of good descriptors of Powell: "firey-headed captain," "triple-threat Wildcat," and "what makes a Wildcat wild." The best game of Powell's career came in 1926, his junior year, against Clarendon College in which the Wildcats pummeled the Bulldogs, 28–7. Powell scored all 28 of ACC's points—4 touchdowns, including a 50-yarder, and 4 extra points from the quarterback slot. In the same season, the Ralls "flashing runner" used his toe to beat Sul Ross, 3–0, with an 18-yard field goal with five minutes left to play. At the end of his career, he had earned four letters in football, four in basketball, three in baseball, and two in track and field, and he was twice honored as an all-TIAA athlete in football and basketball. An *Optimist* writer in Powell's senior season wrote, "A cleaner sport has never attended Abilene Christian College."

Beyond sports, he illustrated his versatility playing the character of Walter in the senior play, *Children of the Moon*, and shared the leadership of the social club Sub T-16 with his best bud and roommate Dalton Hill, a star himself. Hill was Sub T-16 skipper, and Powell was first mate. A member of the Greatest Generation, Powell served during World War II with the U.S. Navy as a first class petty officer based in Cleveland, Ohio. After the war, he opened a sporting goods store in Marietta, Oklahoma, fourteen years after he finished college. He died unexpectedly in his store in April 1949 at the age of forty-five.

The storybook game of Bugs Morris's career was played in 1933 against McMurry, which was Homecoming Saturday for both teams, in front of a crowd of five thousand at Eagle Stadium. The Wildcats intercepted five McMurry passes. In the third quarter, "Bert Ezzell, cotton-headed place kicking specialist of the Wildcats, entered the lineup for a single down to boot a goal which sent the underdog Purple and White into a 3–0 lead," wrote Prexy Anderson in the *Abilene Reporter-News*. The victory was uncertain until defenders Jake Gray and Sammy Bryan stopped McMurry a few inches from a touchdown on the game's final play. Ezzell was assigned the nickname "Golden Toe," and today his son, Johnny, can recall more sports data than most any other Wildcat sports laureate. A pothole popped up in Morris's road in 1936, right in the middle of the Great Depression and the Dust Bowl. ACC had a new president, James F. Cox, from the Bible faculty, a tall, tough, distinguished gentleman. As a youth, he was sickly but overcame that to become a star on the University of Texas track and field team with a best of 10

In 1928, Theo Powell was considered the best all-around athlete that the Wildcats had ever produced.

▲

Lee Powell played tackle and served as team captain of the 1932 Wildcats.

▼

flat in the 100-yard dash. "I thought I was flying," he said. Track nuts of the era were speculating about when 10 flat would be broken. As successor to Batsell Baxter, he faced the possibility that the college would fail. Cox, however, took this attitude: "If I have to get down and crawl on my knees, I will do it to keep Abilene Christian College going." The school survived, but apparently some wanted to "chuck athletics out altogether," according to the *Lubbock Morning Avalanche* of June 16, 1936. The impeccable source for this story was B. Sherrod, a young ACC trustee and businessman from Lubbock who had just returned from a board meeting in Abilene. However, in the other side of the story, Sherrod pointed the writer to the trustees' desire "to build a new stadium, replenish its coaching staff (with former Wildcat Garland Keyes) and bring more and bigger athletes to the institution." The headline could not have been more alarming to Morris and his staff: "Keyes offered Abilene Post: ACC Board of Directors votes to go in strong for sports and build new stadium; to offer Keyes directorship."

Tension existed in 1936 between the trustees and the administration, mainly focused on the leadership of the board by Chairman John McKinzie, described by Dr. John C. Stevens in his book, *No Ordinary University*, as "a dominant personality . . . wearing out his

An All-TIAA quarterback, Garland "Goober" Keyes was a clever, elusive runner who regularly broke free for long gains.

welcome as board chairman." In the board's February meeting, T. A. Russell, a long-time backer of the athletics program and father of one of the 1919 football team members who was later murdered, made the motion to elect banker W. H. Free to a one-year term as board chairman. In 1937, five members of the local board, all Abilenians, resigned. The "pothole in the road" came along in the middle of this period of tension. Coach Morris, however, had Rebecca at his side; Guy Scruggs as his number two man; 1919 veteran W. R. Smith on the board; Don H. Morris in the vice president's role; R. H. McKay, Rebecca's father, on the board; J. C. Reese, uncle of Ogle and Sewell Jones, on the board; and James F. Cox, the early century sprint ace from the University of Texas, in the office of the president.

Garland Keyes from Cisco was unique. His attraction to a small part of the Board of Trustees can be understood. A coach whose identity is hidden by the fog of time once looked at Keyes and said, "Why, son, you're not bigger than a peanut." Translated to "Goober," that became his lifetime nickname. In high school, if he had rocks in his pocket, he weighed a little more than 100 pounds.

Under the tutelage of Bugs, this slight young man was named all-TIAA quarterback in 1929, and in a 1930 shutout of McMurry, he scored three of the Wildcats' four touchdowns. His total talents pointed him into coaching, and by 1936, he had coached at Cross Plains, Cisco, Albany, and Lubbock High School, where Head Coach Weldon Chapman told the Lubbock paper, "He is an able man and has been a great help" and that "no doubt would accept" the ACC offer. "Keyes has been in communication with ACC authorities all spring." The Lubbock paper also noted that Keyes "rejected early offers." Sherrod summed up the Wildcat offer in the article; Keyes "probably would be invited to become director of athletics, head basketball coach and assistant football coach." The *Abilene Reporter-News* didn't spend any ink on this story, nor did *The Optimist*. The student newspaper did report that at the 1937 homecoming bonfire and pep rally for the annual McMurry game, Goober, head coach-to-be at Lubbock High School, made one of the speeches.

The trustees followed through on the stadium plan and dedicated Morris Stadium in mid-October 1937, a 2,400-seat structure located about where the Mabee Business Building is today. Then, it complemented Bennett Gymnasium, built in 1931, which was the biggest and best facility of its kind between Fort Worth and El Paso at that time. Athletics Director Morris had arranged a sweet home schedule for his new stadium, three games on his home turf, the first time ACC had played on a home field since moving from the old campus on North First Street. First, the Wildcats played the Southwestern University Pirates at the new $8,000 field in a "rough and tumble game," according to *The Optimist*. The Wildcats lost the

inaugural game in the stadium, 9–6, in spite of a 16-yard off-tackle run by Bernard "Mouse" Shelansky. He and Helmut "Red" Stromquist were the anchors on a mostly freshman team. Then it was Howard Payne Yellow Jackets 14, Wildcats 6, and then Austin College Kangaroos 6, Wildcats 0. One-score losses all around. In fact, the whole year was a bummer as the Wildcats finished 0–9.

An upshot of the pothole experience was the return of Tonto Coleman to the campus in 1938 as assistant football coach and head track and field coach. J. Eddie Weems, English professor and head track coach from 1924 to 1937, had built a national level track and field program; he left Abilene for Pepperdine College to work as track coach from 1937 to 1942 and from 1946 to 1950.

Bugs's own evaluation of his best football team ever was his 1939 bunch of boys. ACC had moved into the Texas Conference and shared the championship with St. Edwards. Hal Sayles wrote, "Morris admits he's had better individuals in the past, but he cannot recall the time he has seen the Cats play better than in the four games in November." It was a 6–2–1 season, but the late games were ACC 32, Austin College 6; ACC 6, Daniel Baker 2; ACC 14, Howard Payne 0; and ACC 26, McMurry 0. By this time, Coleman was his assistant in football, and this pair motivated unexcelled teamwork. The big stars were "Red" Stromquist, Little All-American mention; Tyson Cox, Little All-American mention; Garvin

Beauchamp, who would coach the 11–0 undefeated 1950 team; cocaptains Wesley Cox and Graham Orr; and Bill "Mighty Mite" McClure from Abilene High School, who would coach the backfield of the 1950 undefeated team. The other 1939 lettermen included Buster Dixon, Sewell Cox, Harold Persky, Stanley McKeever, Gene Sosebee, Pat Wyatt, Howard Lumley, Dane "Sticks" Lovelace, Forrest Beaver, Bob James, Pleasant Hazard "P. H." Hill, Lloyd Connell, Lillus Virden, Durell Sanders, Thurmon "Tugboat" Jones, Chesley McDonald, Joe Bob Sparks, Johnny Owens, and Cy Young.

Bugs and Tonto sent the first two Abilene Christian boys to the NFL from the 1939–40 and the 1941 teams. The first was Little All-American second-team fullback Tugboat Jones, who had "explosive terrestrial moves," wrote Prexy Anderson of the *Abilene Reporter-News.* Anderson went on in his description: "A line smasher from way back, 'Tugboat' is a broken field runner too, in his individual way, which consists of (1) rolling off tacklers and (2) running over tacklers." He was the leading scorer in the Texas Conference with 49 points in 1939 and 76 in 1940 as one of the nation's leading scorers. Tugboat played for the Brooklyn Dodgers in 1941 and 1942. His favorite story from the pro experience was about jubilant Dodger owner Dan Topping when his team beat the New York Giants. "Well he finally got around to me, and said, 'great game, Tugboat, keep up the good work.'" The former Wildcat chuckled as he remembered the meeting,

saying, "I never got off the bench that day." As head coach of Hardin College (now Midwestern State) in 1947, Tugboat came up against his old coach Tonto Coleman and the Wildcats' Greatest Generation running back V. T. "Vitamin" Smith Jr. and came away on the short end of the 28–0 shutout before ten thousand fans in Wichita Falls. Jones would go on to a colorful coaching career in Texas high schools, leading Highland Park High School in 1957 as they broke Abilene High School's 49-game winning streak.

The other NFL player came to Coach Morris and Coach Coleman in the summer of 1941, one of the best pigskin surprise gifts they ever received, especially with some of their boys already leaving college to join the war. Tipp "Bow" Mooney was born in Shamrock, Texas, in 1918. The *Wellington Leader* said in 1937 that Bow was headed for West Texas State College. Instead, he enrolled at Oklahoma Baptist College, where he was named to the Associated Press All-Oklahoma Collegiate team in 1940 as a junior. The AP said he was better than any halfback at Oklahoma, Oklahoma State, or Tulsa. Mooney's journey changed again in 1941 when he, Oliver Jackson, and James McWhorter, who had been named to the AP's All-Oklahoma team at tackle, transferred to ACC. Little did Bugs understand the profound effect this transfer would make in the history of Wildcat football and track and field. He already had all-time great Tugboat Jones on his roster.

The *Optimist* said Mooney was like "greased lightning." Earl West, sports editor of the student newspaper who became a distinguished church historian, mused in his column "Wildcat Wanderings" that "Tugboat Jones and Tipp Mooney could have beaten any team in the state." In the 1941 victory, 20–7, over McMurry, Mooney scored 2 touchdowns. Oliver Jackson would go on to coach the line of the fabulous, unbeaten, 11–0, team of 1950, including Little All-American players Wally Bullington and Les Wheeler, and to mentor Wildcat Olympians Bobby

Morrow and Earl Young in track and field. Mooney would go on to play in the NFL for the Chicago Bears in 1944 and 1945, and afterward went into the coaching ranks, including the staffs of Texas Tech and Baylor University.

For the 1942 season, Bugs and Tonto traded coaching positions, which meant that Bugs filled his last football coaching assignment that fall and Tonto turned in his first college head coaching performance. Interestingly, he heard the advice of two great coaches, Frank Leahy of Notre Dame and Wally Butts of Georgia, as they

Several players from the 1940 team that tied for the Texas Conference crown, including Garvin Beauchamp (top row, second from left).

conducted the Texas high school coaching clinic in Abilene just before the 1942 season opened. This last pre-World War II Wildcat team racked up a notable 6–2 season, outscoring all opponents 169–36 and placing four players on the 1942 all-Texas Conference team—senior end Hulen Stromquist, junior tackle Dick Stovall, junior guard Joe Akins, and freshman running back Bert Brewer. The latter, a flash from Eden, also ranked as top scorer in the conference with 51 points. Maybe the most exciting part of the 1942 season for Tonto was sharing it with his seven-year-old son, Dickie. In the 1942 team photograph, Dickie was sitting cross-legged on the ground in front of the team with the football in his lap.

Texas Conference football disappeared in 1943 until Germany and Japan surrendered and the world could begin to reclaim some degree of normalcy. The armed forces and home front heavy war materials factories needed volunteers and draftees to defeat enemies in Europe and in the Pacific, and football players were already in good physical condition. Late in the 1942 football season, the first Wildcat to die in World War II, Sewell J. Cox, twenty-six, perished when a steel plate fell on his chest at the Basalt shipyards in Napa, California, while working on a navy salvage vessel. His widow, Margaret, and a nine-month-old baby survived him. Two brothers, Tyson and Wesley Cox, also were tough Wildcat football players. Sewell was president of

his senior class and was honored as the outstanding player of the 1939 team.

At least once a month, crushing news from battlefields stunned the campus community and the families of alumni and students who hadn't finished college—a total of thirty-nine death messages throughout the war. Even the coaches left the campus to render military service. Coach Morris received a navy commission as a lieutenant and was sent to the Iowa Naval Pre-Flight School's Athletics Department in Iowa City, Iowa. He was ideally suited to operate the program that shaped the bodies of young pilots for military service. Coach Coleman was commissioned a lieutenant in the Army Air Force at Randolph Field in San Antonio, and his specific assignments were likewise well matched—chief scout for the Randolph Ramblers in San Antonio, and line coach of the AAF Training Command Spymasters in Fort Worth.

The blackest day, unrelated to war, for the family of Tonto and Ann Coleman came soon after they settled in San Antonio. The scourge of polio, the worst of the three strains of the virus, invaded little Dickie's body, and within two days their son died. Don H. Morris, Walter H. Adams, and Leonard Buford led Dickie's memorial in Sewell Auditorium on October 17, 1942. The auditorium was almost packed, particularly with former players of Coach Tonto. Dickie was buried in Cedar Hill Cemetery across Cedar Creek, where his parents also lie today. Then, killed-in-action messages and training-death letters began to arrive on campus more often, particularly in 1944. The total of thirty-nine combat deaths averaged about one per month, but in some months the mood of the campus was pushed even lower. Headlines would appear in the *Abilene Reporter-News* such as "31st ACC Man Dies in Action." Bugs and Tonto lost fourteen of their boys in combat or in training accidents, beginning with Sewell Cox.

Lt. Roy B. Kendrick of Clyde died December 26, 1942, in New Guinea. He was piloting a B-17 takeoff when, at thirty feet in the air, the left engine blew up and all eleven aboard were killed. Lt. James Emmett Lee of Abilene, a navigator-bombardier, was one of the casualties when a B-26 Marauder medium bomber on a training run crashed January 8, 1944, near Kellogg Field in Battle Creek, Michigan. Lt. Henry Barrett Roberson of Abilene died in a plane crash in July 1943 on an island off South Carolina. He was the center on the 1941 and 1942 football teams and the son of Charles H. and Katherine Roberson. Charles was chair of the Bible Department. Like the death of Dickie Coleman, it was a crushing blow to the entire campus.

Lt. Curtis Dane "Sticks" Lovelace of Fulton, Kentucky, was piloting a B-17 on a bombing run near Munich on July 16, 1944, when enemy fire downed the plane and all were killed. Sticks, an end on the 1941 team, and his copilot had earned the Air Medal on another mission. President Don H. Morris characterized the Kentuckian "as one of the most likable and versatile" students on campus. Lt. Hulen Leroy "Red" Stromquist was killed July 31, 1944, on Tinian, where the *Enola Gay* lifted off for Hiroshima. Ed Leach, one of Hulen's Marine friends, wrote this about Stromquist: "When I went ashore I saw a young enlisted man wearing my friend's helmet liner, which had 'Stromquist' and a gold bar on it. Lt. Hulen Stromquist would not need the liner any further. I found him later in the Second Marine Division cemetery." Ray DeBusk of O'Donnell, a kicking specialist on the 1939 team and a navigator on a B-17 crew, was killed in the first bombing run on Ploesti oil field in Romania in August 1944, a critical attempt to shut off oil supplies to Germany.

Pvt. Gene Allen Scruggs, son of Coach Guy and Bess Scruggs, reached Belgium on March 15, 1945, as a replacement soldier with five weeks of infantry training. He was killed in action on April 1 near the Remagen Bridge during some of the most brutal fighting of World War II. Coach Scruggs wrote Secretary of War Henry L. Stimson with a plea "that others may be spared by being given adequate training before they are sent into combat service." Their grief could not be requited for their son, a Texas badminton champion.

Cpl. C. W. "Snakey" Johnson, a center on the 1941 team, died on Okinawa, June 21, 1945, with the Sixth Marine Division. Shortly before his death, he wrote to the college alumni office, "For a long time I've nursed a yen to return to the alma mater, and I'm sending these [six yen of military currency] for you to hold until I can redeem them in person." Five other football players who died during the war were Robert King of Abilene, who was killed at Manila on February 16, 1945, with his cavalry unit; Perry Hunter of Canyon, who was a reserve on the 1942 team; J. W. Burns of Olden, a center on the 1942 team; Capt. Willie Wyatt Oliver of Nolan, in September 1944; and Seaman First Class Al Hunter of Llano, who died in a car wreck in June 1944 in California.

Harold Ratliff, Associated Press sports editor, wrote a column in January 1945 based on a survey of Texas college athletics programs and the number of "athletic sons" who died for their country. He reported one hundred or more deaths and the heaviest losers as the University

of Texas, Southern Methodist, and Baylor with thirteen each. As this story shows, Abilene Christian's losses were near the top with fourteen football players at the end of the war.

The college and the community gathered in Sewell Auditorium early in the evening of February 5, 1946, to remember all the alumni and students lost in World War II, the injured survivors, and every man and woman who served their country in that dark time, including the football players who had died. Speakers were President Don H. Morris; President Emeritus James F. Cox; student Jack Fogarty, who served as chaplain in the war; Maj. Landon Hill, who was one of Coach Morris's boys; and Dr. Paul C. Witt, chair of the Chemistry Department. The A Cappella Chorus

The 1946 ACC football team with Head Coach Tonto Coleman (second row, left), along with assistant coaches Oliver Jackson (top row, left) and Garvin Beauchamp (top row, right).

performed four songs directed by blind conductor Dr. Leonard Burford.

When the coaching staff returned after the war ended, Bugs had only three jobs: director of athletics, head basketball coach, and chair of the Physical Education Department. Tonto became head football and head track and field coach. Two of their boys—Garvin Beauchamp, a veteran of the California shipbuilding operation, and Oliver Jackson, a veteran intelligence officer—started their Purple and White coaching careers. "Beech" was the B-team basketball coach and head tennis coach, while Oliver became an assistant football coach. Guy Scruggs became the head baseball coach. Tonto had taken advantage of his service in the Army Air Force to school himself on the T-offense, which he installed at ACC. Of all the T's he studied, he believed Wally Butts at the University of Georgia ran the best.

The Greatest Generation, represented by the Wildcats of Abilene Christian and the Southwestern Tech Bulldogs from Weatherford, Oklahoma, returned to the gridiron on September 14, 1946. Hal Sayles of the *Abilene Reporter-News* gave credit to "Abilene Christian's tricky T-formation" for the 28–0 shutout at Fair Park Stadium. The first touchdown of the post-World War II football era came on a 1-yard run by Buster Dixon. The new guy in Purple and White, V. T. "Vitamin" Smith Jr., was a fast, smooth running back who led the Wildcats to an 8–1–1 season. Southwest Texas State beat ACC for its only loss, and Southwestern University was the tie. ACC outscored all opponents 228–53. Five men made the all-Texas Conference: back V. T. Smith, tackle Willard Paine, center Moose Stovall, back Buster Dixon, and guard Charles Floyd.

Tonto put in two more winning seasons as the Wildcats' head coach (6–3 in 1947 and 5–3–1 in 1948), with Smith as his featured and three-time All-Texas Conference back. Vitamin would go on to considerable fame with the Los Angeles Rams, and Tonto's 1949 record without

The Wildcats run through pre-game warmups behind the end zone before a 1946 game at Fair Park, which served as the Wildcats' home field until 1959.
◄◄

After serving his country during World War II, "Vitamin" T. Smith Jr. graduated from ACC in three years. He went on to play in the NFL, becoming the first former Wildcat to play in an NFL title game.
◄

him was 3–6. Two more players earned All-Texas Conference during Coleman's tenure: end Billy Joe McKeever in 1947 and end Pete Ragus in 1949. Vitamin was a continuation of the forty-years-long line of small, quick, difficult-to-bring-down running backs that began in 1919 with Ogle Jones, then Eck Curtis, Theo Powell, Bernard "Mouse" Shelansky, "Goober" Keyes, Thurmon "Tugboat" Jones, Tipp "Bow" Mooney, Bert Brewer, and Vitamin Smith. The Wildcats moved on the ground in this 1919–1949 era. They were brought to the edge of greatness by their supporting players and their two matchless coaches— Bugs Morris and Tonto Coleman.

Coach A. B. Morris served as the athletic director of ACC from 1924 to 1969. During his time at Abilene Christian, he also served as the head football coach and head men's basketball coach.

Lloyd Jones

Coach Morris is not only the builder of football teams but a molder of men as well. By his constant contact with "his boys," as he calls them, he shapes them into men with strong characters with the will to fight the battle of life as clean as a football game should be played. In the heart of every student with whom he comes in contact is stamped an indelible picture of a real man, filled with love, kindness, and appreciation. —Tribute in the 1935 *Prickly Pear* Yearbook

CHAPTER THREE

THE SINGING CHRISTIANS

When the trumpet of the Lord shall sound, and time shall be no more,
And the morning breaks, eternal, bright, and fair
When the saved of earth shall gather over on the other shore,
And the roll is called up yonder, I'll be there

When the roll, is called up yonder,
When the roll, is called up yonder,
When the roll, is called up yonder,
When the roll is called up yonder, I'll be there
—"When the Roll Is Called Up Yonder"

The 1950 Abilene Christian Wildcats would sing anywhere they were asked. They would sing in the showers or in the dorms, in team meetings or in victorious postgame locker rooms, on buses or trains. They even sang on radio stations just before the biggest game of their season. And their song of choice was the beloved American spiritual "When the Roll Is Called Up Yonder" written by James Black. The group sang so much that it earned them the nickname the "Singing Christians."

"We had great locker room chemistry on that 1950 team," said Wally Bullington, who was a center and linebacker on the 1950 squad, earning All-American honors

that season. "We would have team meetings, and before the coaches arrived we would have a singing session. The whole squad would join in, and Jacque Baker would lead us. He was kind of our unofficial song leader. Sonny Cleere was another song leader, so we had some guys who knew what they were doing leading us. The rest of us just sorta fell in with them and followed along. But we loved to sing together." That group also made sweet music on the field in 1950, overcoming a 3–6 season in 1949 and the departure of their head coach before the season to turn in what remains the only unblemished season in ACU football history.

Garvin Beauchamp led the Wildcats to national fame in his first season as head coach.

and finishing the season on a four-game losing streak that included a 21–0 loss to crosstown rival McMurry, which featured future College Football Hall of Fame selection Brad Rowland at running back. But according to one player from that era, that 1949 season—coupled with the ensuing off-season put in by the upperclassmen and a talented group of freshmen who would be sophomores in 1950—set the tone for the following season. "The season we had in 1949 was the catalyst that made us into what we eventually became in 1950," said end Pete Ragus, who later became a highly successful coach in Texas and is a member of both the ACU Sports Hall of Fame and Texas High School Coaches Association Hall of Honor. "We had lost a lot of great athletes off those teams the two years prior to 1950, so I don't think we had a lot of great athletes on the team in 1950."

But even without Smith and other standouts from teams of the late 1940s, the Wildcats had their fair share of standouts on the 1950 team. "We didn't have any V. T. Smiths or [Richard] 'Moose' Stovalls in 1950," Ragus said, "but we had a bunch of really good athletes. There's a difference between a good athlete and a great athlete, and we had a roster full of good athletes." The 1950 season probably didn't begin to come into focus until after spring training came to an end in April 1950 when Head Coach Tonto Coleman gathered his team and informed them that he was leaving Abilene for Gainesville, Florida, to become an assistant coach at the University of

In 1948, the ACC Wildcats captured the program's third Texas Conference title, finishing the season 5–3–1 overall and 3–1–1 in the league as all-everything running back V. T. Smith Jr.—perhaps the first great star of the Wildcat football program—earned Little All-American honors. The Wildcats, however, sank back to a 3–6 record in 1949, finishing 1–4 in the Texas Conference

Florida. In his place, former ACC football standout Garvin Beauchamp—future father-in-law of Dewitt Jones, who would play at ACC in the early 1960s and then lead the Wildcats to the 1977 NAIA Division I national championship—took over as the head coach after serving on the staff at Midland High School. "In his farewell speech to the team, Coach Coleman told us to stick together because we had the makings of a good team," Bullington recalled. "He had done a great job recruiting freshmen the year before, and he told us we'd like the new coach [Beauchamp] and to play hard for him."

Bullington, however, was already thinking about a way to get back home to Alabama after his freshman season in Abilene. "Coach Coleman was the man who recruited me to come to Abilene Christian, so when I heard he was leaving, I began making plans to transfer," said Bullington, who was set on transferring to either Auburn or Alabama, two of the schools that had recruited him out of Athens, Alabama, just one year earlier. "I was still in touch with my coach, and I got a summer job pouring concrete on a football stadium in Pulaski, Tennessee." However, as the summer came to a close, two of Bullington's teammates, Rob and Dub Orr, made a stop in Athens on their way from Nashville back to Abilene. "They told me to pack my bags because we were going to Abilene," Bullington said with a chuckle. "So I didn't really have a choice, and looking back, I'm glad they stopped to get me." Bullington and the other freshmen in 1949

The four Orr brothers—(left to right) Graham Orr, W. C. "Dub" Orr, Rob Orr, and Forrest Orr—all played center at Vernon High School before playing center at Abilene Christian.

In 1955, Head Coach Garvin Beauchamp (left), Line Coach Oliver Jackson (center), and Backfield Coach Bill McClure (right) ready the Wildcats to play in the Gulf Coast Conference.

didn't know their new head coach, but he was a familiar face to some of the upperclassmen, and that helped to ease the transition to the new head coach.

"Coach Beauchamp was easy going and had workouts that were very organized down to the last detail," Ragus said. "Everybody knew exactly what they were to be doing every minute of practice. He knew the athletes and put them in position to have success. And [assistant coaches] Oliver Jackson and Bill McClure were great coaches as well. Everybody knew what their role was that year and we didn't deviate from that plan." Jackson and McClure are best known in the annals of ACU athletics history for their prowess as track and field coaches. Jackson is widely considered one of the greatest coaches in U.S. track and field history, and McClure followed him and was an assistant coach on the 1972 U.S. Olympic Team in Munich, Germany. But they were also solid, fundamental football coaches in the 1940s and 1950s.

"Oliver Jackson was a great coach," Ragus said. "He could coach anything. He had a way about him. He was organized, reasonable, and honest. And he knew what it took to get athletes prepared and ready to compete. The thing that guided Oliver Jackson, along with everything else, was hard work. He worked hard and expected everyone under him to do the same thing. He would have been a great head football coach if he had chosen to purse that as a career." Tommy Morris, who would come to Abilene Christian a little bit later as both a football player and track and field athlete, saw the same things in Jackson that Ragus and other student-athletes saw in him. "If you can coach, you can coach anything," said Morris, whose father, Don Morris, was the president of ACC from 1940 to 1969. "I think it's all about how you inspire

people. Can you motivate them? Can you inspire them to do more than they think they can do? It carries over, so it doesn't much matter if you're coaching football or track and field. Coach Jackson was a brilliant coach."

McClure, meanwhile, is one of the most underrated coaches in Abilene Christian athletics history. After he left ACC, he went on to serve as the head track and field coach at both LSU and South Carolina. He passed away in 2009 at the age of eighty-six. "Bill McClure was sensible, honest, straightforward, organized, and always did the reasonable thing," Ragus said. "The players had confidence in him, and he had confidence in them. Each of us knew where we stood with Coach McClure."

With the new head coach in place and a strong group of 1949 freshmen ready to turn into 1950 sophomores, the Wildcats were thinking about returning to the top of the Texas Conference. "There was a chemistry that the 1950 team found that was special," Ragus said. "Alton Green and I were cocaptains, but neither of us were really vocal guys in terms of talking to the team. But there was no need for any inspirational talks with that team. We had a confidence and a work ethic and a camaraderie with one another on and off the field that was unusual." However, most of the college football prognosticators of the day didn't take any of that into account when looking at the 1950 season. McMurry was the preseason pick to win the Texas Conference title and beat Abilene Christian for a fourth straight season. "Here's the thing: even with all of the hard work and the camaraderie and the relationships that were forming, we had no idea that 1950 was going to turn out like it did," Ragus said. "Putting together that kind of season is never anything you think about going into the season. But the work ethic and the will to be competitive and win was there because of what had happened in 1949. And then we started winning and that just bred more and more confidence."

The Wildcats started that 1950 season with easy back-to-back shutout wins over Eastern New Mexico (39–0) and Sul Ross (34–0) before their first true test of the season. On September 29, the Wildcats ventured east to Chattanooga, Tennessee, to take on the Moccasins of Tennessee-Chattanooga in a nonconference tilt. ACU's defense—the lynchpin of that season's team—held the Mocs to just 72 yards of offense in a game that wasn't really as close as the 13–7 final score indicated. Then came the October 7 trip to Georgetown, Texas, to take on Southwestern University in the closest game the Wildcats would play all season. The Pirates scored in the first quarter, but E. J. "Tiny" Moore threw his 290-pound frame into the extra-point try and blocked it to leave the Southwestern lead at 6–0. The game stayed that way until the second quarter

As a sophomore, offensive guard E. J. "Tiny" Moore opened holes for the Singing Christians and was an honorable mention All-American.

▶

A member of the 1950 All-Decade team, Jerry Mullins was a dazzling back with great speed. He also returned kicks, played defensive back, and was the team punter in 1951 and 1952.

▶▶

when Bill Ayres came to the rescue, returning an interception for a touchdown and
kicking the extra point to give the Wildcats
a 7–6 lead. That stood up as the final score
and helped push the Wildcats to 4–0 on
the season, topping the team's win total in
1949. "Southwestern was our worst game,"
the late Jerry Mullins said in an interview
back in 2000 for a story about the team
written by the late *Abilene Reporter-News*
sportswriter Bill Hart. "Twice I was to get
a pitchout, and one of the officials ran into
me. Also, one of our running backs, Sam
Davidson, broke his leg in the game."

After another shutout win, this
time a 19–0 whitewashing of then-East
Texas State (now known as Texas A&M-
Commerce), the Wildcats hosted their
crosstown rivals from McMurry at Fair
Park Stadium. Rowland had another big
night, but it wasn't enough as the Wildcats
topped the Indians, 26–14, to improve to
6–0. "We were thinking one game at a time,"
Bullington said, "but we were also thinking

about games 10 and 11. You can't help but
think of those games when you get halfway
through the season and you're unbeaten.
After we beat McMurry, we could see we
could play with about anybody on the
schedule. We had good size for the time,
and we had great speed with Don Smith,
Pete Ragus, Bill Ayers, Ray Hansen, Jerry
Mullins, and [quarterback] Ted Sitton. We
had some guys that could have played anywhere. Fortunately, they were Wildcats."

After another shutout victory over
Midwestern State (13–0), the Wildcats
returned home to take on Texas A&I (now
known as Texas A&M-Kingsville). The
Javelinas took a 3–0 lead at halftime before
watching the Wildcats outscore them 20–0
in the second half to remain unbeaten.
Two more wins followed as the Wildcats
beat Austin College (33–14) and Howard
Payne (27–6) to finish the program's first
perfect regular season. That 10–0 regular-season record and Texas Conference
championship earned the Wildcats an

During his playing
career, Don Smith
was a receiver, a
rugged fullback, and
in 1952, he was hon-
ored as an All-Texas
defensive back.

James Lyda, a halfback in 1950, would go on to serve as an assistant coach for ACC under head coaches Les Wheeler and Wally Bullington.

▲

Don Smith later served Abilene Christian as an assistant coach from 1968 to 1981 and was inducted into the ACU Sports Hall of Fame in February 1998.

▶▶

invitation to Evansville, Indiana, where they would take on Gustavus Adolphus in the Refrigerator Bowl on December 2, 1950. The city of Evansville rolled out the red carpet for both teams as fire trucks met them at the airport and provided them with an escort into town. Because the Wildcats were from Texas, players were given cowboy hats to wear on the ride into town. "I didn't have any boots, so I borrowed some," Bullington recalled. "We dressed up like cowboys and rode that fire truck into town and right down the main street of Evansville with people coming out of the stores to see what was going on."

Not long after their arrival, the Wild-cats became celebrities in town when several of them made an appearance on a local radio show and were asked to sing their theme song. "So we sang 'When the Roll Is Called Up Yonder,'" Bullington said. "We sang two or three other songs [including 'Goodnight Irene,' recorded by The Weavers] and really put on a show for them. We were only supposed to sing a few songs, but they had us stay on for the whole hour. We later heard that the station got a lot of phone calls asking if we had a record out because people wanted to buy it."

While the Wildcats didn't have a record to sell, they did have a perfect record to protect in the game against the Gusties. Playing on a field covered in water left behind by a torrential thunderstorm and in cold and blustery weather, the Wildcats turned to Sitton and the running game to handle Adolphus. Sitton was a magician with the ball in his hands, and one play in the game stands out in the history of Wildcat football. Sitton faked a handoff to Alton Green and then handed off to Bailey Woods on a reverse. However, the officiating crew from the Big 10 Conference went for the fake, blew the whistle, and ruled the play dead when Green was tackled. At the time, Woods was streaking down the sidelines before being knocked out of bounds at the 2-yard line. But the play was dead with the long run being negated by the inadvertent whistle. Sitton then told the officials to watch the ball because the Wildcats were going to run the same play again. Sitton was abruptly told by the referee to take care of the playing and he would take care of the officiating, sending the Stamford, Texas, native back to the huddle for the next play. Sitton and the Wildcats didn't need the help of the officials that night in Evansville as they beat the Gusties, 13–7, on a late touchdown to finish what is still the only unblemished season in program history.

The men on that team went on to become some of the most influential in the life of ACU athletics as Bullington, Sitton, and Les Wheeler each became the head football coach at their alma mater. Don Smith, Mullins, and James Lyda were

assistant coaches at ACC. Ragus coached Corpus Christi Moody to a state football championship, while Bullington was an assistant on the great Abilene High teams of the 1950s, winning three straight state championships from 1954 to 1956 before becoming the Eagles' head coach and then moving on to become the Wildcats' head coach in 1968. Smith was a longtime assistant coach for the Wildcats and coached Abilene Cooper High School to a state track and field championship before joining the ACC coaching staff, and Sitton did the same at Graham High School.

The surviving members of that team continue to gather every few years to reminisce and reflect on the undefeated season of 1950. "As time passes, you don't really remember specific games or plays, but

The 1950 ACC Wildcats became one of just nine colleges to win the Refrigerator Bowl, along with teams like Arkansas State and Delaware.

▲

Les Wheeler, a first-team All-American in 1951, would return to ACC as head coach of the football team, a position he held for six seasons.

◄

The 1950 Wildcats, with their sterling 11–0 record, became one of just eight undefeated and untied football teams in the nation at that time.

moments," Bullington said. "You remember 'Tiny' Moore blocking an extra point against Southwestern that allowed us to win that game. You remember Ted Sitton and how he handled the ball. You remember the great coaches who put it all together. You remember friendships that were made that have lasted a lifetime. Those are things that time can't take away."

Note: Parts of this chapter were adapted from a story written in 2000 by the late Bill Hart, an Abilene Christian graduate and longtime sportswriter for the Abilene Reporter-News. The story he wrote appeared in the October 28, 2000, ACU football game program as the 1950 team gathered to celebrate the fiftieth anniversary of its undefeated season.

COACH WALLY BULLINGTON

Author's Note—*Wally Bullington passed away suddenly on Friday, July 20, 2018, after a short illness. Bullington was perhaps the central figure in ACU Athletics since 1950, having served his alma mater for thirty-nine years as a football player, assistant football coach, head football coach, and athletics director before retiring in 1988. He began fundraising work as director of athletics emeritus in 2002. Though Coach Bullington never read the final version of this book, he didn't really need to read it; he had lived most of it. Rest well, Coach.*

It's hard to imagine what ACU athletics in general and ACU football in particular would have become if not for Wally Bullington. Sure, someone would have come along and filled the role of head coach from 1968 to 1976 and director of athletics from 1969 to 1988. But his former players and student-athletes in general would be hard-pressed to imagine someone else making the kind of impact on them or the university that Bullington made. And it's not just about his role as coach or director of athletics. It's about his role as player, teammate, confidant, campus leader, community leader, church elder, husband, father, and friend that has made such an impact on ACU and Abilene for almost seventy years. It's not that other great men and women haven't made impacts on the ACU campus. It's just that no one in the history of ACU athletics has impacted more young men and women than has the man with the deep voice that still has the hint of an Alabama drawl when he speaks. And when he speaks, you can make sure that most people are listening.

In a rare color photograph from his first year as ACU head coach, Wally Bullington (left) talks on a phone to his staff in the press box during a 1968 home game at Shotwell Stadium.

▶

April Anthony stops to talk with Wally Bullington and his wife, Valrie, during ACU Sports Hall of Fame festivities in September 2017.

▼

Paul White

The old coach doesn't get around the way he did when he was a regular every weekday morning for a round of golf at Shady Oaks Country Club in Baird with old friends Ted Sitton, Rip Ripley, and Willard Tate. Too many years of playing, coaching drills in practice, and standing on sidelines have left him tethered to his ever-present scooter. The golf cart he drives to ACU football practice at Anthony Field at Wildcat Stadium provides him a place to sit and watch the Wildcats work every day. It also provides shade, an extra seat for a friend or acquaintance to sit and talk football, and, if he sees something he doesn't like, a way to quickly escape the field and head home.

The pain in his hips and knees from multiple surgeries keep his gait a little bit slower than it was when he led the Wildcats. And the fiery pain from neuropathy in his feet makes it feel like hundreds of needles poking into the bottoms of his feet when he stands to walk. But he's still Coach. He still answers to it. Still loves to be called by that moniker. Still considers himself a coach, even though his last game was in December 1976. He still loves to be around other coaches, whether they be ACU head football coach Adam Dorrel, women's basketball coach Julie Goodenough, or any of the other men and women leading Wildcat programs. And when asked his opinion, get ready, because he's going to give the unfiltered truth.

For example, his opinion on ACU's move from NCAA Division II status to NCAA Division I affiliation? "It's been up and down so far, but I'm still glad we made the move," he said. "When [ACU president] Dr. Phil Schubert met with me and asked me if Division I athletics at ACU would work, I told him we could continue to do really well on a national level at Division II, but that success at the Division I level would be a question mark. But I also told him that if we're going to do it, we have to fund it the right way and give our coaches the resources they need to be successful, and I believe we're doing that. I still believe we'll have long-term success at the Division I level, but it's going to take time, and I hope our fans understand that. We've made a number of facilities improvements, including the football stadium, that will be such a big part of our success because those things attract recruits. I still believe we made the right decision to move up."

Or how about his decision to give up the head coaching position in 1976 after a 9–2 season and with a loaded team returning in 1977 in what would be a national championship season for the first-year head coach, Dewitt Jones? At the time, Bullington was the head football coach, director of athletics, fundraiser, church elder, and a member of the Abilene Independent School District school board. "I can't say I regret the decision, but it's certainly something I look back on and think that I might have done something differently," he said. "I probably would have given up either the school board or

ACU Director of Athletics Emeritus Wally Bullington holds a microphone while serving as a third commentator on the radio broadcast from Shotwell.

the director of athletics position. I really loved mixing with the guys on the practice field, in the locker room after practice or after a big win, and trying to be a positive influence in their lives. You felt like you'd been in battle together, and I really missed that." And it was in those postpractice or postgame locker rooms or in behind-closed-doors talks with young men where Bullington had his most profound effect on his players. "I always thought I was Wally's favorite," former ACU wide receiver Pat Holder said with a laugh. "But what made him so great is that we all thought we were his favorite. That tells me that he has a way of making people who come into contact with him feel good about themselves, and a lot of that is his discipline, his God-given ability as a communicator, and his values. You know that Wally Bullington is going to do the right thing and he's going to be consistent and fair."

Holder gives credit to Bullington for leading him in the right direction both on and off the field during his time with the Wildcats. "I had a great father growing up in Azle," Holder continued. "I was meant to play football at Abilene Christian because of Wally, and he ended up being like a second father to me. I remember one night during warm-ups before a game, I was catching punts and Coach comes up to me and asks, 'Holder, would you rather be doing this anywhere else?' I told him, 'No, sir. This is what I was destined and meant to do.' He looked right at me and said, 'I knew you would say that. You were

meant to be here for things bigger than football.' I've never forgotten that, and he was exactly right. The thing we all knew playing for Coach is that football wasn't the most important thing. The most important thing was that we were going to honor God, and we were going to do the right thing, and we were going to grow into men. That was a given. When I was in high school, I knew nothing about Abilene Christian or Abilene Christian football, but I went to a lot of track meets at Elmer Gray Stadium when I was a kid and I remember watching Earl Young run, and he was such a beautiful runner. I just came to the realization that Abilene Christian was where I needed to be, and the decision to play for Coach Bullington is one of the best I've made in my life."

"Wally Bullington IS Abilene Christian University athletics."
—former ACU running back Wilbert Montgomery

In the fall of 1948, Foy Wallace Bullington was a star prep football player in Athens, Alabama, who caught the attention of not only the state's two biggest college football programs at Alabama and Auburn, but also most of the Southeastern Conference and more than twenty other schools across the country. To some, it was a foregone conclusion that the young Bullington would stay home and play for the Tigers of Auburn because his two older brothers were enrolled at Auburn. But those who thought that had never spoken to Bullington's father, Clifford Bullington, who a few years before Wally began catching the attention of recruiters had helped start Athens Christian Bible School, a private Christian school in Athens. Wally went to school at Athens Christian from seventh grade through tenth grade before talking his parents into letting him transfer to Athens High School as a junior, where he played his final two seasons.

It was at Athens High School where his prowess as a multiposition athlete began to earn him some attention from colleges across the country, and coaches from those universities came calling to the Bullington home in hopes of luring the strapping young Wallace Bullington to their campus. He eventually agreed to a scholarship offer from Auburn, but his father's words to visiting coaches always stuck in the back of his mind. "My dad always wanted me to go to a Christian school, and Abilene Christian was about the only Church of Christ school playing football at the time," Bullington said. "My dad was a very strong leader in the church and was an elder for more than forty years. Every time a coach came into our living room—be it a coach from Vanderbilt, Ole Miss, LSU, or wherever—my dad would tell them what he really wanted was for 'Wallace'—he always called me that—to go to a Christian school. He got that in every time."

Abilene Christian was on Clifford Bullington's mind because he had spent one year (1911) at the tiny school in West Texas before falling ill and returning home to Alabama. But that one year made an impression on him, and soon he would take matters into his own hands to make sure his youngest son would make his way west to learn about God, life, and football. "My dad contacted [Abilene head football coach] Tonto Coleman and had him send me a telegram offering me a scholarship," said Bullington, who had earned first-team all-state and first-team All-Southern States honors as a senior. "I had a four-year offer to Auburn, and I thought that's where I was going to go because my two older brothers were in school at Auburn. But when I got that telegram from Abilene Christian, I knew that's where I was going to go to school. I always remembered my dad telling those coaches he wanted me to get a Christian education, so because of that and my respect for my dad, I chose to go to Abilene Christian." So, the offensive lineman/linebacker/punter from Alabama dropped Auburn and settled on a small school he'd barely heard of in a place he'd never been. Sounds about right.

"I had a 1928 Model A Ford that I drove from Athens, Alabama, to Abilene, Texas, without stopping," Bullington recalled. "Bob Cobb was also from Athens, and he was going to Abilene Christian, so we drove together. I'd never been to Texas, and it sounded pretty exciting." But when he arrived in the middle of a drought in the summer of 1949, he didn't exactly find the oasis he was promised. "I was told there were trees out here," he said with a laugh, "but I couldn't find any of them. Someone pointed some out to me, and I told them those were bushes, not trees." Bullington didn't find any trees on the sparse Abilene Christian College campus, but he did find the groundwork for a group of men who would have a lasting and profound impact on ACU athletics and ACU football. Men like Ted Sitton, Don Smith, Pete Ragus, Les Wheeler, Ray Hansen, Jerry Mullins, Tommy Morris, Don Hood, James Lyda, E. J. "Tiny" Moore, Bob Davidson, James

Wally Bullington played three positions in his first season, including punter.

Lloyd Jones

Cobb, and James Muns. "I loved the guys I met on that squad," Bullington recalled. "They made me feel at home and really took me in. I remember looking around the practice field and realizing we had a lot of great talent and that I could play on their level. It was unusual at that time for a freshman to play much, but I earned quite a bit of playing time." And Head Coach Tonto Coleman had to find creative ways to make sure his talented freshman didn't leave Abilene and head home to the South, where any number of SEC schools would have taken him onto their teams. Bullington had been receiving calls from his brothers back in Alabama about returning home, putting pressure on him to leave Abilene. But Coleman took care of that in the season-opening game at Texas Tech when he had Bullington kick off, in effect putting to an end any thoughts of transferring.

Bullington played center, linebacker, and was a punter as a member of the 1949 squad that finished 3–6 overall and 1–4 in the Texas Conference, a disappointing season for sure considering the Wildcats had won the Texas Conference title in 1948 with a 3–1–1 record. The season had also been tough both physically and emotionally on Coleman, who had suffered a broken leg in a fall from a roof and was still recovering from the death of his son, Dickie, in 1942. More disappointment hit the Wildcats when Coleman gathered his team on the practice field in the spring and told them he was leaving Abilene

Lloyd Jones

for Gainesville, Florida, where he would be an assistant coach at the University of Florida. "When he told us that, I made my plans to transfer because he was the coach who got me to come to ACC," Bullington said. "I was still in touch with my high school coach, so I decided I was going to go home and play for either Alabama or Auburn. I got a job that summer in Pulaski, Tennessee, pouring concrete on a football stadium." But as the summer drew to a close, Bullington received a visit from a couple of classmates from Abilene, Rob and Dub Orr, who had been visiting a brother in Nashville, Tennessee, and were returning to Abilene for the start of the fall semester. On their way back, they swung through Athens, Alabama, and told Bullington to pack his bags and get in the car because they were taking him back to ACC. Bullington was now 0-for-2 in trying to get out of Abilene. "I've thought a lot about how my dad basically sent me out here and then how Rob and Dub stopped

by and picked me up, and it was clearly the plan the Lord had for my life," Bullington said. "So I ended up coming back, and I've never regretted that decision."

What he found upon his return was a new head coach in Garvin Beauchamp, who had served as an assistant under Coleman, but who had also left Abilene before the 1949 season to be a high school coach in Midland, Texas. Bullington was assured by the Orr brothers that he would love playing for Beauchamp, and it didn't take Bullington long to realize they were right. "Beech knew that encouragement is the greatest motivator someone can use," Bullington said. "We used that to our advantage and the guys on our team really played hard for him. He knew people and how to reach them." As the Wildcats began preparing for the remarkable 1950 campaign, it's doubtful any of them could have imagined what awaited them. Nor could they have realized they were on the precipice of leaving a mark on the history

Wally Bullington lines up with Von Morgan. While at ACC, Morgan was a two-time All-American and a track standout.

of ACU athletics and ACU football that would last into the twenty-first century.

The 1950 Wildcats—or the Singing Christians, as they were called—turned in the only unblemished season in ACU football history to date. The Wildcats went 11–0 (5–0 in the Texas Conference), allowed just 57 points all season, and beat Gustavus Adolphus, 13–7, in the Refrigerator Bowl in Evansville, Indiana, to cap the undefeated season. "I go back to the spring before that season when Tonto gathered us together and told us he was leaving for Florida," Bullington recalled. "He told us we had the possibility of having a great team and great season if we worked hard

and trusted each other. I think some of the things he went through with his fall and his son passing away that he and his family needed a change, a new place to live and start over. But he left us with the thought that we could have a great team. And we did." Bullington played for two more conference championship teams in 1951 and 1952, but those titles weren't his greatest accomplishment during those years. It was, without a doubt, convincing Valrie Darden to marry him.

Valrie grew up in Port Arthur, Texas, and her connection to Abilene Christian goes all the way back to 1908 when her grandfather, H. C. Darden, served as the

Before a home game at Fair Park in 1952, (in white, from left) Don Smith and Wally Bullington represent ACC as captains.

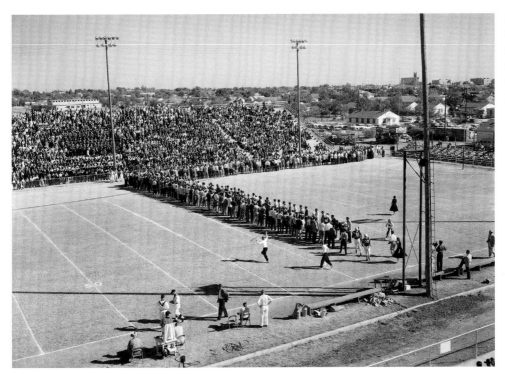

university's second president (1908–1909). After a semester at North Texas State University in Denton, Valrie returned to Abilene Christian in the spring of 1951. Wally and Valrie met that spring and have been together since, a partnership that in more than sixty-five years has produced three children—Brenda Bullington-Dickson, Laurie Muns, and Brad Bullington—and six grandchildren. They were married on December 20, 1952, and began their married life living in the old hutments that the school purchased from Camp Barkley after World War II and moved to the campus.

The Wildcats won those other two Texas Conference titles in 1951 and 1952 with Bullington on the team and again in 1953 after Bullington and many of the men who were on the 1950 team had graduated. The Wildcats would win a Gulf Coast Conference cochampionship in 1955 under the direction of N. L. "Nick" Nicholson, the first-year head coach, but it was the program's last conference title for almost two decades. When Bullington thinks back on his playing days, he thinks about the coaches and the relationships built more than he thinks about particular games. "That coaching staff that we all played for—Tonto, Beauchamp, Oliver Jackson, Bill McClure—all of those guys knew how to motivate us," Bullington said. "They had some talented players, but they weren't afraid to do some new things. When I thought about going home after

Tonto left, Dub Orr told me, 'You'll love playing for Garvin Beauchamp,' and he was right. Beech used positive reinforcement and guys played hard for him. He knew people and he knew kids, and that's what made him a success." It would be those attributes—and others he learned at the feet of one of the greatest coaches in Texas high school football history—that would guide Bullington through the rest of his career.

If it took Bullington's father to get him to Abilene the first time, Dub Orr to keep him there a second time, and marrying Valrie to make him stay for another few years, it's only fitting that it would take someone else to make him return for a fourth and final time.

After graduating from Abilene Christian in 1953, Valrie accepted a teaching job in Weatherford and Wally accepted a coaching job. They then went to Denver City where Wally worked in the oil field for Shell Oil Company in the summer to make some money for him and his young bride. While they were there, Wally received a call from head football coach Chuck Moser offering him a job on his new coaching staff at Abilene High. Wally and Sitton had spent the spring of 1953 as volunteer assistant coaches under Moser, and he liked what he had seen of both of them. But he only had one opening at the time, and he called Wally to offer him the job. However, he didn't exactly offer him a football job. He offered him a job coaching basketball

because Shorty Lawson—another ACC graduate and assistant coach at Abilene High—couldn't coach basketball because he was a Southwest Conference basketball official during the winter months. So Bullington was hired to help coach basketball with Head Coach Nat Gleaton, assist with track under Head Coach Bob Groseclose, and work with the football team under Moser. "And he also graded film," Valrie recalled. "All of that and he taught four classes for $2,800 per year."

"Oh, we were rolling in high cotton," Wally said with a laugh. "Valrie was making $2,400, and I was making $2,800, and we thought we were rich. We haven't had that much money since." What Wally found when he came back to Abilene again and joined the AHS coaching staff was a bond similar to the one he found among the coaches at Abilene Christian. He also found in Moser a man who would teach him just about everything he would end up using throughout the rest of his life. "He was a stickler for detail," Bullington said of Moser. "If you were going to teach something, we went over how you were going to teach it and why you were going to teach it that way. He was also a great organizer. Every minute on the practice field was detailed. And everything we did in practice was under gamelike conditions. Nothing half speed. I'd say 80 percent or more of what I learned and used in my coaching career came from Chuck. Every practice we worked on basics—blocking and tackling—and I carried that through the rest of my coaching career. He also said the toughest coaching is after you've lost two in a row. You can't lose three, so how do you react to that? Do you have what he called 'bounce-back skill?'"

Fortunately for Moser, Bullington, and the Eagles, they didn't have to incorporate that skill very often. Beginning early in the 1954 season after an unsightly loss to Breckenridge—after which Moser said the Eagles were about to "separate the men from the boys and get down to the serious business of winning football games"—the Eagles embarked upon a 49-game winning streak that made them legendary.

Abilene High won Class 4A state championships in 1954, 1955, and 1956, setting records and creating stars out of players like Glynn Gregory, Jimmy Carpenter, Twyman Ash, Rufus and Boyd King, David Bourland, Stuart Peake, Jim Millerman, and many others. The Eagles played in front of capacity crowds in every city they played in, becoming so popular that fans across West Texas would wait at stadiums through the night for the chance to buy a ticket to watch the Warbirds run roughshod over the opponent. They won. And they won some more. And they kept on winning. For almost four full seasons, they did nothing but win, outscoring their opposition by the insane figure of 1,773 to 276. The Eagles pitched 19 shutouts in the 49-game streak and allowed 1 touchdown or less in 19 other games. They were so dominant that most of the starters rarely played in the second halves of games.

They were such a force that more than forty years after the streak came to an end, the *Dallas Morning News* tabbed the Eagles in December 1999 as the Texas high school football "Team of the Century."

"Those teams had some outstanding players," Bullington recalled. "Not all of them were college prospects, but each one of them learned to give great effort. The great thing about being part of those teams wasn't just the winning but that the entire town was behind the Eagles. Old Fair Park Stadium where we played had about ten thousand seats and we'd fill that thing up every time we played at home. We'd take a train to Midland to play Midland High and fill up the train." The Eagles filled up trains and the "W" column with regularity, until one Saturday afternoon in Dallas when they didn't do the latter. The Eagles' streak ended in a stunning 20–20 tie against Highland Park in a state semifinal game on December 14, 1957, at the Cotton Bowl. The Scots advanced to the state championship game—which they won easily over Port Arthur—based on "penetrations": an antiquated system used to break ties before overtime came into play which was based

"I know I'm following one of the best coaches Texas has ever had, and I just hope I can do a creditable job."
—twenty-eight-year-old Wally Bullington in the January 16, 1960, edition of the *Abilene Reporter-News* after being named to replace Chuck Moser as the head coach of the Abilene High Eagles

on how many times one team moved inside the opponent's 20-yard line. Such was the magnitude of the tie that in the *Fort Worth Star-Telegram* the next day, the story called the stalemate a "stunning victory" for Highland Park. And that was it. The Eagles under Moser would go on to finish 10–2 in each of the next two seasons, but there would be no state championship runs in either 1958 or 1959. And then came the real stunner in late 1959 when Moser decided to resign as head coach and become the school district's director of athletics just as Abilene Cooper High School was coming online.

Into the void left by Moser stepped Bullington, who, at twenty-eight years old, took on the challenge of replacing the man who is still widely regarded as the greatest coach in Abilene High football history and one of the greatest in the history of Texas high school football. "Well, that was pretty tough," Bullington said of replacing Moser, "but he made it easy. He never came to practice unless I invited him. He didn't want anyone to think he was there to second-guess. Even more than sixty years later, he's still influencing people. The men who played for him will tell you that he's one of the greatest role models they've ever known." Bullington coached the Eagles from 1960 to 1965, putting together a very solid record of 40–19–1, but never led the Eagles to the playoffs. In those days, only one team from each district reached the state playoffs in each classification, making a district championship and playoff berth

almost as difficult to earn as a state title. "I count myself as a pretty competitive person, so not making the playoffs in any of those seasons was tough," Bullington said. "It was tough watching the teams that went to the playoffs knowing that some of those kids that were playing at Cooper could have helped us win some games and get into the playoffs ourselves." But while he was coaching, Bullington also had something else on his mind—working with kids and spreading the gospel.

Bullington began working with the Herald of Truth national radio and television program in the summers, and when officials from the national office approached him with the offer to become the national coordinator for the program, it was an opportunity to follow a calling.

Bullington talks to the Wildcats at halftime during a 1968 home game against Howard Payne, a contest the Wildcats would win, 50–49.

"I wasn't burned out on coaching at all," Bullington said of his decision to resign his job at Abilene High. "It was more about the opportunity to reach people and spread the gospel of Jesus Christ. I probably did more traveling in my job with Herald of Truth than I did with football." But on January 11, 1968, just one week after Les Wheeler resigned as the Wildcats' head football coach, ACU President Dr. Don H. Morris announced that Bullington, who was also serving as the director of the university's Alumni Association, had been hired as the new head football coach. In the "contract" that Bullington signed on January 15, 1968, Morris wrote to Bullington, "We look forward to years of very pleasant association with you and your family as you assist in the great work of building Abilene Christian College." Bullington made $1,066.67 per month for the nine months of the school year and $800 each month during the summer months for a total compensation package of $12,000.03 per year.

Bullington's first assignment in his new role was to appoint his coaching staff, and he hit a home run. He hired James Lyda to coach the defense and the defensive line, K. Y. Owens to coach the defensive backfield, along with two former teammates—Sitton to coach the offensive backfield and run the offense, and Don Smith to coach the offensive line. All four of those assistant coaches are enshrined in the ACU Sports Hall of Fame, and the staff probably goes down as the greatest in the history

Bullington yells instructions from the sidelines at Shotwell Stadium during the 1968 season, his first as the Wildcats' head coach.

of ACU football. "Wally hired some great men to coach under him, and there was no doubt about where they stood," said Dub Stocker, who was recruited by Don Smith out of Fort Worth Arlington Heights High School. "They were very strong Christian men. I wouldn't have ended up at ACU without Don Smith recruiting me to go there, and there are literally hundreds of others who could say the same thing."

After getting his coaching staff hired, Bullington used a bit of what Moser used early in the 1954 season and began separating the men from the boys and those who wanted to stay and play and those who didn't. "When I got the job in January, I could tell we had some guys that hadn't done anything in the offseason and they didn't want to work," he said. "That didn't fit at all into our plan, so we went to work

for every ACU quarterback who would follow him.

But before Jim Lindsey could begin to rewrite the college football record books, the Wildcats had to install a passing offense. To do that, Bullington and his offensive coaches met with pro football passing game guru Sid Gillman of the San Diego Chargers, as well as the coaching staffs of the Dallas Cowboys and the Florida State Seminoles. "We had some pretty good receivers in 1968 [Bob Bearden, Bill Lockey, Kenny Roberts, and quarterback-turned-receiver Pat Holder], and we had a quarterback in Jim Lindsey who could really throw the ball," Bullington said. "He had a great arm and we saw that pretty quickly. The biggest thing with Jim was how quickly he was able to pick up the offense and how quickly and accurately he could read defenses. Of course, Ted worked with those guys at all hours and it got to the point where Jim was coaching the team on the field. If teams tried to blitz us, he would hit the 'hot' receiver and just kill people. Most of the teams we were playing weren't throwing the ball much, so they had no idea how to defend it."

Coming off a 3–6 campaign in 1967, the Wildcats improved to 4–5–1 in Bullington's first season in 1968, and from there went 8–2 in 1969 and 9–2 in 1970, competing for the Southland Conference title each season, only to finish second to Arkansas State in both seasons. The passing combinations of Lindsey to Holder and Lindsey to Ronnie Vinson helped the

Coach Bullington speaks with quarterback Jim Lindsey on the sideline during a game in 1968.

even harder and we had seventeen quit that spring. That was fine with me because you can't win with players who don't want to work hard." It hadn't taken very much film study for Bullington and Sitton to determine something had to change in order for the Wildcats to be successful because they didn't have the personnel to bludgeon opponents with a running game. So they decided to take to the air in the fall of 1968. It was a fortuitous decision. That's because the one thing the Wildcats did have on their roster was a quarterback: a blonde-headed sophomore from Sweeny, Texas, who would become the benchmark

Wildcats light up scoreboards across the Southwest, and it also enabled Lindsey to finish his career as college football's all-time leading passer with 8,521 yards in four seasons. And while the offense was humming, the defense in those seasons was being led by a hulking behemoth of a linebacker from Denver City, Texas, named Chip Bennett. The six foot three, 225-pounder finished his career as ACU's all-time leading tackler with 374 stops (he's now fourth on the list) and was named the Defensive MVP on the ACU Football All-Century Team that was selected in 2005. But it's his single-season and single-game marks that might never be topped. He recorded a school-record 184 tackles in 1968 and 161 more in his first-team All-American season of 1969. He also owns four of the top five single-game tackle marks, including a ridiculous 27 in a 1968 game against Howard Payne. Bennett was the type of player Bullington loved to coach: a hard worker who expected nothing in return. He was a walk-on to the program who didn't even play as a freshman. But Lyda moved him from defensive end to linebacker before his sophomore season and the rest is ACU football history.

After Lindsey graduated following the 1970 season, the Wildcats had a couple of lean seasons while Sitton searched for the team's next great passer. He appeared in 1971 as a freshman from Littleton, Colorado, and while he would eventually go on to make a name for himself on a much bigger stage than Abilene, no one knew at the time that Clint Longley was the player who would lead the Wildcats to their first football national championship. After a 1972 season that saw the Wildcats finish 3–8, the team went back to work in the offseason, determined not to let that kind of season happen again. Of course, it also didn't hurt when a running back from the Mississippi Delta walked onto campus in August 1973 and began a career that would lead him straight into the College Football Hall of Fame.

—

If the first five years of Bullington's ACU coaching career were good, the final four would have to be considered wildly successful. The Wildcats were 29–22–1 in his first five seasons, but were 33–10–1 with one Lone Star Conference championship, one NAIA Division I national championship, and one Shrine Bowl victory to their credit in his last four campaigns. Following the 1972–1973 athletics season, Abilene Christian made the decision to leave the Southland Conference and the NCAA and drop to the NAIA level, where they would be paired with programs like Angelo State, East Texas State (now Texas A&M-Commerce), Texas A&I (now Texas A&M-Kingsville), Sul Ross State, Sam Houston State, Stephen F. Austin, Southwest Texas State (now Texas State), Tarleton State, and Howard Payne in the Lone Star Conference.

But if those outside the program thought the competition level would drop, they were sorely mistaken. From 1968 to

1979, a team from the Lone Star Conference was represented in the national championship game, and from 1969 to 1979, a team from the league won the title, with A&I winning it in 1969, 1970, 1973 through 1976, and 1979, ETSU winning it in 1972, ACU winning the title in 1973 and 1977, and Angelo State winning it in 1978. "There were some great teams and great players in the Lone Star Conference at that time," Bullington said. "The top teams in that league were every bit as good as the teams in the league we had just left, if not better. We knew we had to keep recruiting and getting players that could help us win games and reach our ultimate goal." The missing

Wally Bullington in 1973, the year he led his team to its first NAIA Division I National Championship.

piece in 1973 was a running back named Wilbert Montgomery, whose electric play on the field was in stark contrast to his quiet demeanor off the field. But it wasn't just the play of Longley or Montgomery or anyone else. The 1973 team developed an attitude after what had happened in 1972. "I don't know that many people realize we were 3–8 in 1972 and it was a very tough year," Stocker said. "Coach Bullington tried to run off as many players as he could in the offseason. We had dropped down to the NAIA level and lost several scholarships, so those became a precious commodity. We had a very tough spring, but I believe that hard work had a lot to do with our success in 1973."

The Wildcats went to Jonesboro, Arkansas, for the first game of the 1973 season, but did so without making Montgomery the starting running back. It didn't take him long to make an impact. The first time he touched the ball, he went 39 yards on a screen pass for a touchdown in a 56–46 loss to the Indians. "Wilbert ran through the entire defense," Bullington said. "And I got on the headset with Ted and I said, 'Bear [Sitton's longtime nickname], I believe we got a good one.' We weren't smart enough to start him that day, but we were smart enough to never take him out again." Montgomery continued to run through defenses that season, finishing with a then-school-record 31 touchdowns in the regular season before adding 6 more in two playoff victories, the last of which was a win over Elon (North

Carolina) College in Shreveport, Louisiana, in the national championship game.

Longley made a surprising move after the 1973 season and entered the NFL supplemental draft. He was selected in the first round by the Cincinnati Bengals, who then traded him to the Cowboys, setting him off on his wild path in the NFL. Jim Reese took the reins at quarterback for Bullington's final three seasons as the head coach, guiding the Wildcats to a record of 22–9–1 and a tough win over Harding in the 1976 Shrine Bowl in Pasadena, Texas, in a game that marked the end of the careers for Reese and Montgomery and other key players like wide receiver Johnny Perkins, fullback Hubert Pickett, and tight end Gary Stirman. It also marked the end for Bullington, who shocked his own team on December 16, 1976, when he suddenly announced his resignation. "It was like somebody slammed a door or something," one player told the *Abilene Reporter-News* the day of the resignation. Longtime sports information director Garner Roberts said of the day, "Everybody's chins dropped on their chests." Many around him thought that the forty-five-year-old Bullington would coach again, that he simply needed to recharge his batteries. It turns out they were wrong. The last game Bullington coached in an official capacity was the 22–12 win over Harding on December 4, 1976. "I'm not retiring," Bullington told *Abilene Reporter-News* sportswriter Mark McDonald. "We just need to gather more shekels. With spiraling costs, it will take

Bullington with running back Wilbert Montgomery.

somebody full time to gather the support we need to do the things we want facility-wise."

Looking back some forty years later, Bullington gives in somewhat to a feeling of regret for giving up the gig on the sidelines. "I can't say I totally regret it, but I would have done some things differently," he said. "I was serving on the Abilene school district board of trustees at the time, so I probably would have given up either that or the director of athletics job and continued to coach a little bit longer." Bullington would spent the next twelve years as the full-time director of athletics; and while the 1977 team won the NAIA Division I national championship behind John Mayes, Kelly Kent, Cle Montgomery, Ray Nunez, Chuck Sitton, John Usrey, and the new head coach, Dewitt Jones, the program soon began a downturn that would last most of the next twenty-five years.

While the football program was struggling, it was the Wildcats' legendary track and field program that became the athletic program's bell cow, led first by Don D. Hood and a slew of world-class athletes, and then followed by a lanky ACU graduate from Rule, Texas. Perhaps one of the most overlooked victories in Bullington's tenure at ACU—whether it be as the coach or director of athletics—was to spot the coaching talent in a twenty-two-year-old Wes Kittley and hire him to coach the women's track and field team. Kittley had run track at ACU for Hood and was working as his graduate assistant one afternoon in 1983 when he saw Bullington ambling toward him.

"Coach Bullington pulled me aside and asked me if I was ready for one of the greatest opportunities of my life, and I asked him, 'Well, Coach, what do you have in mind?'" Kittley said. "He asked how I would feel about coaching the women's track team, and I about passed out. I had never dreamed of coaching women at that point because I was just a GA for Coach Hood. But he had watched me and thought I might deserve that opportunity." Bullington didn't offer the young track coach much in terms of salary or benefits, but he offered him a chance to build a life and career in collegiate athletics. "He offered me $10,000 and the chance to be the dorm director at Morris Hall, which was the student-athletes' dorm," Kittley said. "What he did for me meant everything. I was just a young man who was probably going to coach high school when I finished my master's at ACU. But it's amazing the route that I've been able to travel because he came down to the track one day and saw something in a young man that I didn't even see in myself. That tells you a lot about him and his insight into people."

Kittley would go on to win twenty-nine NCAA Division II national championships as the leader of the Wildcats' program, eventually becoming the head coach for both the men's and women's programs. He's now in his twentieth season as the head of the track and field program at Texas Tech University, where he's led the Red Raiders to the best seasons in program history. But none of it would have happened had Bullington not made the fateful decision to throw him to the wolves when even Kittley didn't know if he was ready. And even after Bullington retired as the director of athletics on February 1, 1988, he was still encouraging his men.

"I went to him and [former men's basketball coach] Willard Tate for advice all the time," Kittley said. "They would always tell me, 'Kittley, pound for pound, you're the best coach we've ever had here.' Now, I only weighed about 135 pounds back then, so they always got a good laugh out of that. But he was always so proud of Wes Kittley, and that meant so much to me then, and I can't even begin to say how much it means to me now. I still get phone calls from him just checking on me, and I'll bet a lot of his former players get those same phone calls. When he calls me, he doesn't want to know anything besides how fast our 4 x 400 relay is going to be that year. It's his way of encouraging his men. It's incredible how much love and respect I had for him when I was working at ACU, and that's only multiplied in the years since I've been away because he's the man who gave me the first opportunity I had in this business to do what I love to do."

There were other victories for Bullington during his years as the director of athletics: national championships in track and field, the revitalization of the men's golf program, and numerous Lone Star Conference championships. His biggest victories, however, were always in the men he coached and the men and women he led as the director of athletics, helping them to become better people and making certain their experience at Abilene Christian was always grounded in faith. And that's what he wants people to remember about his more than half century at ACU. "We always preached God first, team second, and self third," he said. "I want people to know that I was a team player and that I always wanted the young men who played for me to be able to say that God was number one on our team, that we had a spiritual emphasis, and that they're better people for having been at ACU. You forget about the wins and losses; they don't stay with you. It's the relationships you build that stay with you for a lifetime."

Bullington gets the ride of a lifetime after the Wildcats beat Elon in Shreveport, Louisiana, and win the NAIA Division I National Championship.

Bullington stands next to the bust of himself that was placed in the foyer of the renovated Teague Special Events Center in September 2017. ▶

Paul White

"Coach Bullington has been a big part of so many aspects of my life. It's hard to believe the impact he's had on so many people and that he was only the head coach for nine seasons. He never once stopped thinking about the importance of having a Christian university and one that was intentionally Christian in every way. Most of us showed up as eighteen-year-old young men under his care and left as twenty-one or twenty-two-year-old young men changed forever because of his love and devotion to Jesus Christ."

—former ACU defensive lineman Dub Stocker

Bullington tips his hat to the crowd at Shotwell Stadium as part of a halftime ceremony in 2001 that marked the 25th anniversary of Ove Johansson's world-record 69-yard field goal. ▶▶

he last prowled the sideline, Bullington is still the person many of those men—now older than Bullington was when he coached them at ACU—still turn to for fatherly advice.

"It's hard to find the words to describe Wally Bullington," Montgomery said. "It's hard to say what he really means as one of his former players. When I think of Wally, I think of a man who has a master's degree in loving people and getting the best out of people. Wally is always straightforward with you, right or wrong. If he said something, you could believe it was the right thing at the right time. He never misleads people, and he always gives you information that helps you, no matter what the situation might be. I can't say it enough: Wally Bullington is Abilene Christian University athletics. And he always will be."

To this day, many of the young men whom Bullington coached or led as the ACU head football coach or director of athletics still call him for advice. They ask about how to deal with their families, business prospects, financial difficulties, and marital issues. Time might have taken him away from the sideline, but he's never stopped coaching. Even more than forty years after

WILBERT MONTGOMERY

Wilbert Montgomery still sees the cotton. Can still feel it in his hands. Can still, even fifty years later, remember the backbreaking labor that came with picking it from dawn to dusk every day. He still remembers the fields of the white fluffy bolls stretching as far as he could see as a young man growing up in segregated Mississippi. He can still feel the sun beating down on him on those unbearably hot summer days in the Deep South. He can still feel the canvas bag slung over his shoulder as he picked cotton for twelve hours a day, along with most of the rest of his family. "Growing up in Greenville, Mississippi, and in the South was very difficult," Montgomery said of his youth spent in 1960s segregated Mississippi. "If you were a black man, you stayed on your side of town. Everyone knew their place. My mother worked two jobs just to put food on the table for my brothers and me.

My older brother Alfred was a tremendous athlete who had more talent than the rest of us put together. He grew up when we had Willie and Gloster Richardson [both of whom went on to play in the NFL] and George Scott [former Boston Red Sox first baseman] all living within a few miles of our house. We knew them and saw them playing in college and then in the NFL and the major leagues and we wanted the same opportunities to get out of Greenville. Where we lived would now be called the ghetto, but we didn't call it that then because we didn't know how to define the term 'poor.' We just knew we didn't have what some other people had. But we also knew that if we went out and worked hard that we would have opportunities down the line to get some of those things we didn't have."

Still, though, there were unending rows of cotton, as well as the ever-present racism, which was a way of life in the South of that era. "I picked so much cotton when I was a young boy that I just thought that was going to be the way it was for me my entire life," he said. "Some people have asked me if we could see the light at the end of the tunnel in those days. Well, there was no tunnel. There was only cotton. From 6:00 A.M. all the way until 6:00 P.M. Every day."

But he always believed that he would make it out of the cotton fields. Make it out of Greenville, Mississippi. He believed he would make it to a place where skin color didn't matter. He believed he would make it to a place where he could show off his rare athletic gifts. More importantly, he believed he could make it to a place that offered a better life. What he couldn't have imagined was that place was about six hundred miles to the west in Abilene, Texas.

Greenville, Mississippi, sits hard on the western half of the Mississippi Delta with only the mighty Mississippi River separating it from Arkansas. A small finger reaches off the east side of the Mississippi River to form Lake Ferguson, which was created in the 1930s when an S-shaped curve in the Mississippi River was straightened. Three years before that, in 1927, a disastrous flood—at the time the most destructive river flood in U.S. history—inundated almost thirty thousand square miles with almost thirty feet of water. After the flood caused what was estimated to have been $347 million in damage at that time—the

equivalent of a staggering $4.8 trillion in 2017—Congress ordered the U.S. Army Corps of Engineers to build or improve the world's largest system of levees, dams, and floodways, including more than two thousand miles of mainline levees from the heartland of America (Missouri) all the way to the mouth of the Mississippi River in Louisiana. What those levees also did was provide "the Hill" for aspiring athletes in Greenville.

The Hill was one of the levees designed to keep Lake Ferguson in its banks, but it did more than that. It provided a training ground for the Montgomery brothers, as well as for other athletes in the area who wanted a way out, future Tampa Bay Buccaneers tight end Jimmie Giles among them. Wilbert Montgomery—along with his brothers Alfred, Cleotha, Willie, Jerry, Lenny, Anthony, Tyrone, and Fred—trained on the Hill. Legend has it that the Hill was approximately fifty feet high and set at a ridiculous angle. That's where the Montgomery brothers learned to work hard and push themselves to get out of Greenville.

"We ran that thing over and over," Montgomery said. "I saw running that levee as a way to get into shape for track and football. I didn't lift weights at all. When I went to the NFL Combine after my senior year at Abilene Christian, I did six reps of two hundred pounds, and I thought I'd really done something." Despite the fact that Montgomery wasn't going to wow anyone with his work in the

Born to Roosevelt and Gladys Montgomery, Wilbert grew up in Greenville, Mississippi. At only 5 feet 10 inches and 195 pounds, Montgomery thought that his future might be in baseball.

playing football. When Montgomery told him it was because he had an after-school job at a local laundromat, Payton told him he would put him to work at school setting up the cafeteria if he would play football. Agreeing to do that, Montgomery then met Dempsey, his high school coach at Greenville High School, who turned him loose on the rest of the state over his final two seasons. In 1971 and 1972, Montgomery was all-conference, all-state, all-Southern, and All-American. He clocked times of 9.7 seconds (100 yards) and 21.4 seconds (220 yards) in track and field and also starred on the baseball team. And as a defensive back, he intercepted 12 passes in nine games his senior season.

But it was as a running back where he excelled, and it was his prowess there that led to a pitched recruiting battle for his services at the collegiate level. Such was Montgomery's shyness during those years, however, that he committed to virtually every school that sent a coach to visit him. "Wilbert was heavily recruited by almost every school in the South," his younger brother, Cleotha "Cle" Montgomery, recalls, "and he never learned how to say 'no.' So Wilbert committed to just about every school that recruited him and promised to sign with each one of them." And these weren't your average college football programs. They were the cream of the crop at the time: Alabama, Nebraska, Arkansas, Tennessee, and every program in Mississippi. He committed to each and every one of them. He also committed to Jackson

Greenville High School weight room, he quickly made a name for himself on both the football field and baseball diamond. In fact, baseball was how he first thought he would make it out of Greenville.

"My first love was baseball and my other love was running track," he said. "I didn't really pursue track because I preferred baseball over everything else. I didn't even play football my sophomore year of high school. I was done with football at that point of my life." Until Arthur Payton and Gary Dempsey intervened and set Montgomery on a path that would lead him to Abilene Christian, the Philadelphia Eagles, and, eventually, the College Football Hall of Fame. Payton was a vice principal at a junior high school in Greenville who pulled Montgomery aside one day and asked him why he wasn't

State University and Head Coach Bob Hill, who dreamed of pairing Montgomery in the same backfield as Walter Payton, who grew up in Columbia, Mississippi, and was going to be a junior in 1973 just as Montgomery would be enrolling as a freshman. But what neither Hill nor the rest of the college football world knew was that out in Abilene, Texas, a head coach looking for a spark for his program had fielded a call from a man who had married his niece and had a tip on a pretty good player.

"Jimmy Vickers lived in Greenville, Mississippi, and had played football at Mississippi State, so he knew football," said former ACU Head Coach Wally Bullington (1968–1976). "He called me one day and said, 'Coach, I've seen the best high school running back that I've ever seen.' As a coach, you hear that and you discount it a lot of times. I said, 'Jimmy, that's good. Can you get me some film?' He got me some film and sent it to me and it didn't take me long to figure out that he was right." It was about that time that longtime ACU assistant coach and recruiting guru Don Smith was in Meridian, Mississippi, looking at a wide receiver named Evan Jennings. That's when fate intervened on behalf of the Wildcats.

"The football coach at Meridian told Coach Smith that if he wanted to see the best football player in Mississippi, he needed to go to Greenville and see that kid wearing number 30," Wilbert Montgomery said. "That Saturday I was going to sleep in, but Coach Dempsey called and asked if I could make it over to the high school because there was a coach there who was

From 1968 to 1981, Coach "Smitty" (Don Smith) recruited Wildcats from all over the country, including Wilbert Montgomery, who was arguably his greatest catch.

coming to talk to me. That's when I first met Don Smith." During that same time period, Bullington was putting the hard sell on Montgomery's mother, Gladys, as well as his grandfather, William, who was the male role model in Montgomery's life. "I talked a little bit to Wilbert, but I really talked to Gladys and to his grandfather, who was the male mentor in the family," Bullington said. "I told Gladys, 'I don't know how great Wilbert can be—he can be really great—but if he'll come to Abilene Christian, I can promise you that he'll be a better man.' That struck a nerve with her because the part about becoming a better man was as important to her as the football part, and I think that had something to do with him eventually ending up in Abilene." It wasn't without a fight, however.

Montgomery was almost too scared to tell Hill that he wanted to play collegiately in Texas, and because of that he showed up at Jackson State for the first day of camp on August 1, 1973. Going into the second week of camp, Montgomery was a starter in the defensive backfield before Payton went down with an injury and Hill moved Montgomery to running back. "Now I'm working both sides of the ball and I was tired," Montgomery said. "At an all-black university, they worked you extra hard back then. If you're getting a scholarship, they wanted to make sure you were earning every bit of that scholarship. Plus, they were always scared I was going to leave Jackson State. Every time we had down time, someone was following

me, whether it was to the cafeteria, to the bathroom, my room, whatever; someone was following me. It was almost like I was in a prison." Then one Saturday a couple of weeks into camp, Montgomery broke out of prison. Percy Brady, Montgomery's cousin, traveled to Jackson State to visit his brother, Charles, who was Montgomery's roommate. Wilbert snuck out of the dorm window, hunkered down in the back seat of Percy's car, and covered himself with clothes and blankets so no one would see him as Percy left campus. "And we got back to Greenville," Montgomery said, relief still in his voice more than forty years later. "It was 120 miles to my front door, and as soon as I got inside the house, I called Coach Smith and told him I was ready to go to Abilene and be a Wildcat." It wasn't that easy, though.

As soon as Hill and his coaching staff realized their prized freshman recruit had gone AWOL, they began searching for him. They eventually called the Montgomery home and told Wilbert they would be sending someone to pick him up and haul him back to Jackson State. At the same time, Smith was on a plane from Abilene to Mississippi in a race to get to Wilbert first. "I was praying that Coach Smith would get to me before the Jackson State coaches got to the house, and he did," Wilbert said. "Coach Smith was in the back room of the house with me and Cle when the Jackson State coaches knocked on the front door."

Cle remembered the scene this way: "That's when Wilbert was ready to run out

Lloyd Jones

The Offensive MVP of ACU's All-Century team, Montgomery is ACU's all-time leading rusher.

touchdowns en route to an NAIA Division I national championship in 1973], Darrell Royal at Texas was trying to get me down to Austin. But then he signed Earl Campbell and that was the end of that." But it was just the beginning of an unparalleled ACU football career.

Wally Bullington gets a twinkle in his eye when he thinks back to the spring of 1973 and watching film of a kid named Wilbert Montgomery play football for Greenville High School, imagining what he could do for his team, which was coming off a 3–8 campaign in 1972 and needed a jolt of energy. "I was shocked at how fast he could get started," Bullington said. "He played 7 yards behind the quarterback, but he was so quick that he was into the hole quicker than anyone I'd ever seen. He could really catch the ball out of the backfield, too. He made catches high school kids don't make. He returned punts on special teams, and he was a great defensive back. He could have been a terrific cornerback and could have played in the NFL as a defensive back."

of the back of the house and leave everyone behind. But my grandfather said, 'No, sir. You're going to make your mind up right now where you're going to play and you're going to stick with it.'"

So Wilbert left the house via the back door while Smith walked out the front door, right past the coaches from Jackson State. "I met him [Smith] down the street at the corner, got in the car, and the rest is history," Wilbert said. "Jackson State didn't leave me alone the first two years I was at Abilene Christian, though. They were always calling and telling me I had to come back home, but that obviously never happened. After my freshman season [31

But when he got to Abilene in August 1973, Hubert Pickett was the starting running back and Wilbert settled in as the backup. However, that didn't keep Bullington and offensive coordinator Ted Sitton from plotting ways to use their fabulous freshman. "Wilbert was a difference-maker, and we were going to get him on the field," Bullington said. "He could do so many things with the ball in his hands.

He was just electric in the open field." But he didn't make much of an impression on then-assistant coach K. Y. Owens, who coached the defensive backs. Montgomery was a notoriously slow walker, which didn't much impress the hard-nosed Owens. One day at the end of a summer practice before the 1973 season-opener, Owens said to his fellow coaches, "I heard this guy [Montgomery] was supposed to be a good football player, but I haven't seen him get out of a slow walk yet." You might say that Montgomery was a "gamer." "When the pads came on and those lights switched on and it was game time, I was ready to go," he said. "When that happens, most people run as fast as they can. I ran as fast I needed to run."

In 2007, after rushing for one of his 39 touchdowns, ACU runnng back Bernard Scott, who had a habit of coasting into the end zone, came to the sideline where he was greeted by then-Head Coach Chris Thomsen. "Why don't you run hard all the way into the end zone," Thomsen asked Scott in a not-too-friendly tone of voice. The running back answered, "I run as hard as I need to run." That was the end of the conversation. Poetically, Scott ended up playing for the Baltimore Ravens for part of the 2014 season where his running backs coach was Wilbert Montgomery. Presumably, they ambled slowly to the practice field together each day.

Wilbert, however, didn't start the 1973 season-opener at Arkansas State in Jonesboro, which didn't sit too well with the player who had never sat on the bench in his life. "My family drove to Jonesboro, Arkansas, from Greenville to see me play, and I honestly said I wasn't going back to Abilene with the team after the game," Wilbert said. "I was going to go home to Mississippi and I was going to be finished with football. Somehow Coach Bullington got wind of it and told [offensive coordinator] Ted Sitton to get me in and see what I could do." The first time he touched the ball as a college football player, he went 39 yards on a screen pass, and he was off and running. The Wildcats lost that first game at Arkansas State, but they wouldn't lose again.

With an offensive attack led by quarterback Clint Longley, Montgomery, tight end Greg Stirman, wide receiver Richard Williams, and offensive linemen Don Harrison, Bob Harmon, Clint Owens, and

Fullback Kelly Kent leads Wilbert Montgomery downfield in the Wildcats' 1976 win over rival East Texas State.

Milton Taylor

Garry Moore, the ACU offense pummeled opponents into submission.

The Wildcats averaged 38.8 points and 478.2 yards per game and had a 3,000-yard passer in Longley (3,167 yards), a 1,000-yard rusher in Montgomery (1,181 yards), and a 1,000-yard receiver in Williams (1,054), a feat that wouldn't be accomplished by another ACU team until 2007 when Billy Malone (3,914 passing yards), Bernard Scott (2,165 rushing yards), Jerale Badon (1,034 receiving yards), and Johnny Knox (1,158 receiving yards) matched the feat first performed by the 1973 squad.

And the defense—led by the likes of Chip Martin, Dub Stocker, Charles Hinson, Reggie Hunter, Chuck Lawson, Richard Lepard, Ken Laminack, Monty Tuttle, and Jan Brown—kept improving throughout the season, limiting three Lone Star Conference opponents to 7 points or less and holding Langston (6 points) and Elon (14 points) to a combined 20 points in two NAIA Division I playoff victories, the latter of which was a 42–14 win in the national championship game in Shreveport,

Louisiana. "Our defense kept getting better and better," Bullington said. "We weren't great to start the season, but we had some good players on that side of the ball, and they kept getting better." Montgomery earned first-team NAIA Division I All-American honors on his way to scoring 37 touchdowns and 224 points, marks that would stand as school records until Scott came along and broke both records in 2007 (39 touchdowns and 234 points).

The 1974 season held the promise to be even better than the previous year because the Wildcats returned several starters, and the team added future star receivers Johnny Perkins and Cle Montgomery. Cle had no intention of joining his brother in Abilene, instead preferring to further his football education in Norman, Oklahoma,

Montgomery is inducted into the ACU Sports Hall of Fame in 1989, joining fellow inductees of that year: John Ray Godfrey, Earl Young, Robert McLeod, Garland "Goober" Keyes, Dalton Hill, and Glenn Terhune.

under the tutelage of Barry Switzer, the second-year head coach. However, Cle had warmed to Abilene during the 1973 Christmas break when he returned to West Texas with Wilbert and Dick Felts, who, along with his family and several others, had taken to Wilbert. Felts had driven Wilbert home to Mississippi—a strict no-no in today's NCAA world—and brought Cle back to Abilene for a visit. "I was with them for about seventeen days, and I kind of fell in love with that family," Cle said of the Felts family. "I ended up meeting Tommy Morris and his family, Thurman Andrews and his family, and Rip Ripley and his family. I met tons of great people. We're talking in the early 1970s, and with race relations the way they were in Mississippi at the time, I couldn't believe how nice everyone was and how kind they were to me. I met the Ray McGlothlin family, and of course, Dr. John Stevens was

the president of the university at the time, and he was super, super nice. And, boy, there wasn't a nicer person in the world than Dr. [Robert] Hunter.

"It got to the point where I was thinking, 'maybe this wouldn't be a bad school for me,'" Cle said. "Wilbert had a great year in 1973 and they won the national championship, and I was still leaning toward Oklahoma. When I got back home, I told my mother, Gladys, that I thought I was still going to OU because ACU is a good school and Wilbert is going to be fine. Even though Wilbert was older than me, it appeared that I was the older brother because I always did the talking for him. Mother wanted me to go to Abilene with Wilbert, and I wanted to go to OU; and when she started crying, I couldn't say no, and that's how I ended up at ACU." Those relationships that swayed Cle sustained Wilbert during his four years in

Abilene and beyond. He still counts as his own family the Felts and Morris families, among many others. "It didn't take me long to understand the people at Abilene Christian cared about me for more than football," Wilbert said. "When I first arrived, I wondered why everyone was so nice and what they wanted. But you didn't have to be very smart to realize that I didn't have anything to give them, and that made me understand that they cared about me as a person. I wasn't used to people hugging me and telling me they loved me and they cared about me. But within the first few weeks, you got that feeling from everyone who lived on the Hill."

Wilbert practically lived with the Felts family during the 1974 spring semester, and that's when he began to visit more and more with the Morris family, who lived across the street. "We began to really get to know Wilbert during the spring of his freshman year when he would come over to the house with Ricky Felts," Tommy Morris said. "We loved him and he was comfortable at our house. He would get down in the floor and play cards with our kids, and it was something that was just a natural fit for all of them. That connection started at that point and it's still strong today. He calls us 'mom' and 'dad' and will text us and ask how 'mom' is doing or what is 'dad' doing."

All those families played a vital role in the growth of not just Wilbert and Cle, but a host of ACU athletes during those years. And Wilbert, for one, has not forgotten.

"Tommy and Martha Morris and their family are unbelievably generous and engaging," Wilbert said. "I was so proud to be part of their family. They wrapped their arms around me and embraced me. But it wasn't just me, but a lot of other students, and not just student-athletes. I happened to be one that their kids latched on to as well, and we spent a lot of time together. They'll always have a special place in my heart and in my family."

The men that Wilbert spent the majority of his time with while at ACU were the coaches who led the Wildcats to that 1973 national championship. "That was a great group of men, but they were all different," Wilbert said. "Wally Bullington was the head coach, but he was the master motivator of the group. He would bring [ACU graduate and noted author and motivational speaker] Ron Willingham in to talk to us during the season, and those two men were strong forces for our team. Ted Sitton was the head coach of the offense. Coach Sitton would try to make you think he was mean and hard, but deep down you knew he was a bear cub. He was full of laughter. He knew how to make you feel good about yourself and your abilities. And he always made you feel like you'd be a big part of what he was doing. And then Coach [Don] Smith—he was a tough guy. I like to think of him in terms of the actor, Dan Blocker, who played Hoss Cartwright on *Bonanza*. He was a guy who would whistle and slap his hands together and get upset when things weren't done the

Wilson remembers without hesitation how many miles it was from ACU to Montgomery's house in Greenville, Mississippi. "Six-hundred-one miles exactly," Wilson recalled when thinking about the numerous trips he made with Montgomery in the early 1970s. "I made that drive every Thanksgiving and Christmas when Wilbert was here so he could go home for the holidays. We were in the NAIA back in those days, and you could do things like that. It was a different time in a lot of ways." Wilson made those drives with Wilbert and other members of the Montgomery family, even though he had his own family at home in Abilene enjoying the holidays without him. "Those drives back and forth were special to me," Montgomery said. "Every time we passed through Dallas, he would point out the Texas School Book Depository where Lee Harvey Oswald assassinated President Kennedy. I asked him every time how many times he was going to show me that. After a while, I think he did it just to get under my skin. I think about those drives a lot, especially now when I'm taking my kids different places. I think about Jerry driving Cle and me up and down the road and leaving his family behind. These were holidays and the time he gave up to make sure that we were happy tells you everything you need to know about Jerry Wilson."

Wilbert Montgomery scored 76 touchdowns in his ACU career, which set the college football record for career touchdowns at that time and still stands as the ACU record.

way they were supposed to be done. But off the field, he was a gentle giant and a great man."

But the one coach Wilbert truly latched on to during his ACU days was Jerry Wilson, who coached on the defensive side of the ball. They hit it off instantly, forming a bond that goes beyond friendship. "Jerry Wilson was truly my 'brother from another mother,'" Montgomery recalled. "We spent so much time riding up and down the highways together just talking about life. When people ask me to define a 'player's coach,' I always think of Jerry. He could speak to us on a different level. His wife, Diane, became like a sister to me, and their children [Greg and Jimmy] became like my nephews."

The final three seasons of Wilbert Montgomery's ACU career didn't pan

Montgomery battles for extra yards against the Sam Houston State Bearkats.

out exactly how he or those around him thought they might. He still had some big games, but he was hampered by injuries and defenses whose sole focus was to take him out of the games, either literally or figuratively. "Before I got to college, I was playing on both sides of the ball, so if a team tried to take me out of the game on offense, I could make my presence felt on defense," Wilbert said. "I had never been a part of what happened the last three years where teams were focused on taking me out of the game. Jim Hess, the head coach at Angelo State, would tell me that their goal was to eliminate me or get me out of the game. Gil Steinke at Texas A&I [now Texas A&M-Kingsville] told me the same thing." Wilbert, though, still led the Wildcats in rushing in 1974 and 1976 and scored 16 touchdowns as a sophomore. And on October 16, 1976, he went into ACU's game against East Texas State (now Texas A&M-Commerce) with a chance to become college football's all-time

leading touchdown scorer. That afternoon at Shotwell Stadium, Montgomery played against the Lions in a game that became famous not for what he did, but for the exploits of a then-unknown kicker named Ove Johansson, who set a still-standing world record with a 69-yard field goal in the 17–0 win over the Lions.

But Wilbert did set college football's all-time touchdown record, scoring his 67th touchdown with 3:40 left in the first half on a 1-yard run. That touchdown, ironically, broke the previous record of 66 set by Walter Payton, the man who was supposed to be his Jackson State team-mate. And despite the attention Johansson received that day—and still receives some forty years later—Montgomery said he's never felt overshadowed, going so far as to say he never even thinks about records or stats. He would go on to be selected in the sixth round of the 1977 NFL draft by the Philadelphia Eagles and eventu-ally became the Eagles' all-time leader in rushing attempts, rushing yards, rushing attempts in a season, rushing yards in a season, career 100-yard rushing games, 100-yard rushing games in a season, and touchdowns in a game. In 1979, Wilbert led the NFL with 2,012 all-purpose yards (rushing, receiving, and returns), and over his nine-year career, he accumulated 6,789 rushing yards and 45 rushing touchdowns to go along with 273 catches for 2,502 yards and 12 receiving touchdowns. He would earn two Pro Bowl invitations (1978, 1979), and in 1980, he led the Eagles to their first

Super Bowl appearance when they reached Super Bowl XV in New Orleans. To get to that game, the Eagles beat their archnemesis, the Dallas Cowboys, 20–7, at bitterly cold Veterans Stadium in Philadelphia as Wilbert ran for 194 yards and 1 touchdown, a 42-yard score in the first quarter. The Eagles, however, would lose to the Oakland Raiders, 27–10, in Wilbert's only Super Bowl appearance as a player.

Several years after retiring from the NFL in 1985, Wilbert received his highest personal honor when he was inducted into the College Football Hall of Fame as part of the Class of 1996. In a final, fitting bit of fate, Montgomery was inducted into the hall the same year that Payton was inducted. Two men who were to have been teammates at Jackson State still ending up together among college football's immortals. They were joined that year by, among others, quarterback Terry Bradshaw (Louisiana Tech), running back Charles White (USC), linebacker Hugh Green (Pitt), receiver Billy "White Shoes" Johnson (Widener University), and quarterbacks Marc Wilson (BYU) and Neil Lomax (Portland State). "We had a great trip up to South Bend, Indiana, for the induction," said Bullington, who suffered a dislocated hip on the trip, which didn't dampen his enthusiasm for the proceedings. "When you think about the group of men he was inducted with, you quickly realize that we had something pretty special going on." Montgomery then spent

Steve Butman

Garner Roberts with Montgomery outside the College Football Hall of Fame.
◄◄

Montgomery (left) stands with Walter Payton after their induction to the College Football Hall of Fame. Both received commemorative rings as part of their recognition.
◄

Wilbert Montgomery speaks to a Teague Center crowd in October 2016 during an ACU Wildcat Football Legends luncheon event.

▲

ACU President Dr. Phil Schubert and Wilbert Montgomery at the ACU Sports Hall of Fame induction in 2017.

▶

the next eighteen years in the NFL as an assistant coach, first in St. Louis for his old head coach, Dick Vermeil, who revived the Rams and won Super Bowl XXXIV over Tennessee, and later in Detroit, Baltimore, and Cleveland. He was the running backs coach in Baltimore in 2013 when the Ravens beat San Francisco in Super Bowl XLVII in New Orleans. He retired after the 2015 season and says his coaching days are behind him.

However, he and his wife of twenty-four years, Patricia, now have a son, Derron, in the coaching world at Georgia, and two children, Brendan and Breana, enrolled at ACU. The Montgomery legacy lives on at ACU. "There are moments that turn around an entire program," said former ACU quarterback Jim Reese, who was the starter during Wilbert's final three seasons. "And Don Smith going to Greenville, Mississippi, to pluck Wilbert Montgomery out of there and bringing him to Abilene is one of those moments. Without him, there's not a national championship. We don't win two national championships.

There's no legacy. Wilbert is *the* defining player in ACU football history."

And Wilbert is happy that he represents his alma mater in the College Football Hall of Fame. "The day I was enshrined, I thought about all of the people who were enrolled at ACU during my four years there, and I went into the hall of fame that day for all of them," Wilbert said. "It was for all of the professors. It was for all of my teammates and coaches and friends and family. It was for the city of Abilene and the support the people there gave all of us when we were students. I have never looked back and regretted for one second my decision to play at Abilene Christian. I'm a firm believer that the good Lord put our eyes in the front of our head because we should all be interested in where we're going and not looking back to see where we've been. I've been extremely blessed, in large part because of Abilene Christian, and I would never take that back."

NATIONAL CHAMPIONS

One of the greatest periods in the history of ACU football was a short five-year window when terrific players merged with terrific coaches to create a startling run that was bookended by a pair of national championships. It also left the players on those teams with an unbreakable bond that still exists more than forty years later. From 1973 to 1977, ACU's rosters were dotted with All-American players like quarterback Clint Longley, running back Wilbert Montgomery, wide receivers Johnny Perkins and Cle Montgomery, defensive lineman Chip Martin, defensive back Chuck Sitton, and many other greats like quarterbacks Jim Reese and John Mayes, running back Kelly Kent, linebacker Ray Nunez, defensive back Glenn Labhart, defensive tackle Dub Stocker, linebacker Reuben Mason, linebacker John Usrey, tight end Greg Stirman, and offensive linemen like Greg Newman, Garry Moore, Bob Harmon, and Don Harrison.

They were coached by a Who's Who of ACU football coaches, men like head coaches Wally Bullington and Dewitt Jones and assistant coaches Jerry Wilson, Ted Sitton, Don Smith, and others. All of those men led the Wildcats to a combined record of 44–11–2, two Lone Star Conference championships (1973 and 1977), a 9–2 record and a win in the Shrine Bowl at the end of the 1976 season, and two NAIA Division I national championships (1973 and 1977). Those were the days when Shotwell Stadium was filled to

This group of coaches is generally considered the greatest coaching staff in Abilene Christian football history—(from left to right) assistant coaches K. Y. Owens, Jerry Wilson, Don Smith, Ted Sitton, and Head Coach Wally Bullington.

Chuck Sitton, the son of coach Ted Sitton, was an All-American safety who died tragically in a house fire in November 1980. Chuck Sitton Tower at Wildcat Stadium is named in his honor.

near-capacity each home football Saturday afternoon so fans could catch a glimpse of an offense that ran up and down the field on opponents and a defense that pitched six shutouts and held opponents to just one score seven more times in fifty-six total games. Those were the days when college football didn't saturate the television landscape and the ACU Wildcats were the most popular game in town on Saturday afternoons. The games were must-see events, and the players on the field provided the entertainment the masses were seeking. However, no one saw the five-year burst coming. But when it happened, it was hard to not stop and watch.

The 1972 Wildcats were a fairly nondescript group, a team that finished 3–8 overall and 1–4 in the Southland Conference, its final season in the league that it helped start until the ACU program returned to the conference in 2013–2014. ACU's only wins that season were against old rival East Texas State (now Texas A&M-Commerce), conference foe Arkansas State, and future Lone Star Conference rival Eastern New Mexico. The only two all-Southland Conference performers on the team were center/placekicker Sonny Kennedy and tight end Greg Stirman. Sophomore quarterback Clint Longley threw for 2,062 yards, but he also threw 21 interceptions compared to just 9 touchdowns, leaving Wildcat coaches perplexed as to what exactly they had on their hands at the most important position on the team. But a tough spring training following that 1972 campaign was, according to one Wildcat, the impetus for the turnaround in 1973. "I don't think many people remember that we were a 3–8 football team in 1972," former all-conference defensive tackle Dub Stocker said. "Coach Bullington tried to run off as many players as he could in the off-season. We had a very tough spring, but I believe it made us tougher and had a lot to do with our success in 1973."

Longley spent the summer in Abilene working with his receivers and building a rapport that would help him throw for 3,167 yards and 28 touchdowns in 1973, becoming the first ACU quarterback to ever throw for more than 3,000 yards in a season. What no one outside the ACU football program knew, however, was that there were some other pieces that were beginning to fall into place that had the potential to make the 1973 season a special one. And the biggest piece to the puzzle was about six hundred miles to the east and being recruited by several NCAA Division I programs. After a recruiting battle against Jackson State, several trips back and forth between Mississippi and Abilene, and one finely tuned escape plan, Wilbert Montgomery was an ACU Wildcat.

But his commitment to ACU didn't stop coaches from virtually every school in Mississippi from trying to poach him. Those were the days when NCAA enforcement of recruiting rules was, at best, lax and most times nonexistent. The Southwest Conference was widely known as the leading offender, but the Southeastern Conference wasn't far behind. "One day after Wilbert arrived in Abilene in August of 1973, I got a phone call from someone telling me that two Ole Miss alums were on their way to Abilene to get Wilbert," Bullington recalled. "They got to Elmer Gray Stadium, and I met them down there before they could get much further onto campus. I introduced myself as the head coach and asked them where they were from."

Bullington proceeded to ask if they were in town for a casual visit or if they were in Abilene to try to take his prized recruit back to Mississippi. When they wouldn't answer, Bullington told them he was headed back to his office to make a phone call to the NCAA. "I told them that when I made the phone call that if they were still here, I was going to report that they were recruiting on our campus," Bullington said. "I told them, 'That's not going to go over very well in the NCAA offices,' and one of them said, 'We were just leaving, Coach.' That was the last time I ever saw them in Abilene."

But just because Montgomery was on campus didn't necessarily mean that he would start at running back. Hubert Pickett was the starter on September 8 when the Wildcats took on Arkansas State in Jonesboro, Arkansas. But it didn't take Montgomery long to make an impact. He scored from 39 yards out on a screen pass the first time he ever touched the ball in a college football game, and he didn't stop scoring touchdowns for four seasons. ACU lost that game, 56–46, but it found its

A Lone Star Conference first-team linebacker, Ray Nunez was a team captain and a leader of the defense that helped ACU win the 1977 NAIA Division I national championship.

Milton Taylor

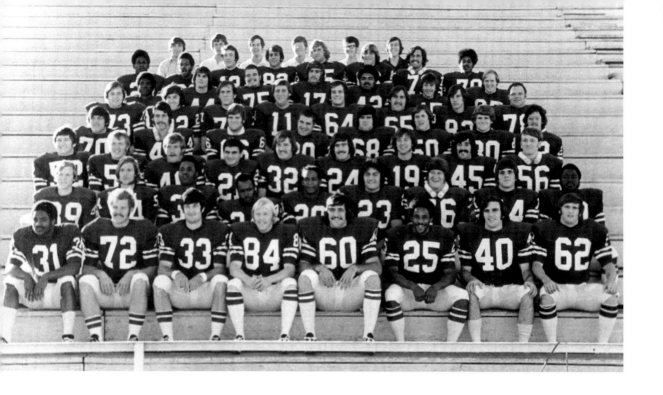

greatest star and wouldn't lose again the rest of that season. "We weren't used to starting freshmen for a couple of reasons, mainly because we didn't want to put that much pressure on them," Bullington said. "But Wilbert was so calm and cool that I don't think he ever felt any pressure. But he showed us something in that game. He had such great moves and from then on he was our guy. Hubert filled in well, and the chemistry between those two guys was never an issue."

After that loss, ACU reeled off eleven straight wins, and after surviving a wild 57–50 win over Stephen F. Austin, the defense only allowed more than 15 points once in the final eight games. The Wildcats beat teams like East Texas State that featured defensive stalwarts Dwight White and Harvey Martin, who would go on to win Super Bowls with the Pittsburgh

Steelers and Dallas Cowboys, respectively, and a supremely talented Texas A&I (now Texas A&M-Kingsville) team. East Texas State, in fact, was the defending NAIA Division I national champion in 1973, and after ACU won the title that season, Texas A&I would win three straight titles. The teams in the newly expanded Lone Star Conference were no pushovers. "We never played a game where we were out-coached or didn't have a game plan that was superior to the teams we were playing," Stocker said. "Our coaches were visionaries. Most teams were just running the ball out of the wishbone set, but we were running everything out of a pro set and throwing the ball all over the field."

And as much as the ACU offense gets credit for the national championship season, Bullington believes the defense deserves a pat on its collective back as well.

"That was a great team in 1973, the best I've been around," Bullington said. "The biggest key to the season was that our defense got better. We weren't very good to start with, but we had some really good players and they got better. Guys like Chip Martin and Dub Stocker and Chuck Lawson and on down the line. They just got better and better on that side of the ball."

The Wildcats won the Lone Star Conference championship by blistering their last five opponents—Sul Ross, Angelo State, Tarleton State, Sam Houston State, and Howard Payne—by the combined score of 193–44 to finish the season 9–1 overall and 9–0 in the conference. On December 1, 1973, the Wildcats hosted unbeaten Langston (Oklahoma), which featured linebacker Thomas "Hollywood" Henderson, who would go on to fame in the NFL with the Dallas Cowboys. Langston's defense made no bones leading up to the game that it knew it had to stop Montgomery if it was going to leave Abilene with a win.

The Tigers couldn't do it.

Montgomery was stopped on the first play, but took a pitchout on the second play of the contest and ripped off a 71-yard touchdown run. An early 7–0 lead turned into a 20–6 halftime lead and a 34–6 victory. Montgomery ran for four touchdowns, Martin had 10 tackles and 2 sacks, and Richard Lepard had two interceptions. Montgomery never needed prompting to play hard, but he got his motivation for the semifinal game in the form of trash-talk aimed at him throughout the week and in the moments before the game started. "Langston had a very good defense, and some people outside of Abilene thought Langston would win the game because of that defense," Montgomery said. "When I was introduced before the game and I ran down the hill to the field, I held up my index finger and waved it over my head. That was the first and only time I ever did that at ACU, and I did it for a reason. I wanted my team to know we were going to fight."

The next week's national championship contest against Elon wasn't a fair fight as the Wildcats rolled to a fairly anticlimactic 42–14 win in the Champions Bowl in Shreveport, Louisiana. Montgomery ran for 159 yards and 1 score, and Longley threw for 341 yards and 1 touchdown in the romp.

Corliss Hudson

As a sophomore in 1977, Kelly Kent was named the Outstanding Offensive Player of the Game in the NAIA semifinal and national championship games.

"Our coaches preached to us from the start of the season that we were good enough to win a national championship," Martin said. "They said it so much that I got tired of hearing it. But as the season wore on, we were cautiously optimistic that we had something. We saw what Wilbert could do, and Longley was always supremely confident, and our defense continued to improve. The team that scared us the most on our schedule was Stephen F. Austin. Once we got past that game [a 57–50 win that saw Martin and Stocker combine for three sacks on the game's final three plays] we thought we had a chance. We got on top of Elon pretty early and it just steamrolled on them. We thought it would happen the next year, but it didn't. But that 1973 season was certainly very special."

There would be no repeat after Longley decided to declare himself eligible for the NFL's supplemental draft in the summer of 1974, giving up his final year of eligibility. And Montgomery would fight through leg injuries the final three years of his career that would limit his availability to the offense. But the Wildcats still put together a 7–4 record in 1974 and a 6–3–1 season in 1975, leading up to a 9–2 campaign in 1976. That season saw three records set that might not ever be broken: Montgomery finishing his ACU career with 76 career touchdowns, a 69-yard world record field goal from Ove Johansson, and a 564-yard passing day from Jim Reese on a sloppy Shotwell Stadium turf.

The 1976 season was also the final one for Bullington as the head coach and Montgomery and other greats like Johnny Perkins and Reese. Bullington retired a few weeks after the Wildcats beat Harding, 22–12, in the Shrine Bowl in Pasadena,

ACU quarterback Jim Reese speaks to the crowd after the Wildcats beat Harding, 22–12, in the 1976 Shrine Bowl in Pasadena, Texas.

David Dillard

Texas, and Perkins and Montgomery were drafted by the New York Giants and Philadelphia Eagles, respectively, in the 1977 NFL draft. By that time, the Wildcats had a new head coach and were aiming for the program's second national championship.

Dewitt Jones was a fine player for the Wildcats in the early 1960s, and he went on to a very successful high school coaching career that saw him serve as an assistant at Abilene Cooper, Highland Park, Midland, and Midland Lee high schools before finally getting his chance to become a head coach. In five seasons as a head coach, he put together a sterling 44–11–2 record with a Class A state championship at Troup in 1973 and two zone titles at Class 3A Liberty Hill. In February 1976, he was hired to be the head coach at Class 4A Abilene High and led the Eagles to a 4–6 record that fall. He was as surprised as anyone when Bullington announced his resignation as the head coach after the 1976 ACU football season; but looking back, he thinks he knows the real reason.

"Well, he lost Wilbert Montgomery, Jim Reese, and Johnny Perkins after 1976 and that would make anyone want to resign," Jones said with a laugh more than forty years later. "We had just moved to Abilene early in 1976 to raise our family. I was the head coach at Abilene High, and after the season, Wally called and asked if I'd be interested in the job. I told him I'd be right over. We had a great coaching staff

Corliss Hudson

in place with Ted Sitton, Don Smith, Jerry Wilson, and Bob Strader, and I'd have been crazy to change that. I just walked in the door and told them to keep doing what they had been doing and we were going to be fine. I talked with Bear [Sitton] and told him I'd learn the offensive terminology and reserve the right to make some changes as I saw fit. We made a few in the running game and the short passing game that turned out to be beneficial, and then we turned everybody loose."

Jones and his coaching staff spent the spring evaluating what they had on hand to replace the departed Reese, Montgomery, and Perkins. What they found they had were stars-in-waiting in John Mayes, Kelly Kent, and Cle Montgomery. Alex Davis was also in the backfield, and a slew of other standouts were already in place. Defensively, middle linebacker Ray

Kelly Kent receives his award in recognition of being voted the Outstanding Offensive Player in ACU's 1977 NAIA Division I semifinal win over Wisconsin-Stevens Point at Shotwell Stadium.

Nunez—who led a defense that pitched four straight shutouts in 1976—returned, as did defensive back Chuck Sitton (a first-team All-American in 1977), defensive back Glenn Labhart, and linebacker Reuben Mason, who would end his career as the program's all-time leader in sacks, a mark he still holds forty years later.

"We didn't have a proven running back, although we had Kelly and Alex," Jones said. "But we had Kirby Jones at tight end and Cle at wide receiver, so I thought we could do some things with those two guys. John Mayes turned out to be as good as anyone could have ever hoped, especially for a guy without much experience. Then we brought in Tim Purnell to play opposite of Cle and we were ready to go offensively. Defensively

Named to the All-Century Wildcat team, Glenn Labhart was a feisty safety who recorded a 92-yard interception return against Northwestern Oklahoma, one of the longest scoring plays in school history.

we had a really good nucleus with Nunez, John Usrey, Labhart, Mike Lively, and Reuben Mason. I felt good about our defense, and based on what we saw from John Mayes in the spring, I thought we had a chance to be very competitive. From the beginning of the season, we talked about winning a national championship. We had to have a dream and a goal, and we couldn't be afraid to talk about it."

But before they could worry about winning a national championship, they had to dig themselves out of a rather large midseason hole. The Wildcats won their first four games of the season rather handily and had a 25–0 lead over three-time defending national champion Texas A&I in the fourth quarter in Kingsville before the bottom fell out on the Wildcats. The Javelinas rallied for 25 fourth-quarter points to earn a tie in a game that felt much more like a loss for the Wildcats. Then the next week, ACU dropped a 21–14 decision to Angelo State, and suddenly the Wildcats were 0–1–1 in Lone Star Conference play and on the verge of not even qualifying for the NAIA Division I playoffs.

"The Monday after the Angelo State loss was as tense an environment as I'd been around at ACU," Labhart said. "It was not a pleasant practice field or film room. But that's when everyone came together and really started gelling and getting focused and raising the intensity level. We knew what had happened, and we knew whatever it was couldn't happen again. We had to take the intensity up a couple

David Dillard

to wins over East Texas State, Stephen F. Austin, and Sam Houston State before he and the Wildcats ran into trouble at home against Southwest Texas State. ACU fell behind 20–6 at halftime, knowing a loss would put an end to their hopes for a national championship. "I got on the headset with Ted [Sitton], and he asked me what I wanted to do," Jones recalls. "I told him I was going to put John Mayes into the game, and we were going to win. And that's what happened. He put on one of the greatest passing performances I'd ever seen."

Mayes completed 21 of 40 passes for 403 yards and 2 scores in a little more than two quarters, rallying the Wildcats to a 36–30 victory. The next Saturday, they fell behind Howard Payne, 24–7, at halftime, but rallied for a 42–24 win, securing a spot in the NAIA playoffs. "We had a great will to win," Nunez said. "We dug ourselves a

Kelly Kent (left) and Greg Newman (right) celebrate ACU's 1977 Apple Bowl win in the Kingdome in Seattle, Washington.

◄◄

ACU President Dr. John C. Stevens (left) and Head Coach Dewitt Jones (right) celebrate on the field with the Wildcats after ACU beat Southwestern Oklahoma State to win the 1977 NAIA Division I national championship.

▼

of notches and we did. We didn't lose after that Angelo State game, and it's because we had a tremendous will to win and passion to play the game at a high level."

ACU reeled off five straight wins to end the regular season, doing so with backup quarterback David Hansen playing a key role after Mayes injured his throwing hand against Angelo State. Hansen led the team

David Dillard

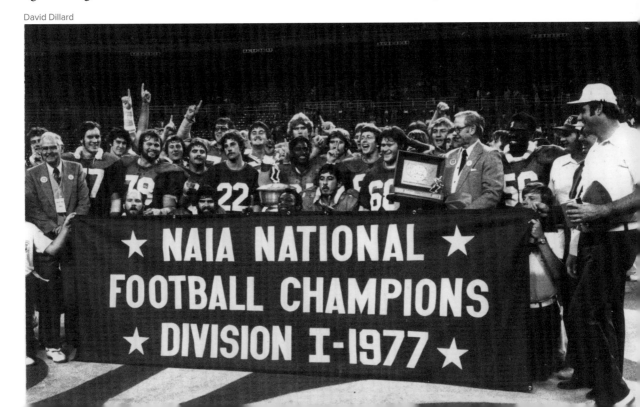

Corliss Hudson

hole to start the conference season, but we learned to take the next practice, play, and game and work hard. At the time, nobody had any inkling that we couldn't win the national championship. When we got into the playoffs, it was a done deal. We knew no one was going to beat us. I don't want that to sound cocky, but in our minds, the other teams were playing for second place."

Cocky or not, Nunez was right. ACU dominated Wisconsin-Stevens Point, 35–7, in a home semifinal game, and then flew to Seattle, Washington, to take on No. 1-ranked Southwestern Oklahoma State in the Apple Bowl. The Wildcats laid waste to the Bulldogs, winning the national championship with a 24–7 victory in the Seattle Kingdome. "When we got to Seattle, we were so jacked up and ready to play that Southwestern Oklahoma really had no chance," Labhart said. "Every player took their game up a notch. We were running around hitting people as hard as we'd ever hit anyone in our lives. We all rallied after that bad start to conference play because we had to rally. We watched more film. We practiced longer. We practiced harder. We lifted more weights. Everybody did what they needed to do to win that national championship."

Two national championships, two conference championships, three bowl wins, and forty-four victories in a five-year span speak volumes about ACU football from 1973 to 1976. But there was more to those teams than just what went on in the locker room or the weight room or on the field. Those teams have somehow managed to form a bond that continues to this day. Their ranks include doctors, lawyers, leaders of industry and finance, coaches, and teachers. They are some of the largest donors to ACU and ACU athletics, and they probably keep in touch with one another more than any other group of former players. And it doesn't matter if they played together or not. Players who might have last played in 1973 have a connection to 1977 championship players because they might have shared teammates. They certainly shared assistant coaches. And they all shared in the ACU experience. "I played for a state championship team at Odessa Permian High School in 1972, and we don't even stay as close as those 1970s teams from ACU," Nunez said. "Part of it is just ACU and the Christian atmosphere and how nobody is afraid or embarrassed to show love to one another."

Reese—the quarterback who was the backup on the 1973 championship team and then started from 1974 to 1976—said the tone for that era was set by the coaching staff that drove, pushed, prodded, cajoled, and loved on each player in the locker room. "It was those men who coached us who brought us together," he said. "Coach Bullington is the catalyst to the whole thing because he was the orchestra director. He's the one who put it all together. That coaching staff created an atmosphere

Paul White

David Dillard

1977 Team captains Ray Nunez (left) and John Usrey (right) were reunited in 2017 when the team celebrated its championship with a forty-year reunion.
◀◀

Head Coach Dewitt Jones (left) celebrates the Wildcats' 1977 national championship victory with Assistant Coach Jerry Wilson.
◀

and you get good recruits and you win a couple of championships and you create lasting memories and great friendships, and forty years later they continue. The perfect storm came together for our program, really from the late 1960s when Jim Lindsey showed up through the late 1970s. You don't know how lucky you are at the time you're going through it, but then you look back and reflect on the great experiences and you realize we had it pretty good for a while."

THE KICK HEARD 'ROUND THE WORLD

The sound. Not the kick itself, but the sound of it is what Ove Johansson's teammates and coaches remember about his field goal near the end of the first quarter of ACU's 17–0 win over then-East Texas State on October 16, 1976. ACU quarterback Jim Reese said it was unlike any sound he's heard before or since. Head Coach Wally Bullington said Johansson's foot hitting the ball that day sounded like the loud crack of a rifle on a cold November morning at the start of deer season in Texas. It was a sound that resonated throughout not only Shotwell Stadium that day, but also the world of college football. That's because it was the day that a little-known placekicker from Abilene Christian University put his stamp on the history of a game he'd only been playing for a few months. It was the day that Johansson made "The Kick Heard 'round the World."

To understand how improbable it is that Johansson would ever do anything of significance in the game of American football, one has to go back a few years and a few thousand miles to his hometown of Gothenburg, Sweden, where he grew up playing soccer and dabbling in music. When he was just fifteen, his father told him he needed to take his talents to the

Six weeks before his world-record kick, Johansson had never played in a football game.

United States, and, eventually, he would. At twenty, he joined the Swedish Navy, and a teammate on his crew's soccer team who had played professionally for the Dallas Tornadoes invited Johansson to join him in the Metroplex to help him begin an arena league. After a road game in Colorado, a coach from Davis & Elkins College recruited Johansson to play for the small Presbyterian school in West Virginia but with no guarantee of a scholarship. He returned to Texas to mull his options when a woman named April Bankes muddied the waters.

Johansson had noticed Bankes, who would later become April Johansson, in the stands at one of his games and asked her out on a date. After they had been dating for several months, Johansson's visa expired and he had to return to Sweden. While there, however, Johansson received both a visit from Bankes and a most welcome piece of mail from the Davis & Elkins coach, who offered Johansson a scholarship. Bankes informed him her family was moving to West Virginia so that her father, R. H. Bankes, could take a preaching job. Johansson played one season at Davis & Elkins, earning all-conference honors and helping the Senators reach the NAIA national championship game. But when Bankes had the opportunity to enroll at ACU in 1975, Johansson encouraged her to go and followed her to Abilene. He attended every ACU home football game in 1975, but never really watched the action on the field. He was there to see his future wife play the clarinet in the Big Purple Band at halftime and then go home.

"There was no sport for me in Abilene, plus I was starving to death," Johansson said. "I told April that I had to go back to Sweden. I just had no money. My mother would send me 18-karat-gold soccer ball necklaces that I would sell for $20 and that's what I would use to eat." Somehow Johansson endured, and during Christmas 1975, he was watching a televised football game and the commentators were talking about University of Arkansas placekicker Steve Little and his lengthy field goals. That planted a seed in Johansson's head, and a few months later that idea began to take hold. "In January 1976, I was walking near the football practice field and saw a guy kicking a football," Johansson said. "I asked for a couple of footballs and [former ACU professor] Dr. Dwain Hart gave me a couple and I started to kick. I was so poor I couldn't afford to buy a tee so I used the cap on a shaving can. People thought I was going to the nuthouse, but that's how it got started."

His future teammate, Greg Stirman, spotted him practicing one day and went to Bullington, who agreed to the tryout. "I had worked four or five months for this opportunity and I didn't want to blow it," Johansson said. "The first kick went all the way into the parking lot. From that point, I was on the team." And it wasn't long after his audition that Johansson put together a list of goals for what would be his only season of college football. "I was in the cafeteria one day, and I asked a guy about the longest field goal, and he told me 63 yards [by Tom Dempsey of the New Orleans Saints in 1970]," Johansson said. "I made a goals board, and I finally got Coach Bullington to take a look at it one day. I started to panic a bit when I started to talk to him, but I wanted him to know that I was serious about it." Johansson settled the role as the Wildcats' placekicker and was part of a team that started the season 2–2 before reeling off wins in its last seven games of the season to finish 9–2, defeating Harding, 22–12, in the NAIA Shrine Bowl in Pasadena, Texas.

The 1976 team might be the best team in ACU history to not win a conference championship. The squad was loaded with standouts like running back Wilbert Montgomery, linebacker Ray Nunez, wide receivers Cle Montgomery and Johnny Perkins, tight end Gary Stirman, quarterback Jim Reese, defensive linemen Chuck Lawson and Mike Lively, and defensive backs Chuck Sitton, Glenn Labhart, Mike Belew, and Harold Nutall. And while Montgomery, Reese, Perkins, and company garnered a lot of the headlines, it was the defense that did the heavy lifting late in the season, pitching four straight shutouts as the Wildcats finished 5–2 in the Lone Star Conference, qualifying for the bowl bid.

The first of those four straight shutouts came on October 16, 1976, when the Wildcats hosted longtime rival East Texas State (now Texas A&M-Commerce) for homecoming at Shotwell Stadium. The game was set to be a record-breaking day for Wilbert Montgomery, who needed to score just one touchdown to make him college football's all-time touchdown scoring king. No one inside or outside ACU football thought that it would be anything other than a crowning day for the greatest running back in Wildcat football history. No one, that is, except for one kid from Sweden. Bullington likes to tell the story of Johansson walking into his office the day before the game and repeating—while using his best Swedish/Texas/Alabama accent—what his kicker told him was going to happen in the next day's game. "Coach, on Saturday, Wilbert will set a national record for touchdowns in a career," Johansson told Bullington. "And if you give me the opportunity, I will kick a world record field goal." Because of course he would.

Through the first five games of the season, Johansson was 3 of 6 on field goals and 17 of 19 on PATs with a long field goal of 43 yards in a 21–16 loss to Southwest Texas State (now Texas State). Bullington didn't give his kicker's statement much thought after he left the office, but he did remember Johansson's leg speed and tucked that away in the back of his mind as he continued preparations for the next day's game. Never could he have imagined where that would lead.

—

The morning of Saturday, October 16, 1976, dawned partly cloudy and cool and with about a 15-mile-per-hour wind out of the north that would linger into the 2:00 P.M. kickoff time against the Lions. During pre-game warm-ups, Bullington took notice of his placekicker, who booted a couple of 70-yard field goals that were good with plenty of room to spare. He made a mental note of Johansson's range that day but didn't think much more about it. Johansson, however, knew he had that length in his leg that day. "I talked to a guy who played for East Texas at a seminar many years later, and he asked me if I remembered kicking two from 70 yards, and he asked if I saw what the East Texas players did," Johansson said. "He told me, 'We ripped our helmets off and told our coaches that if ACU gets to its own 40-yard line, they're going to kick a field goal.'"

ACU got the scoring started with 3:24 left in the first quarter when Cle Montgomery scored on an 11-yard touchdown pass from Reese, and Johansson's PAT gave the Wildcats a 7–0 lead on the Lions in front of about thirteen thousand fans at Shotwell. As with many home-coming contests across the country, the majority of the crowd was mingling with old classmates, renewing acquaintances with long-lost friends, and making postgame plans. The only thing that caught their attention during the first quarter was the news over the public-address system that Texas A&M sophomore kicker Tony Franklin had kicked a 64-yard field goal in College Station to give the Aggies a 6–0 lead over Baylor with 10:03 left in the second quarter. It was the first of two field goals from 60 yards that day for Franklin, who kicked a 65-yarder with 9:07 left in the third quarter. The fans didn't have much else to get excited about in the first quarter until the Wildcats, on their third possession of the quarter, stalled out at their own 48-yard line and Bullington had a notion that he'd give his Swedish import a chance to mark off one of the items on his goal sheet: kick a world-record field goal. ACU was moving toward the south end zone and Johansson would have the breeze behind him. He'd also be kicking off a 2-inch tee used by every kicker in college football, including Franklin and the other collegiate kicking giants of the day—Russell Erxleben of Texas and Steve Little of Arkansas.

Along with the inherent advantage that Johansson had with his powerful right leg, he'd also have a bit of a breeze behind him and a tee to help give the ball needed trajectory to quickly get in the air and over the outstretched arms of defenders. He also had a rule of the game working for him. In 1976, a field goal attempt was very much like a punt in that an attempt could be fielded and returned, or it could be downed. It could also be a touchback if it was downed in the end zone, bringing the ball out to the opponent's 20-yard line for the start of the drive. Bullington

Johansson earned his spot on the 1976 roster by impressing Head Coach Wally Bullington in a summer tryout, landing the starting spot before the season started.

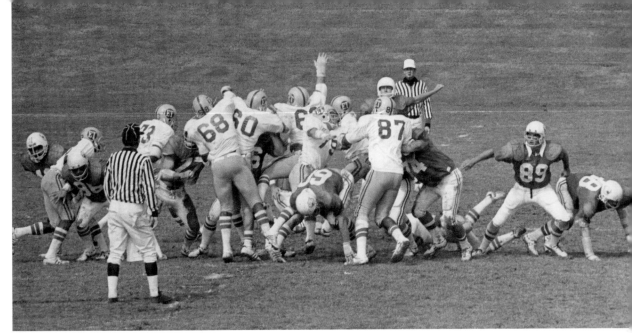

Milton Taylor

believed Johansson would at least force a touchback, meaning he really had nothing to lose with the long attempt. "In today's game where if you miss from there the other team gets the ball at the line of scrimmage, you'd never try a field goal of that distance," Bullington said. "But that day we had nothing to lose and a whole lot to win."

Most of the Wildcats on the sidelines figured they would be punting, including a couple of members of the punt team. "I was on the punt team, and I ran out on the field because I was thinking, 'We have to punt this,'" Labhart said. "Then I look behind me, and I see Ove out there and I'm thinking, 'What are you doing? Are you crazy thinking you're going to kick this thing?' Then I heard everybody yelling at me to get back to the sidelines, so I hustled my butt off the field." It was in those moments when Labhart was trying to figure out what was going on that Bullington turned to

Johansson and simply said, "Well, there it is. Go get it."

The words from his head coach shook Johansson a bit before he eventually ran onto the field, not exactly sure what was going on. "I was a little taken aback when he said that," Johansson said. "When I was running onto the field, my brain was going wild. I could barely spell the word 'football,' but I knew I had an opportunity to do something that no one has ever done in the history of the sport. To have the chance to do something special like that was unbelievable. In those 30, 45 seconds from

East Texas State's defenders attempt to block Johansson's 69-yard field goal attempt.

▲

Dean Low easily handles a bit of a high snap from Mark McCurley and places it for Johansson.

▼

sideline to kick, I just remember looking at [holder] Dean Low, [long snapper] Mark McCurley, and the rest of my teammates, and I thought about the opportunity we all had to do something special." McCurley wasn't a natural snapper, but because he was the center on the offensive line, the job basically fell into his lap. The most important snap of his life was a bit high but handled easily by Low, who put the ball down on ACU's own 41-yard line as Johansson began sweeping his right leg toward the ball with soccer-style motion. And then:

"That foot hit the ball, and I mean, it was as loud a crack as you've ever heard in your life," Bullington said. "It was like a deer rifle. The guys on our sideline were in awe that we'd even attempt a field goal from there. We had a little wind behind us, and I thought he'd have a chance to make it because he was fairly accurate." As the ball climbed higher and higher and traveled farther and farther, it became clear

that Bullington's gamble just might pay off. Just a few seconds after Johansson's right foot sent the ball toward the south goalpost, the ball cleared the bar with ease, creating bedlam in the stadium.

Sixty-nine yards.

With ease.

A world record.

As it became clear the field goal was good, Johansson whirled to his left to face the ACU sideline, which at the time was on the east side of the stadium. He stood ramrod straight with his arms in the air signaling "good," just as the officials under the goal post did the same. His teammates sprinted off the sideline and engulfed him, while the East Texas players trudged to their sideline in disbelief that the Wildcats had not only attempted a 69-yard field goal, but also that Johansson had made the dang thing. "I think East Texas State thought we were going to fake it, even though they'd seen him make a couple from 70 yards

Johansson is mobbed by his teammates on the field after his field goal clears the crossbar.

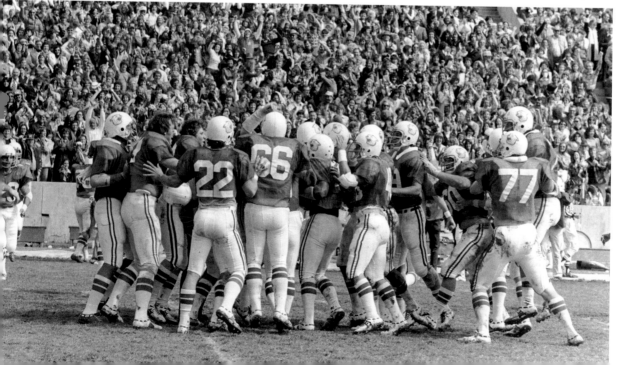

Milton Taylor

in pregame warm-ups," Bullington said. "They couldn't believe we were going to try it, and then they couldn't believe what they saw. I talked to [longtime East Texas State head coach] Ernest Hawkins after the game, and all he kept saying was, 'That was unbelievable. Just unbelievable.'"

But it had really happened, even though some of Johansson's teammates hadn't seen it. Because he was sprinting to get off the field before ACU was penalized for having too many men on the field, Labhart wasn't quite sure what was going on. "I had just gotten off the field and all of a sudden I turned and saw the kick, and I said, 'Oh [wow], we just kicked a field goal,'" he said. "Then I asked somebody how long it was because I couldn't believe we'd kick one from that far away. Amazing." Word quickly spread that a kicker from Abilene Christian had just topped Franklin's kick by five yards, and that left Bullington to answer postgame questions from reporters at major media outlets across the country. And in the days before the Internet or social media, that meant he was doing telephone interviews. And answering the same question: Why would you attempt a 69-yard field goal?

"A reporter from the *Philadelphia Inquirer* called and asked me why I'd try a 69-yarder, and I told him that he'd made two from 70 in pregame warm-ups so I figured 69 yards would be easy," Bullington said. "Of course, Ove always tells people the reason we kicked it is because we needed three points." Those three points

with 2:13 left in the first quarter gave ACU a 10–0 lead and had the crowd buzzing. The players on the field, however, had to quickly move past it because there was still a game to be played and won. "I didn't think very much about it being something really special at the time," McCurley said. "It was a field goal attempt. I did recognize it was a crazy long one, but I didn't understand *how* crazy long it was at the time. We were in the game and didn't have time to think about it, so it didn't really hit me until after the fact." And there was also a record to get for Montgomery, who had suddenly become overshadowed for about the only time in his wondrous ACU career.

With 3:40 left in the first half, Montgomery scored on a 1-yard run and Johansson added the PAT to give ACU a 17–0 lead and make Montgomery, at the time, the leading touchdown scorer in college football history with his 67th career TD, breaking the old record of 66 set by Walter Payton of Jackson State (Mississippi). Montgomery was glad to give up the spotlight for once and never begrudged

Gerald Ewing

On the 25th anniversary of his 69-yard field goal, a 53-year-old Johansson kicked a 53-yard field goal during the halftime of the Wildcats' Homecoming contest against Tarleton State.

Johansson for taking the spotlight away from him on a day that was supposed to celebrate the greatest touchdown-scorer in college football history. "I never thought about individual achievements," Montgomery said. "I thought the reason you played the game was for your school and your teammates. I just wanted to come out of the game with the win. There was a lot of excitement during pregame because we all watched him kick from 70 yards and make them with ease. We knew if we got close enough, we'd go for it. When the time came, we liked the odds, and because of the rules at the time, it was a win-win situation for us. I never felt overshadowed by the field goal. I honestly never knew anything about records or stats. I never thought about them. My only goal was to win games and that's what we did that day."

Johansson went on to lead the Lone Star Conference in scoring by a kicker in his only season of college football,

earning first-team all-conference honors. He injured his knee in the season-ending game against Harding—an opponent Reese called the "dirtiest" he played against during his ACU career—and spent a few years in the NFL bouncing around between the Philadelphia Eagles, Dallas Cowboys, and Houston Oilers. He eventually settled in Amarillo with April and their children, Annika and Stefan, and found success in corporate America. He traveled the country as a motivational speaker for audiences at schools, business conferences, and civic clubs. He talked about confidence and setting goals and following through on them. "That kick was not a fluke," he said in the Fall 2001 edition of *ACU Today*. "I didn't know much about American football, but I found out what the world-record field goal was, and I planned to break it. People who win and succeed, they plan it. It takes hard work, dedication, and commitment."

And the import from Sweden has shown plenty of that in the forty-plus years since he set a record that is still the longest field goal ever kicked in a game at any level of football. "I am the poster child for the American Dream," Johansson said. "When it comes to married life, children, business life, etc., I've been so blessed. I think of all of the kids who never had the chance to play college football or put on an NFL jersey, and here I am a kid from Sweden who didn't know anything football, and I had the chance to do those things. I have so much to be thankful for in this life."

GUNSLINGERS

A few years ago, Abilene Christian University commissioned a poster with illustrations drawn by art and design professor Jack Maxwell depicting each of the eight greatest quarterbacks in program history—Ted Sitton, Jim Lindsey, Clint Longley, Jim Reese, John Mayes, Loyal Proffitt, Rex Lamberti, and Billy Malone. The poster was completed before Mitchell Gale had even begun his career, one that ended with him breaking the ACU and Lone Star Conference record for passing yards in a career from 2009 to 2012. Or before John David Baker authored perhaps the greatest season by a quarterback in program history when he accounted for a school-record 40 touchdowns in 2013, ACU's first season as an independent Football Championship Subdivision (FCS) program. Or before Parker McKenzie passed for 3,084 yards—including 403 yards and 4 touchdowns on August 27, 2014, in his first career start, and ACU's first game as a member of the Southland Conference after more than forty years in

the LSC—in 2014. It could be argued that the poster needs to be redrawn with a few additions.

That's because the top ten career passers in ACU history by yardage—Gale, Malone, Lindsey, Lamberti, Proffitt, Mayes, Longley, Reese, Dallas Sealey, and McKenzie, in that order—threw for 78,756 yards (nearly forty-five miles) in their time in the Purple and White. Those ten also threw for a combined 589 touchdowns and led their teams to twenty-two winning seasons in their combined thirty seasons as the primary starting quarterback. They also led the Wildcats to four Lone Star Conference titles (1973, 1977, 2008, and 2010), two perfect regular season records (2008 and 2010), two NAIA Division I national championships (1973 and 1977), and six straight NCAA Division II playoff appearances (2006–2011). And in 1950, it was Sitton who quarterbacked the Singing Christians to the only undefeated, untied record in school history as the team finished 11–0 with a win over Gustavus

Adolphus in the Refrigerator Bowl. And to top it off, after Malone finished his four-year career with 12,012 career passing yards, Gale came along and topped him, finishing his four-year stint with 12,109 yards, helping ACU become just the fourth program in NCAA history—following Louisiana Tech, Houston, and Hawaii—to have back-to-back starting quarterbacks throw for at least 12,000 yards in a career.

In short, many schools claim the title of "Quarterback U," but few have the overall credentials to back it up. ACU, which was throwing the ball all over the yard when most programs in Texas were content to run the ball up the middle three times and then punt, is on the short list of programs that can actually prove their worth in being mentioned with the elite in the country when it comes to a history of great quarterback play. Here are the stories of the greatest gunslingers in ACU football history.

↝

It's pretty easy to tell when ACU went from a three-yards-and-a-cloud-of-dust running offense to a light-up-the-scoreboard passing attack. The line of demarcation is between the 1967 and 1968 seasons, when Wally Bullington took over as head coach and brought with him Ted Sitton as his offensive coordinator. In short order, they figured out the Wildcats no longer had the personnel to be a running team and had to immediately change their offensive personality. They couldn't line up and run over anyone, so they had to recruit

players who could fit a more finesse offensive style, a style that was pretty much foreign in the rough-and-tumble world of southern football. It was the great Darrell Royal who once said of the passing game, "Three things can happen, and two of them are bad," referring to incompletions and interceptions.

Bullington and Sitton, however, adopted a different philosophy. "We knew we had to throw the ball, and we were going to figure out the best way to do it and get about the business of winning football games," Bullington said. And in Sitton, Bullington had the perfect coach to teach the new offense.

↝

Ted Sitton wasn't a great passer in his days as the Wildcat quarterback in the early 1950s. What he was, however, was one of the finest people and finest coaches to ever

Though he was quarterback for the undefeated team of 1950, Ted Sitton's greatest impact came as a coach.

step foot on the ACU campus. Sitton grew up in Stamford, Texas, and played high school football for the Bulldogs before joining the team at Abilene Christian in 1949. He led the Wildcats in passing in 1950 and 1951, throwing for 482 yards and 5 touchdowns in the undefeated season of 1950 and 464 yards and 6 touchdowns in 1951. Those meager numbers belied his leadership on and off the field, and neither do they tell the story of the man who became known as "Bear."

He graduated from ACU in 1954 and went on to coach at Graham High School and Abilene High School before joining the ACU staff. He coached Abilene High to the 1961 state track and field championship. From 1968 to 1994—serving as offensive coordinator from 1968 to 1978, 1985 to 1986, and 1993 to 1994, and then head coach from 1979 to 1984—Sitton coached six quarterbacks who threw for at least 2,000 yards in fifteen different seasons. He coached the first ACU quarterback to throw for 3,000 yards in a season (3,167 by Clint Longley in 1973), and he helped four quarterbacks earn first-team all-conference honors and one earn first-team All-American honors. But he was more than a coach. He was also father to four children that he and his wife, Gloria, raised in a home not far from campus.

"It's hard for me to talk about my dad without talking about my mom," said Ted's son Gary, one of four Sitton siblings, along with the late Chuck Sitton, Cara Sue Sitton, and Jani Freeman. "We were very fortunate,

and I've realized this more and more the older I've gotten, to have had an unbelievable mom and dad in every way. They were involved in everything we were interested in doing, whether it had anything to do with football or not. At a young age, my interests became more and more directed at outdoor activities like hunting and fishing instead of football. As a result of that, my dad always made sure we had a place to hunt and fish. He loved to go do those things with me, and we always had a great time together. In his later years, I reversed that. Anytime we went whitetail deer hunting, I always made sure he had a spot to go hunting, and he loved going with us."

The Sittons' life was turned upside down, however, on November 9, 1980, when Chuck was killed in a house fire in the Abilene home of one of his former high school classmates, Scott Huddleston. The fire started about 2:00 A.M. in a room near where Chuck was sleeping. Fire officials reported that he was awakened by the fire, but passed out from the extreme heat and died of smoke inhalation. Ted Sitton was the ACU head coach at the time, and Chuck's death was a blow to the family, the team, the campus, and the Abilene community.

"I don't know how my parents dealt with that," Gary Sitton said. "I know they leaned heavily on their faith and the knowledge that there has to be an answer for it somewhere and we'll figure it out one of these days." Ted Sitton and his family were able to survive the loss of Chuck not only because of their faith, but because of the men Ted had surrounded himself with from an early age in Stamford and through his coaching career. "My dad surrounded himself, and as a result of that, we were always around good people who were his good friends, and Coach Bullington was certainly one of those men," Gary Sitton said. "But the one that stands out to me is Rip Ripley. I can remember Rip being at our house when my dad got his first coaching job in Graham. And guys like Rip and Mose McCook and Wally Bullington and Les Wheeler and a never-ending list of guys who surrounded us. My dad's best friend growing up in Stamford was Ray Hansen [who also starred on the 1950 team], who named one of his twin sons after my dad. When I think about my dad, he was a very loving, caring man who was passionate about his family and football."

That passion was on display in the spring before the 1968 season when Bullington and his offensive coordinator decided they needed a new offense. "We went down to Houston and looked at what the University of Houston was doing and then visited with [head coach] Sid Gillman of the San Diego Chargers," Bullington said. "It was after those visits that we knew we had to throw the football. It turned out to be a good decision because we could recruit quarterbacks and receivers who could thrive in that style of offense." Turned out they already had one on campus in a lanky, mop-haired blonde kid from Sweeny, Texas, who showed

up in Abilene and helped speed up the program's transformation. Jim Lindsey became the first quarterback in ACU history to earn first-team All-American honors (1970), and when his playing days were finished, he was the all-time leading passer in both ACU and Southland Conference history with 8,521 yards. That mark stood as ACU's career record until 2008, when it was broken by Malone and subsequently by Gale. "Ted was the best quarterbacks coach I've ever been around," said Bullington. "He didn't just teach fundamentals; he taught leadership qualities. He wanted those quarterbacks to be leaders off the field and in the classroom as much as on the field and in the huddle."

Aside from Lindsey and Longley, Sitton also tutored John Mayes (1974–1977), Loyal Proffitt (1981–1984), and Rex Lamberti (1993). In the sixteen years ACU was in the Lone Star Conference while Sitton coached at ACU, Wildcat quarterbacks led the league in passing ten times. "Coach Sitton believed in me and that made me want to live up to his expectations," Lamberti said. "He was such a godly example to anyone who knew him. He taught me so much about being a good person first, and a lot about being a quarterback."

One of those quarterbacks Sitton tutored said the confluence of elements came together at the right place at the right time for ACU to become one of the nation's top passing teams. "The scheme and the philosophy and the fit of the players at ACU was perfect, and that was because of Coach Bullington and Coach Sitton," Reese said. "We were ahead of our time. We weren't going to overpower people, but we could out-think them and we could throw the ball. The packages we had were similar to what they have now, but in a bit of a limited way. What we did, we did better than anyone at our level. The revolutionary thing was that we were going to throw because we wanted to, not because we had to and not because we were forced to, but because it was what we did. And we had the best teacher showing us how to do it."

The coolest guy in Abilene in the late 1960s and early 1970s was that lanky blonde kid from Sweeny, Texas, who would go on to shatter passing records and establish a reputation as one of the best collegiate quarterbacks of his generation. In covering ACU's October 24, 1970, game against Arkansas State, *Sports Illustrated* columnist Pat Putnam wrote of the ACU quarterback, "Lindsey is a God-fearing riverboat gambler." Lindsey, who died September 9, 1998, at the age of forty-nine, once told a crowd of high school students on the Abilene Christian campus, "I'm not a football player who just happens to be a Christian. I'm a Christian who just happens to be a football player." But make no mistake: he was a killer when he stepped between the white lines on a college football Saturday.

"Jim was a take-charge kind of a guy, and I didn't especially like someone trying to take charge of me," said former ACU wide receiver Ronnie Vinson, who played three years with Lindsey. "Having said that, we respected each other and he was a great friend and he taught me a lot. And on the field he was the boss. He was the field general, and if you didn't do what you were supposed to do, he'd kick you off the field. He demanded that respect and you gave it to him."

Lindsey was a three-time first-team All-Southland Conference quarterback, and at the end of the 1970 season, he was the most prolific passer in NCAA history.

And that flowed throughout the team, whether the player in question was on offense or defense—or a freshman running back who happened to enter the huddle at the wrong time. As the story goes, Dr. David Wallace, an ACU Bible professor, was a 170-pound freshman in 1968 who played running back and also returned kickoffs and punts for the Wildcats. When he finally appeared in the huddle for his first play from scrimmage early in a game a few weeks into the season, Lindsey looked over to the sideline, looked down to the turf, and kicked it in mock disgust before settling back into the huddle. "Well," he said with a laugh while looking at Wallace, "have we already given up?"

Ronnie Vinson had twelve 100-yard receiving games, which is tied for second all-time in ACU football history.

"It was a typical Jim move," Wallace recounted to *ACU Today* in the Winter 1999 issue. "He was such a congenial person. He really said it to put me at ease, to relieve some tension. He probably saw the fright in my eyes. He was an inspiring person, always positive and visionary. He always talked about how many games we could win. He was an ideal leader of people. The kind of person people liked to be around." Pat Holder recalled the story as well years later and still remembered the look on Wallace's face when Lindsey called him out. "Well, we called David 'Bambi,' and I was standing right next to him when Jim said that," Holder recalled. "I just patted him on the shoulder and told him he'd be OK. What else was I going to say?"

Vinson recounted Lindsey's work ethic that kept him and Holder on the field for post-practice workouts most every day. "Jim wanted to keep working out after practice ended," Vinson said. "And so we would stay and work out with him, running routes so that they were perfect by the time the game rolled around. I spent a lot of time lined up at receiver and looking over at Jim and then seeing Pat on the other side. Those were great times." But even in those workouts, Lindsey could be demanding. "I say with all fondness and respect for Jim, but he was never wrong," Vinson said. "He could be wrong, but in his mind, he was never wrong. But that's what you want in your leader. He didn't particularly like it when Pat or I would have pine tar on our fingers, and if he threw a bad pass it was our fault because of the pine tar. We came to accept that because in his mind, he never threw a bad pass.

Holder, who was a five foot eight receiver out of Azle, Texas, became Lindsey's best friend and years later spoke at his funeral. When Holder got to ACU in 1967, he thought he might have a chance to be the quarterback after playing for Azle for three seasons. At that time, ACU played a freshman schedule and both Lindsey and Holder were on the freshman team in 1967 before Lindsey was moved up to the varsity to be the backup, eventually becoming the starter. That gave Holder the chance to start at quarterback on the freshman team, although his coach wasn't very happy about it at the time.

"Coach Sitton came into the locker room and looked at me and he said, 'Well, Holder, we're not really happy about this, but we're going to have to start you at quarterback for this game against Texas-Arlington,'" Holder recalled with a laugh. "I said, 'Well, thank you.' I had a punt return for a touchdown and scored about three more touchdowns, threw for one, and we won pretty easily. Coach Bullington came up to me and asked if I'd like to go with the varsity the next week to Arkansas State and return punts, and I accepted that offer."

Still, though, Holder harbored ambitions of playing quarterback. "The coaches were struggling with whether they should go to a sprint-out or dropback passing game, and so I thought all along that I had a chance because I could throw it on the

Lindsey still ranks among the top ten quarterbacks in Southland conference history in offensive plays, total offense, passing yards, passing attempts, completions, and touchdowns.

run," he said. "We had a great battle for the starting job in the spring of 1968, and when we left for the summer, I was really pushing Jim for the starting spot. When we got back from the summer, I was second behind Jim, and Coach Bullington told me that he polled the coaching staff and it came back that they all preferred Jim to be the quarterback. I went in a few days later and I told Coach Bullington that I absolutely adore the wide receiver position and that my favorite player of all time was [former Arkansas All-American and Pro Football Hall of Fame receiver] Lance Alworth. I really didn't want to be a backup quarterback. I wanted to play and Coach Bullington said, 'OK, we've got several receivers hurt, so we'll give you a chance.'

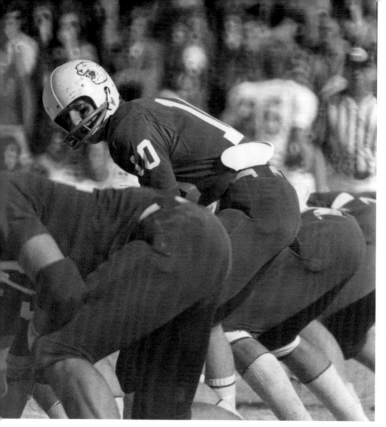

Lindsey was selected as the Southland Conference Player of the Decade for the 1960s.

out to Bullington, who almost fifty years after his first season with Lindsey still considers him the best quarterback in ACU football history.

"His leadership is the thing that sticks out the most," Bullington said. "The way the team rallied around that leadership. He could hold players accountable and they would accept it. Bob Oliver or somebody on the offensive line would miss a block, and he'd get on them and say, 'Hey, Bob, you can do better than that. We gotta have you.' And Jim could do that because his teammates knew that he was going to work as hard or harder than anybody else on the team. Plus, that kind of arm doesn't come along very often. I'd have to say he's still the best we've had here, although we've had plenty of great ones: Clint Longley, Jim Reese, John Mayes. You go right down the line to Billy Malone and Mitchell Gale. But Jim was special."

They gave me that chance, and I never gave it back.'"

Within the confines of a team or a locker room, one player losing a position battle to another can sometimes cause friction between those two teammates. That animosity never developed between Lindsey and Holder, mainly because neither of them allowed it to happen. "I was roommates with Tom Teague my sophomore year, and during that time, Jim and I became good friends, even during the time we were competing for the quarterback job," Holder said. "Jim just came to me one day and said, 'You're going to be my roommate next year,' which was fine, but I asked him who was going to tell Tom." Lindsey's take-charge attitude and ability to connect with teammates are two traits that stuck

And not just to his coaches or offensive teammates, but to defensive teammates who enjoyed the offensive show each week from the sidelines after having to defend him all week during practice. "Jim was everybody's friend and everybody liked him," said Jack Kiser, an All-American defensive tackle for the Wildcats in 1970 who later became an assistant coach and then head coach from 1996 to 1999, and one of Lindsey's closest friends. "Then when he started playing and lighting people up, we realized he could really do it. We didn't have a word for it then, but he had what we call today 'swagger.' I've heard this from guys on the offense, but his favorite phrase in the huddle was 'Hold 'em out and we'll score.' And he believed it. He believed that if he just had that one extra tick he could make a play and score."

That confidence carried through after his playing days. It carried him through a divorce and then a second marriage to Susan (Winkles) Lindsey, to whom he was married when he passed away in 1998. It carried him through business dealings, moves, and the ups and downs that life throws at everyone. The competitive nature also remained. "He was competitive until the day he passed away," Susan Lindsey said. "If we ever went to church in two cars, he would take shortcuts on the way home just to be able to say he had beaten me home. Everything was a competition to him. He'd go outside and play with our daughters [Lauri, Melissa, and Jamie], and I'd tell him that maybe he should let up on them, and he'd say, 'Well, I didn't come out here to lose.'" It was that competitive nature that led him to try to beat Holder back out on the running track after they each had knee surgery. And it was that competitive drive to jog, eat right, and keep himself in shape that led him to hardly miss a day of exercise.

Which is why it's still surprising that he passed away of a heart attack in September 1998 in his home after going for a jog. "He had an appointment scheduled for two weeks later that would have discovered his heart issue," Susan Lindsey said. "We just didn't make it. After he passed away, a lot of his old teammates and ACU guys started getting themselves checked out by doctors, so some good did come out of that."

Still, though, it's not the races home or the competitive nature that Susan still misses twenty years later. "I miss holding his hand during communion at church, which is what we always did," she said. "It's a lot of little things that add up over a period of time. It's a hurt that eventually lessens, but it's not going anywhere.

As a rookie in 1971, Lindsey helped the Calgary Stampeders win the Canadian Football League championship with a 14–11 win over the Toronto Argonauts.

He loved Christmas music, but he couldn't sing worth a flip. But he would always say, 'I can't wait to get to heaven because I know I'll be able to sing.'"

It was that confidence, that faith, that belief, that swagger that carried Jim Lindsey through his forty-nine years on earth. "There weren't many people like Jim Lindsey," said Kiser of the man who introduced him to the woman (the wondrous Kathy Patty) Kiser would eventually marry. "He was so confident and humble at the same time. He was so energetic and positive that anything you want to mention you would say, 'Well, Jim was the best at that.' It's been twenty years, and I'm still not over losing him."

Clint Longley was the first quarterback in ACU history to throw for more than 3,000 yards in a season when he threw for 3,167 yards in 1973.

The man who followed Lindsey as the Wildcats' starting quarterback was his polar opposite. While Lindsey would likely be found in church on Sunday morning after a game, Clint Longley was more likely to be found hunting rattlesnakes in a field. Or wrestling bears in an Abilene bar he once managed. Or perhaps playing guitar in a country band named Shade Tree. He is, without question, one of the two most enigmatic players in the history of ACU football, along with Abilene native Randall "Tex" Cobb. Contact with him by his coaches and teammates over the last forty-plus years has been very sporadic, and he doesn't seem like he wants to be found. It's thought that only one of his former teammates, tight end Greg Stirman, has made any kind of contact with him in at least the last twenty years. In a story written by Matt Mosley for the *Dallas Morning News* in 2005, Stirman said he called Longley's residence (believed to be in the North Padre Island area of Corpus Christi) and Clint actually answered the phone.

"Clint?" Stirman said anxiously.

"Who wants to know?" Longley snarled.

Stirman tried to convince Longley to attend a thirty-year reunion for the 1973 championship team, but Longley wasn't interested. "I think his whole dream was professional football," Stirman told Mosley. "But his dream collapsed, and he didn't have another one."

By now, his story is very familiar to those who follow both the ACU Wildcats and the Dallas Cowboys. He quarterbacked

ACU to the 1973 NAIA Division I national championship and then abruptly decided to enter the NFL's supplemental draft, where he was selected by the Cincinnati Bengals. He ended up being traded to Dallas for a fifth-round draft choice and entered the 1974 season as the backup to future NFL Hall of Famer Roger Staubach. He is best remembered for his performance in the 1974 Thanksgiving Day game against the Washington Redskins when he was forced onto the field when Staubach was knocked unconscious with Dallas trailing, 16–3, in the third quarter. He led three touchdown drives, the last one culminating with a 50-yard touchdown pass to Drew Pearson with less than 30 seconds to play to cap a dramatic 24–23 victory. Cowboys' offensive lineman Blaine Nye said after the game that Longley's effort that Thursday afternoon was "the triumph of the uncluttered mind."

He was on the Cowboys' roster in 1975 when they surprisingly reached Super Bowl X against Pittsburgh where they lost, 21–17, and he entered the 1976 season scheduled to once again back up Staubach. But he got into a fight with Staubach in the locker room before a practice (or, rather, the story goes that he sucker punched Staubach as he was putting on his shoulder pads) and immediately left camp. He was traded to San Diego and stayed with the Chargers for one season before being cut during their 1977 training camp. He spent part of the 1977 season with the Toronto Argonauts of the Canadian Football League before

One of Clint Longley's hobbies was hunting rattlesnakes, which he sometimes kept in a dorm room he shared with fellow quarterback Jim Reese.

signing with the St. Louis Cardinals of the NFL prior to the 1978 season. He didn't stick with the Cardinals, and after a tryout with the Hamilton Tiger-Cats of the CFL in 1980, he was out of professional football.

He then settled into the life of a recluse. Several of his old ACU coaches and teammates have tried to reach out to him over the years with little success. Bullington recalls going fishing with his quarterback when he was at ACU but said he hasn't heard from him in more than twenty-five years. "I've called him several times over the years, but nothing has ever come of it," Bullington said. "You're always disappointed when you lose contact with an ex-player. For whatever reason, he's never found the time to come to any of our reunions, although we've tried to invite him to all of them."

"We just lost him," Bullington told Mosley for the same *Dallas Morning News* article. "But we'd take him back in a heartbeat."

Longley's backup quarterback and roommate at ACU, Jim Reese, has seen virtually every Wildcat quarterback for the last fifty years and insists that Longley's 1973 campaign is still the best season ever authored by an ACU quarterback. That season, Longley completed 195 of 360 passes for 3,167 yards and 28 touchdowns in leading ACU to the national championship. His mark of 3,167 yards stood as the single-season school record until Billy Malone threw for 3,914 yards in 2007. "He just had a great season in 1973," Reese said. "I don't think he gets the credit he deserves for that season because of what Wilbert Montgomery accomplished. But in terms of making plays and results, in my mind it's still the best single season that an ACU quarterback has ever put together."

Watching Longley on the practice field or on game days was one thing. Living with him was another. Reese told Mosley that Longley and his constant sidekick, "Diamond Jim" Sullivan, captured rattlesnakes, which they kept in trash bags inside the dorm. Longley wore boots, a cowboy hat, cutoff jeans, and a holster with two .38 pistols when he was hunting. "Clint always answered the phone with 'This is the Magnificent Clint Longley,'" Reese

said. "Or he would say, 'This is the Purple Vindicator' or 'Longley's House of Pleasure.' He would call girls and say, 'This is Clint Longley, the quarterback at ACU, and I'd like to take you out one night.' And some of those girls would say, 'Yeah, that sounds good.' He's the most talented, most mystical, and craziest person I've ever known. But I'm convinced that 1973 was the greatest year that any ACU quarterback has ever had because no one could stop him. He was just incredible."

Like almost all of Longley's ACU teammates, Reese has not been in contact with Longley in several years. "I've talked to him one time since he left ACU, and that was about twenty years ago," Reese said. "I don't remember how we got together, but at the time, he was a recluse living in Corpus Christi, and I guess he still is. He never really recovered from everything that happened with the Cowboys. We need to keep reaching out to him and try to get him back. It would mean a lot to all of us who played with him."

Once Longley decided to move on, Reese eventually settled into the role as the Wildcats' starting quarterback. It seemed only natural that he would end up at ACU. After all, practically his entire family attended ACU before him, including his father, Leon, who starred as a basketball player and, like Jim, is a member of the ACU Sports Hall of Fame. Jim didn't carry the big arm that Lindsey and Longley did, and his physical attributes didn't compare to the quarterbacks who followed him. But perhaps no quarterback in ACU history ever got more out of his ability than Jim Reese did. And for one day in October 1976, no quarterback ever had a better day under center than Jim Reese did.

On October 16, 1976, ACU's Ove Johansson kicked a 69-yard field goal and Wilbert Montgomery scored his collegiate record 70th career touchdown. Johansson's world record still stands, and Montgomery's exploits earned him a spot in the College Football Hall of Fame in 1996. Two weeks later, playing against rival Angelo State in the mud and muck of Shotwell Stadium, Jim Reese had the single greatest passing day in ACU football history in a win over the Rams. A rainstorm in Abilene during the week leading up to the October 30, 1976, game against Angelo State had turned the natural grass surface at Shotwell Stadium into a mud pit. Perfect conditions, Bullington said, for the Wildcats' quarterback to crank up his throwing arm because, as he put it, "The receivers knew where they were going. The defensive backs didn't, and they were backpedaling, which made it even tougher." Of course.

"We played that day in five inches of mud between the 30s and from hashmark to hashmark because there was no turf in those days, and the Abilene High and Cooper games and then our games had worn out the grass in the middle of the field," Reese recalled. But that didn't stop the senior from Abilene from throwing

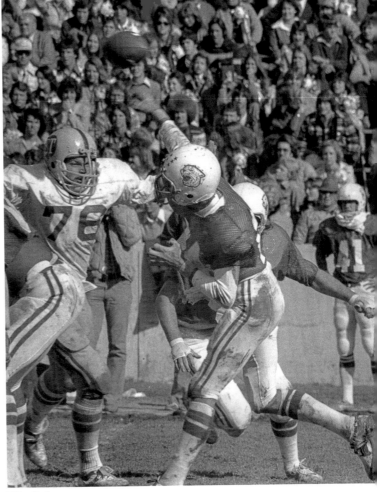

Milton Taylor

39 times and completing 26 of them for a still-standing ACU single-game record 564 yards.

Reese didn't have a Chamber of Commerce weather day to play in, but it didn't matter. He completed 9 passes for 202 yards to Greg Stirman and 4 more for 142 yards and 1 touchdown to silky smooth receiver Johnny Perkins, who would go on to be a second-round pick of the New York Giants in the 1977 NFL draft. "The first play, we ran a bootleg against the top-ranked defense in our division, and we were on. And when you're on, a good defense can't stop you. We went 59 yards on the first play

Jim Reese set the still-standing ACU record for passing yards in a game with 564 yards against Angelo State in 1976.

on a bootleg, and from that point, it was on. We weren't a West Coast offense. We were going for the jugular on every play. We threw the ball down the field, and we had Johnny Perkins, Greg Stirman, Cle Montgomery, and Wilbert Montgomery catching passes." Reese threw for 564 yards and 2 touchdowns in the 26–0 win, and he and most of the other starters exited the game at the start of the fourth quarter. "I try not to be selfish about it, but it would have been fun to see if we could have topped 700 yards that day," Reese said. "It wasn't fair to Angelo State that day because of who we had on the field, but it sure was a lot of fun."

Reese finished his career almost five weeks later when he directed a banged-up Wildcat squad to a 22–12 win over Harding in the Shrine Bowl in Pasadena, Texas. The Wildcats played without several key players that day, including Wilbert Montgomery, who was nursing a leg injury. But Reese threw for 311 yards and 1 touchdown in the game to earn Outstanding Offensive Player of the Game honors, capping a 9–2 season and sending the Wildcats into the off-season riding a wave of positive momentum. That momentum—despite the loss of Wilbert Montgomery, Reese, Perkins, Stirman, and other standouts from the 1976 squad—would carry over to 1977 when the Wildcats would win their second NAIA Division I national championship. It was also the final game in the career of Wally Bullington, who retired as

the head coach a few weeks after the game in South Texas.

Reese later coached in Central Texas and was the head baseball coach at both Cooper High and later Abilene High before returning to ACU in 2000 as the offensive coordinator, a position he held for five seasons. But it's those five years as a player that helped define the man he became. "Those five years I spent as a player are more than memories," said Reese, who is now in his second season as the girls' softball coach at Abilene High School. "It's how those memories changed you in mostly good and profound ways that makes you who you are now. They're the reason I have a wife named Jodi Reese, who put up with me my freshman year when I waited until three days before the football banquet to invite her to go with me because I was an idiot. And it's the reason we have three kids and nine grandchildren and a lot of great things in our life. Words can't express what ACU has done for me, so you just say 'thank you' and move on."

The next great passer in ACU history might well be the most underrated. That would seem to be difficult when all John Mayes did as the starting quarterback for the Wildcats from 1977 to 1979 was win twenty-five games, including one in the 1977 Apple Bowl that gave the Wildcats the NAIA Division I national championship. But he probably didn't have the flair for drama that some before him or after him had, and, outside of one season with Cle Montgomery (1977), he didn't have the weapons at receiver that some of the others at his position enjoyed during their tenures. But John Mayes was a winner, and he did that as well as any quarterback who has ever donned the Purple and White.

"Ted Sitton once told me that John might have been the most accurate passer he'd ever coached," said Dewitt Jones, who coached Mayes and the Wildcats from 1977 to 1978. "John was 'Cool Hand Luke' because absolutely nothing ever flustered him. He could be standing in the pocket with bodies flying around him and it looked like he might be going down, and all of a sudden the ball would come out and it would be on target and we'd keep moving the ball." Jones's faith and belief in Mayes was never more evident than on November 12, 1977, when the Wildcats were playing Southwest Texas State (now Texas State) at Shotwell Stadium. ACU had already tied one game—an infamous 25–25 tie with Texas A&I in Kingsville on October 9 in a game in which the Wildcats led 25–0—and then lost the next week to Angelo State, leaving them no room for error in a bid to reach the national playoffs.

The Wildcats, though, were playing without Mayes, who had broken the thumb on his right (throwing) hand, and were being led by freshman David Hansen, who led ACU to wins over East Texas State, Stephen F. Austin, and Sam Houston State. During that time, the

Corliss Hudson

John Mayes prepares to throw a pass against East Texas State in 1977 while being protected by his All-American tackle Greg Feasel.

Wildcats were clinging to the hope that somehow Texas A&I would lose a game to give them a chance at a playoff berth. And the Javelinas did, falling to East Texas State on November 5 to open the door for the Wildcats to win the Lone Star Conference championship and get to the playoffs. Mayes practiced some during the week but wasn't sure if he would play in the crucial contest against the Bobcats. When the Wildcats found themselves trailing 20–6 late in the second quarter, all questions about his availability were removed. Jones told offensive coordinator Ted Sitton that he wanted to put Mayes into the game to try to rally the Wildcats, which, of course, is exactly what happened. He threw for more than 400 yards in a little more than two quarters to pull out a win that the Wildcats absolutely had to have in their chase for a national championship.

"That game also told me a lot about him," Jones said of Mayes. "He was tough as a boot. And he threw the ball as well in that game as he ever did, probably because he knew he had to if we were going to win. He was a straight-up winner." In the defining performance of his ACU career, Mayes—broken thumb and all—completed 21 of 40 passes for 403 yards and 2 scores in a little more than two quarters, rallying the Wildcats to a 36–30 victory. "Coach Jones turned to me and just said, 'Mayes, warm up,'" Mayes recalled. "We scored the game-winner with about 45 seconds left. We had some things go right for us in that game, including on the game-winning

drive when I got tackled and fumbled and reached out and recovered the ball. If it had been one or two more inches from me, I wouldn't have been able to get it. But I did, and it was just one of those things that has to go right for you during the course of a championship season."

Even the win over Howard Payne in the regular season finale that clinched the Lone Star Conference title and a spot in the national playoffs wasn't easy as the Yellow Jackets jumped on top 24–7 at halftime, setting senior middle linebacker Ray Nunez off on everyone and everything in the halftime locker room. That caught the Wildcats' attention, and while the defense was throwing a second-half shutout, the offense put 35 points on the board to rally for a 42–24 win. The Wildcats crushed Wisconsin-Stevens Point two weeks later in the NAIA Division I semifinals in Abilene, winning 35–7 as the defense shut down Stevens Point quarterback Reed Giordana, who had thrown for almost 10,000 career yards in his career leading up to that game. But he managed just 169 yards against ACU's stout defense, and the Wildcats were on to the national championship game against No. 1-ranked Southwestern Oklahoma State.

"Our defense had a tremendous game against Stevens Point," Mayes said. "We threw the ball early and went down and scored and felt like we had control of the game from that point on. Their quarterback threw one deep down the middle early on, but Glenn Labhart knocked it away to save a touchdown. That was really the only time that they really threatened to score when it was still a game." The Wildcats rode the powerful legs of fullback Kelly Kent to wins over Stevens Point and the next Saturday against Southwestern Oklahoma State in the national championship game. He was named the Most Outstanding Offensive Player in both games, helping ACU to an 11–1–1 finish and the program's second national championship in five seasons. "It was a great feeling to do what we set out to do when the season started," Mayes said. "At some point, you look up and you realize you don't have anyone else to beat. People ask sometimes how it feels, and it really doesn't sink in at that point. It probably means more the older you get as you think back on it and realize that most people never even get a chance to play in a championship game. To play in it was one thing, but to win it was another."

The Wildcats went 7–3 in 1978, losing to eventual national champion Angelo State in San Angelo and also falling at Stephen F. Austin, their only two conference losses. In the off-season, the team not only lost its head coach when Jones decided to retire and enter private business in Abilene, it lost its fullback when Kent died in his sleep on February 7, 1979, just a few months before what would have been his senior season. Mayes also played with Chuck Sitton, ACU's All-American defensive back, who passed away tragically in a house fire on November 9, 1980. "Those two deaths were such tragic events," said Mayes, the

emotion still crackling in his voice almost forty years later. "I sat with Kelly the evening before he passed away, and we were about to go play intramural basketball. The next morning, Coach [Jerry] Wilson came into my dorm room pretty early and told me that Kelly wasn't with us anymore. I asked if he had left, and he told me that he had passed away during the night. It just took a lot out of us and the entire football program. It really makes you understand at that age that life really is a vapor."

And it makes you appreciate everyone who was part of the vapor. Even the most underrated of them.

———

Loyal Proffitt never planned on being an ACU Wildcat. As a senior at Abilene High in the fall of 1980, he was being recruited by Texas, Texas Tech, and Texas A&M and was planning on making one of those schools his home for the next four years. He talked briefly with then-ACU Assistant Coach Jim Breckenridge, but it was a mere formality for both the quarterback and coach. But something strange happened on the way to signing day. He went to Lubbock first and didn't care for Texas Tech. Then came a trip to College Station and a visit with the Aggies. Tom Wilson, the head coach at that time, offered him a scholarship during his visit, but Proffitt told him he was going to Austin the next week to visit with Head Coach Fred Akers and the Longhorns. He never heard back from Wilson and the scholarship offer to A&M was rescinded.

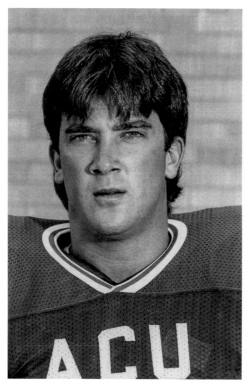

When he graduated, Abilene native Loyal Proffitt ranked second in ACU history in almost every career passing category.

Proffitt had a "horrible visit" at Texas for various reasons, and that led him to begin trying to reach Wilson at A&M and give his commitment to the Aggies. But the phone was never answered in College Station. When Proffitt finally did reach the coaches at A&M, he was told there were no more scholarships available. That's when Akers and the Longhorns came back into the picture, apologizing for the way he was treated on his visit and offering a scholarship. By that point, Proffitt had been talking to some Abilene High teammates and friends who were then at ACU about playing for the Wildcats, and what he heard intrigued him. "After talking to some of my friends, I told my parents I was going to

commit to ACU," he said. "Nobody really expected me to go to ACU after being recruited by some of those other schools. Lanny Dycus from Abilene Cooper had already committed to ACU, too, but he ended up transferring to Sam Houston State." More than forty years after his recruitment, Proffitt has no regrets in how it turned out. He started for the Wildcats for four seasons and is in the top ten in every career passing category in the record book.

"I certainly don't remember being disappointed that I was at ACU because that's not my personality," he said. "I've never regretted being at ACU. I met my wife there, and we have two beautiful grown children now, so how can you regret that?" The Wildcats certainly had no regrets in handing the starting job to Proffitt as a freshman as he led his team to an 8–2 campaign in 1981, one season after ACU had finished 2–8. "I honestly think we caught some people by surprise because we threw the ball so much," Proffitt said. "We had a nine-step dropback pass play, which you never see anymore. The play was called '72 Comeback' where the receiver would go down about 21 yards and come back to the outside, and we used to run that play all the time. Quentin Smith was the receiver that ran the route, and he and I worked on that over and over during the summer before my freshman season."

Proffitt would finish his career with more than 7,800 yards—including 2,306 as a freshman, which is still the most passing yards by a first-year player in program history—and his continuation of the legacy of great quarterback play at ACU is one of the things he still thinks back on. "I'm proud to have continued the quarterback tradition at ACU," he said. "Being in my hometown and in a smaller environment was great for my personality. Those relationships you build are things that you always take with you."

Rex Lamberti's ACU story is one of remarkable comeback. A freshman in 1984, he was one of the Wildcats' most highly touted quarterback recruits in several years after leading state powerhouse Odessa Permian to the Class 5A state quarterfinals in 1983. He saw some playing time in his freshman season (1984) when Proffitt was in his final season, but took over as the starter in 1985. He had a magical season, becoming the

first passer in Lone Star Conference and ACU history to pass for more than 3,000 yards in the regular season and leading ACU to a 5–4–2 record under the direction of first-year head coach John Payne. The next season was the best of his career, and he almost led the Wildcats to the NCAA Division II playoffs.

Lamberti threw for 2,790 yards and a school-record 32 touchdowns and had the Wildcats sitting at 7–1 overall going into the final two weeks of the season. But ACU lost at Texas A&M-Kingsville in the penultimate game of the season, and then lost a big second-half lead in the season finale against West Texas A&M and lost, 32–28, to lose an at-large bid to the Division II playoffs. On a team loaded with offensive playmakers, including Arthur Culpepper and Reggie McGowan—who combined for 24 touchdown receptions—the Wildcats

Wide receiver Arthur Culpepper played with two of the most prolific quarterbacks in ACU history, Loyal Proffitt and Rex Lamberti. Culpepper ended his career as ACU's all-time leader in receptions and touchdown receptions.

had, perhaps, their best team since the 1977 NAIA Division I national championship team. They rolled to a 28–7 lead late in the third quarter before the Buffs rallied to close the gap to 28–26 with 3:01 remaining. A quick, 57-second touchdown drive late in the fourth quarter stunned the Wildcats to give the Buffs their first Lone Star Conference crown. "That was tough because we were really good," Lamberti said. "We got a big lead and then we fumbled it a couple of times and things just kind of came unhinged on us pretty quickly. That was definitely the worst moment of my on-field career."

But the worst moment of his entire career was only about nine months away. The Wildcats were loaded in 1987 with All-American offensive lineman John Layfield—who would go on to win 24 world championships with World

Rex Lamberti was the Wildcats' quarterback from 1984–1986 and then returned in 1993 for his final season. At the end of the 1993 season, he was the Lone Star Conference and ACU leader in career touchdown passes.

Wrestling Entertainment while wrestling as "Bradshaw," "Hawk," and "JBL"—and other standouts like offensive lineman Richard Van Druten, running back Gerald Todd, wide receiver Roderick Johnson, defensive tackle Bill Clayton, defensive end John Buesing, and defensive back Theopolis Hickman. But in August 1987, Lamberti was suspended from school for disciplinary and academic reasons and missed the entire season. A mixture of quarterbacks played the position for the Wildcats with John Paul Webber leading the team in passing with 804 yards on the season, a significant drop in production from just one year before. "That was tough because I let myself down, but also a team that had counted on me for two seasons and was counting on me to help us win a national championship in 1987," Lamberti said. "It was a big hit to my ego, but it also helped me grow up and made me realize my choices didn't affect just me."

The Wildcats limped to a 5–6 finish, and Payne's first two seasons when his teams were 5–4–2 and 7–3 proved to be his only winning seasons as the Wildcats' head coach before he was dismissed following the 1990 season. ACU scuffled again in 1991 and 1992 under Ronnie Peacock, finishing 1–9 and 3–6 in his only two seasons at the helm of the program. Not long after the 1992 season, Peacock resigned and ACU Director of Athletics Cecil Eager set out to find a new head coach. He didn't have to look very far, hiring former defensive assistant coach Dr. Bob Strader, who brought back several familiar faces to ACU fans to coach the squad, including defensive coordinator Jack Kiser, who played for ACU in the early 1970s, and Mark Wilson, who was an All-American defensive back for the Wildcats and assistant coach in the 1980s.

ACU needed a quarterback going into the 1993 season, and Wilson had an idea. "Mark's been a big influence in my life; I consider him to be a brother," Lamberti said. "To this day, we still talk a couple of times a week, so when he called me one day in December 1992, I just thought he was calling to chat." That wasn't the purpose of the call, however. Wilson reminded Lamberti that he had one year of eligibility remaining, and he also told him that Ted Sitton had vowed to come out of retirement if Lamberti agreed to play his final season. "Mark told me they were trying to change the culture and that we were going to win some ballgames in 1993, and that got me interested," Lamberti said. "ACU hadn't been very successful in the time between 1987 and 1993, and I figured this was my opportunity to prove I could come back and overcome."

Lamberti had very little time to get himself enrolled in school, and then he had to start thinking about getting himself in physical shape to play. Fortunately, then as now, Lamberti had continued to throw. "Throwing the ball has never been a problem for me," Lamberti said. "I still throw even today. Getting back in the weight room was the most difficult part about it.

I let that go for six years. It took the full spring for my body to readjust to running and lifting every day. Then when I got back in the summer to start getting ready for the season, everything seemed to just be there. Mentally, I was probably better in 1993 than I was in 1986. In 1993, I was trying to get accustomed to new players and that was tough, but we did OK."

They did more than OK. The Wildcats finished 7–3 and went into the final game of the season at Texas A&M-Kingsville with a chance to tie for the conference championship. But a 26–10 loss to the Javelinas kept them from achieving that goal. Lamberti, though, was outstanding as he completed 156 of 304 passes for 2,052 yards and 28 touchdowns, with 34 catches for 426 yards and 8 touchdowns going to a transfer tight end by the name of Chris Thomsen, who would later go on to some acclaim as the Wildcats' head coach. Thomsen was part of a large group of players who transferred, including his former TCU teammate, offensive tackle Keith Wagner, receiver Angel Alvarez, and defensive end John Douglass, who set the single-season record with 24 sacks that season.

Lamberti's comeback and his success in 1993 garnered national headlines; but when the season ended, he quietly retreated into the background and, because of his age at the time (twenty-seven), never really

Gerald Ewing

Chris Thomsen played his final season of college football in 1993, earning All-American honors as a tight end.

In addition to being voted honorable mention All-Lone Star Conference, Colby Freeman received the Coaches' Purple and White Award in 2002 and 2003 for his spirit and leadership.

had a chance to play the game at a higher level. However, coming back to the game he loved—and to ACU where his greatest defeat had occurred when he was suspended from school—helped Lamberti heal. "It's a good thing I went back because I don't have to think about all of the 'what ifs' that some people have to think about," he said. "If I were fifty years old and only had those two years and had the regret of never going back to finish, it would have left a huge hole. But going back in 1993 helped heal all of that."

After Lamberti's improbable 1993 season, it would be a few years before the Wildcats had the kind of player under center who could take over a game. John Frank had a solid season in 1998, but concussions cut his career short. And Colby Freeman—Ted Sitton's grandson—was a terrific leader after transferring from Texas A&M and led ACU to a share of the Lone Star Conference South Division championship in 2002 before a shoulder injury cut short his 2003 season. But a new head coach showed up in 2005, although Thomsen was a familiar face having played at ACU in 1993 then serving as an assistant coach for the Wildcats from 1994 to 1999. He brought with him his brother-in-law, Ken Collums, as the offensive coordinator, and he would go on to call the plays for some of the best offenses not only in ACU history, but in the history of NCAA Division II football. First, though, they needed a quarterback to turn around a program that had enjoyed just seven winning seasons from 1985 to 2004.

The Wildcats didn't get one. They got two.

THE 12,000-YARD CLUB

Only four programs in college football history have had back-to-back starting quarterbacks each throw for more than 12,000 yards in a career, and ACU is one of them. The first three were Louisiana Tech with Tim Rattay and Luke Cown, followed by Hawaii with Timmy Chang and Cole Brennan, and then Houston with Kevin Kolb and Abilene native Case Keenum. Up until 2007, ACU's all-time leading passer was still Jim Lindsey, whose last snap came in 1970. But from 2005 to 2012, ACU had two quarterbacks who would change the landscape of college football on the Hill and forever etch their names atop the pantheon of great quarterbacks who have worn the Purple and White.

One of the most important meetings in recent ACU football history took place in a quiet office in the hallway of the Teague Special Events Center in December 2005 when then-offensive coordinator Ken Collums summoned his starting quarterback for a make-or-break conversation. The reason the meeting was necessary? Billy Malone's coaches weren't sure what they had in him after he turned in an up-and-down freshman season in 2005. The meeting, however, turned the tide of a program that had been mired in nearly twenty-five years of a mostly losing culture.

Malone showed up at ACU in the spring of 2005 after having committed to Texas and then signing with Tulane, spending a redshirt with the Green Wave. His career in Louisiana, however, was cut short

Gerald Ewing

Billy Malone led the Wildcats to a perfect 2008 regular season and ACU's first Lone Star Conference football title since 1977.

Malone looks for a receiver in the team's comeback win over Northwest Missouri State in the 2008 season opener.

when he was declared physically unfit to play because of a heart murmur. He enrolled at Texas A&M-Commerce with the intent of playing for the Lions before getting a call from a former high school coach who was then coaching wide receivers at ACU, telling him to get to Abilene because the Wildcats and new head coach Chris Thomsen needed a quarterback. So Malone packed up his life—and his then-wife, Ashley, and daughter Cydnie—and moved to Abilene. Not long after the move, he moved into the starting quarterback spot. It was easy to see why, too. He stood at six foot three and weighed about 240 pounds when he showed up and had a cannon attached to his right shoulder. But because he hadn't played in a couple of years, and also because he might be one of the most stubborn athletes to ever set foot on the ACU campus, he was inconsistent and immature in both his on-field and off-field decisions. All of that led to a 4–6 campaign and an off-season "Come to Jesus" meeting with Ken Collums, who would

go on to serve as the Wildcats' head coach from December 2011 through November 2016.

Malone had thrown for 1,749 yards and 14 touchdowns in 2005, but also threw 11 interceptions in just 230 attempts. And he was just as likely to throw for 132 yards (as he did in a loss to Eastern New Mexico) as he was to rack up 343 yards (as he did in a 42–24 loss to Southeastern Oklahoma State the week after the ENMU loss). He was inconsistent because, as Collums put it, "he wasn't putting in the work necessary to be the quarterback we needed him to be." And that's what led to the meeting between the two after the season.

"It's hard to have a relationship with somebody who doesn't do their part, and football-wise in 2005, Billy wasn't doing that," Collums said. "Anyone could see he had a ton of physical ability and that's what was so frustrating to all of us [the coaching staff]. He had the ability to do what we needed to do, but it wasn't coming out in a consistent way. I would tell him after practice almost every day that he wasn't giving us what we needed to have out of the quarterback position. He wasn't yet at a point in his life where he was ready to commit to what we had to have out of him." What they needed was a quarterback who would work hard during the week and be prepared to lead the Wildcats on Saturdays. What they were getting was a player who was just teasing them with the promise of his physical ability. And after that frustrating season, Collums sat down with his quarterback and laid it all on the line for him.

"I couldn't trust him in 2005, and we talked about that," Collums said of Malone. "He went into a shell offensively late in the season because that lack of trust between us ruined everything. If the quarterback and offensive coordinator don't have trust, you have absolutely nothing. We didn't have that trust in 2005, and it put the brakes on everything. Frankly, it scared me because if you don't have a quarterback, you're constantly starting over."

Shortly after the 2005 season ended, Collums sat Malone down and told him that if he didn't make big strides during the off-season, it might not work out for him at ACU. He was told he had to be committed to being better at everything: his faith, being a husband and father, being a student, and being a quarterback. Even more than ten years later, Malone remembers the meeting and the way he felt about the season. "I knew that neither Coach Thomsen nor Coach Collums were happy

with the way I had played that year, and I wasn't either," Malone said. "That season was the most humbling experience of my football life because I just wasn't doing things the right way. It wasn't an issue with athletic ability, but I had been away from the game for two years, and I just struggled."

Time away from the season has helped Malone understand that the results of the 2005 season—and his part in those results—were a reflection of the kind of player he was at the time. "I didn't help myself, though, because I didn't prepare myself during the week like they [Thomsen and Collums] wanted, and I didn't work the way they wanted, either," he said. "I didn't really have any idea about what it took to be a successful quarterback at this level, and I wasn't really listening when they would try to help me with that. But I think I had to go through all of that to get to where I ended up."

Shortly after that meeting, Malone made up his mind that he wanted to be at ACU and that he would become the quarterback that Thomsen and Collums needed to turn the football program

In this 2007 win at Tarleton State, Malone directs the Wildcats to a wild 70–63 win over the Texans.

Gerald Ewing

Malone leads ACU to an NCAA Division II playoff berth in 2007 by directing the Wildcats to a 42–41 comeback win in the regular-season finale at Midwestern State.

▶▶

around. "I knew I could tell them all day long that 2006 was going to be different," Malone said, "but they wouldn't believe it until they saw it. Coach Collums told me all the time that he didn't want me to talk about it; he wanted me to just do it. I knew that 2006 would be different for me and the entire team." And he knew it because he had also finally allowed himself to grow closer to the two men who were trying to groom him into a better man and quarterback. "Looking back, I didn't have a good relationship with either one of them because I didn't really know them," said Malone, who lives and works in the East Texas town of Clarksville these days. "Coach Thomsen always told me I had trust issues, and when he would say that, I would immediately tune him out. But you know what? He was right."

Collums began to notice a difference in the quarterback during spring practice leading up to the 2006 season. "Something

In Malone's final three seasons as quarterback, the Wildcats were 13–4 at Shotwell Stadium.

▼

Gerald Ewing

happened that spring," Collums said, "and everyone noticed. He turned it on and became the kind of player we always knew he could be. Number one, he was more committed and prepared and willing to lead. A successful quarterback has to have all three of those attributes. And number two, he showed up every day ready to work." Just as Malone believed, the Wildcats were much better in 2006, finishing 8–3 and earning the program's first berth in the NCAA Division II playoffs. Malone threw for more than 3,000 yards and 27 touchdowns to lead an offense that would only get better over the next two seasons with him under center. For three seasons, he was the triggerman for an offense that was one of the best at any level of college football.

From 2006 to 2008, the Wildcats played 36 games (winning 29 of them), won the LSC title in 2008, and reached the playoffs in all three seasons. Malone

Gerald Ewing

Gerald Ewing

When he graduated, Malone was the all-time leader in passing yards in Lone Star Conference and ACU history.

directed an offense that put up 18,563 yards of total offense in those 36 games (515.6 yards per game) and scored 1,657 points in those three seasons (46 points per game). He threw for 10,263 yards and 100 touchdowns in that time frame and finished his career with 12,012 yards and 114 career touchdown passes, which were ACU and LSC career records when his Wildcat career was complete. He also has the most 250-yard passing games in ACU history (30), and his 32 career wins as a starting quarterback is the best in program history by two over Mitchell Gale. And in those 36 games between 2006 and 2008, the Wildcats scored at least 50 points in 15 games and at least 40 points in another 13 games.

The game debut of Malone's new focus was on October 19, 2006, when he led 20th-ranked ACU to a 49–33 come-from-behind win over 4th-ranked West Texas A&M in Canyon and in front of a national television audience. Malone threw 6 touchdown passes that night to rally ACU from a 15–0 first-quarter deficit to the victory. In 2007, he helped ACU to a 45–27 road win over then-Southland Conference member Texas State, and an unforgettable 70–63 win at Tarleton State when he threw for 279 yards and 2 touchdowns and running back Bernard Scott—who would win the Harlon Hill Trophy in 2008 as the top Division II player in the country—ran for 283 yards and 6 touchdowns in one of the craziest regular-season games in ACU history. The 2007 season ended in heartbreak as the Wildcats lost a 49–20 fourth-quarter lead at Chadron State (Nebraska) and lost 76–73 in triple-overtime on a clear, cold day in northwest Nebraska. The Eagles outscored ACU 36–7 in the fourth quarter of a game that Malone still recalls as the one that cost the Wildcats a national championship. With receivers Jerale Badon—ACU's all-time

Gerald Ewing

leading receiver in catches (235) and yards (3,311)—and Johnny Knox going for more than 1,000 yards receiving, Scott rushing for 2,165 yards, and Malone throwing for 3,914, ACU became the first football program in NCAA history to have a 3,500-yard passer, a 2,500-yard rusher, and two 1,000-yard receivers in the same season.

The Wildcats continued to run roughshod over opponents in 2008 as the unstoppable trio of Malone, Scott, and Knox did pretty much whatever it wanted on Saturdays in the Lone Star Conference. Rally from two 14-point deficits on the road to beat traditional power Northwest Missouri State in the season-opener? Sure. Outscore your first five conference opponents by a combined 277–49? Why not? That season's defining moment came on

October 18 when the Wildcats went to Canyon to face their archnemesis West Texas A&M in what would be one of the all-time great games in ACU football history. Ranked No. 3 in the nation, ACU jumped all over the No. 4 Buffs, taking a 31–7 half-time lead behind Malone and Knox, who hooked up nine times for 189 yards and 2 scores in the first 30 minutes. WT cut the ACU lead to 10 twice in the second half, but Malone scored the biggest rushing touchdown of his life on fourth-and-goal from the 2-yard line on the first play of the fourth quarter when only he and Scott knew that the quarterback would keep the ball, pushing the ACU lead to 45–28. Then Scott—who left ACU as its all-time leading rusher (4,321 yards) and point scorer (438 points)—finished off the game with a

65-yard touchdown run with 5:54 to play to push ACU's lead to 52–35. Malone threw for 386 yards and 3 touchdowns in one of the biggest wins in program history.

"[WT head coach] Don Carthel on his TV show the Sunday night before we played them said that they were the one team that could knock ACU and they planned on doing it," Thomsen recalled. "That was very motivating for our players. The rivalry was at its peak at that point, and it was very heated. What got overshadowed by all of the offense was how well our defense played, especially in the first half. Our defense came out and punched them in the mouth, and that allowed our offense to really get rolling. From Aston Whiteside

to Bryson Lewis to Fred Thompson to Vantrise Studivant to Alex Harbison and Craig Harris, those guys were tremendous that night. Then Bernard put the game away in the second half. That was a great win and a really good night for our program."

But it only set the table for what was to come between the teams when they met in the second round of the playoffs on November 22, 2008, at Shotwell Stadium in Abilene. Nothing like it had ever been seen before in college football, and one would be hard-pressed to think anything like it will ever be seen again. On a beautiful late autumn Saturday afternoon, the Wildcats and Buffs combined for 161 points,

Wide receiver Johnny Knox torched the West Texas A&M defense with 10 catches, 203 yards, and 2 touchdowns in the Wildcats' win over West Texas A&M on October 18, 2008.

Gerald Ewing

Gerald Ewing

butting heads with the men who mentored and molded him into something he never knew he could become. "Before I became a Christian in September 2004, I wasn't a very self-controlled person," Malone said. "But I grew a lot as a Christian at ACU, and I'm still growing today. Everything that happened to me before I got to ACU—the abnormal heart and everything else—was a blessing in disguise. Tulane wasn't a very good place for me, and I'm very blessed and thankful that I ended up at ACU."

In one of the most remarkable games in college football history, Malone directed ACU's offense for 810 yards to a 93–68 NCAA Division II second-round playoff win over West Texas A&M.

▲

64 first downs, 553 rushing yards, 978 passing yards, 1,531 total offensive yards, and 21 touchdowns as ACU won an impossible-to-explain 93–68 contest against the Buffs. While WT quarterback Keith Null was setting LSC single-game records for passing yards (595) and touchdowns (7) and WT receiver Charly Martin was setting LSC single-game records for receiving yards (323) and receiving touchdowns (5), Scott was setting ACU, LSC, and NCAA playoff and single-game records for rushing touchdowns (6), total touchdowns (7), and points scored (42). All Malone did was direct the offense, completing 16 of 25 passes for 383 yards and 6 touchdowns. Incredibly, the Wildcats needed just a little more than 23 minutes of possession time and only 56 plays to rack up a school-record 810 yards of total offense and those 93 points. As Collums liked to say, the Wildcats' offense was "ginning pretty good." At the helm was the big kid who had grown into a man after spending his first season

Mitchell Gale shares a moment on the field with Rex Fleming, the son of Lance and Jill Fleming, before the Wildcats' win over West Alabama on November 3, 2012.

▶▶

Mitchell Gale spent the 2008 season as a redshirt, watching from the sidelines as Malone directed one of the top offensive units in college football. Then for the first five games of the 2009 season, he was one of three quarterbacks—along with Zach Stewart and Clark Harrell—who saw game action for the Wildcats, who

Jeremy Enlow

had one of the best defenses in the country, but had lost a slew of offensive playmakers off the record-setting 2008 team. Many observers, though, thought it was a matter of "when" not "if" Gale would take over as the starting quarterback. It happened a few days before ACU went to Ada, Oklahoma, to play East Central in a Lone Star Conference matchup when Thomsen told Gale he would get his first career start about 250 miles southeast of his hometown of Alva, Oklahoma. Standing on the field before the game, Malone, who that season served as a graduate assistant coach, was asked what he thought would happen in the game and how Gale would perform. "I think he's going to play great, and he'll start every game the rest of his career," Malone said succinctly.

It turned out Malone was exactly right on both counts as Gale threw for 300 yards and 3 touchdowns in a 43–6 win that pushed ACU to 6–0 on the season. The next week in San Angelo, Gale threw for 218 yards and 1 touchdown in a 38–14 win over Angelo State that elevated ACU to No. 1 in the nation, a first for the program at the NCAA Division II level. In a four-year career that saw Gale embody everything that Thomsen and Collums wanted in a quarterback—toughness, grit, belief, humility, leadership, and faith—the baby-faced kid with the "aw-shucks" grin and Oklahoma twang won over fans, young and old alike. And he won a lot of games, thirty of them to be exact, including an 11–0 regular-season mark in 2010, the best regular-season record in program history.

Billy Malone awaits the snap from center in a 2007 NCAA Division II playoff game at Chadron State.

Gerald Ewing

Gale is the all-time leading passer in ACU football history with 12,109 yards.

▶

Jeremy Enlow

He led the Wildcats to the playoffs in 2009 and 2010, and was part of the program's only road playoff win at the Division II level: a 24–21 win at Midwestern State on November 14, 2009. He also finished his career as the all-time leading passer in both LSC and ACU history with 12,109 yards to go along with 931 completions and 1,513 attempts, both of which are also LSC and ACU career records.

Ken Collums called plays as the offensive coordinator from 2005–2011 and then served as the head coach from 2012–2016.

▶ ▶

But Gale was always about more than wins and losses, and he was never about records. He was the embodiment of what Thomsen and Collums preached during their seven years together at ACU: the program would take players and mold them into better men, husbands, and Christians, and they would have humble hearts and play football at a high level. "I

vividly remember the first conversation I ever had with Coach Collums," Gale said, "because it was different than any other conversation I had with a coach during recruiting. Looking back, I think I recognized the authenticity in his voice and the genuine nature of what he was offering me because what he was offering me was something that I'd never been offered before. I don't even think we talked about a scholarship offer or anything until my official visit. He represented something different to me that matched my personality and matched what was going on in my life at the time. He came to the table with these conversation topics that my heart and mind were searching for at the time. It was so much bigger than football. I got off the phone and I knew immediately ACU was different."

And Gale was different as well. He fully embraced the culture that Thomsen and Collums had developed. "I don't know that I've ever coached a young man with a bigger heart than Mitchell Gale," said Collums, who was Gale's offensive coordinator from 2008 to 2010 and then his head

Jeremy Enlow

Jeremy Enlow

coach from 2011 to 2012. "He understands relationships and people, and that's a trait of a great leader. He could kick his teammates in the tail one minute and then pick them up and love on them the next. Leadership is knowing when you need to do which one, and Mitchell instinctively knew."

But the belief that Collums had in Gale didn't happen overnight. The first year they were together, Collums was calling plays for one of the most prolific offenses in the history of NCAA Division II football while Gale watched from the bench. But what Gale saw was the player he wanted to emulate: starting quarterback Billy Malone. "Billy wasn't a guy who talked a lot, and

that fit my personality as well," Gale said. "He earned respect by the way he carried himself on the field and in the locker room. He was like an old coal miner who took his lunch pail every day to the mine, worked his shift, did his job, and went home when the bell rang. I tried to be the guy who led by example and worked hard."

And as soon as the 2008 season ended, Gale set his sights on becoming the Wildcats' next great signal-caller. "I don't exactly lack confidence in myself, and I thought after Billy left that I was the best quarterback there," Gale said. "After the last game of the 2008 season [a 45–36 loss to Northwest Missouri State in the

Gale directs his receiving corps in a 2011 game at Eastern New Mexico.

Jeremy Enlow

Gale prepares to throw in a 2011 game against West Texas A&M.

▲

quarterfinals of the NCAA Division II playoffs], I thought the job was mine. Then when it wasn't, I would call home and talk to my parents [Steve, his high school head coach, and Pamela, his mother] and tell them that this wasn't what I signed up for and wanted to know what went into transferring."

But by the time the sixth game of that season came around, it was clear that Gale deserved his shot to be the starter. And he never let it go. "As soon as the 2009 season ended, I was back in Abilene pretty quickly after the Christmas break because I couldn't wait to start working out," Gale said. "I was going to do whatever it took. There was no rep I wouldn't take, no weight

After completing his career at ACU, Gale went on to play for the Argonauts, Tiger-Cats, and RoughRiders in the Canadian Football League.

▶▶

that was too heavy, no sprint that was too long. I knew the previous season's struggles happened because of the quarterback position. We had a so-so year [9–4 in the regular season, a No. 1 national ranking, a playoff trip, and the Wildcats' first

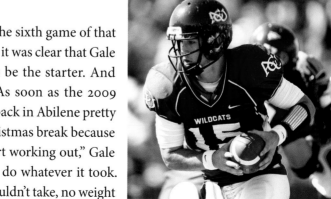

Jeremy Enlow

true road playoff win had become a so-so season at that point in the ACU program] and we had so-so quarterback play. We weren't going to have another season like that because I wasn't prepared. I was going to do everything I could mentally, physically, and spiritually to get myself ready for the 2010 season."

By the time the season rolled around, Gale was entrenched as the Wildcats' starting quarterback. Still, neither Thomsen nor Collums really knew what they had in Gale as the season-opener at Washburn (Kansas) approached. Collums even had a highlight video of Gale's best plays from 2009 put together and showed it to him before the game against the Ichabods. He didn't need to worry. Gale threw for 247 yards and 3 touchdowns in a 34–26 win that got the Wildcats started on a season that saw them go 10–0 in the regular season and win the program's final Lone Star Conference football title. Gale—who played with some of the best offensive players in ACU history in offensive tackles Tony Washington and Trevis Turner, running backs Darrell Cantu-Harkless, Daryl Richardson, and Charcandrick West, and wide receivers Taylor Gabriel, Edmond Gates, Kendrick Johnson, and Raymond Radway—ended up throwing for 3,595 yards and a single-season record 38 touchdown passes against just three interceptions.

"If I had known that Mitchell was going to be as good as what he became, I would have slept a lot better after Billy left," Collums said. "The thing with quarterbacks is that you never know what you have until the guy has to go out on the field and make decisions and plays under pressure. The thing Mitchell had, and so did Billy, was toughness. They were the two toughest guys on the field. Both of them could have played linebacker. They were fierce competitors who had a love for the game of football. If you've got those things, you've got a chance to excel as a quarterback."

Jeremy Enlow

Gale takes off running in the 2012 win over Tarleton State at AT&T Stadium.

And at the end of his ACU career, Gale excelled in more areas than any other quarterback. When he topped the 12,000-yard mark, he made ACU just the fourth program in NCAA football history—joining Hawaii, Louisiana Tech, and Houston—to have back-to-back four-year starting quarterbacks with more than 12,000 passing yards each. "That 12,000-yard mark meant a lot because of the way I knew Billy," Gale said. "I got to watch him play in 2008 and then he was a coach in 2009. He's like a brother to me because we both view things from the same perspective. To be mentioned in the same sentence as him was the coolest thing to me. That was an important number because I wanted the program to be able to boast about it. But it was a neat thing for me because of the journey that it took to get there. To be able to achieve that was a very special thing and something I still appreciate now."

Gale drops back to pass in the 2011 game against North Alabama, the Wildcats' first appearance at AT&T Stadium.

Jeremy Enlow

WILDCAT LEGENDS

ACU has played football for almost one hundred years, which means that somewhere in the neighborhood of five thousand men have worn the Purple and White since the first team in 1919. Of those, a good number were marginal players, hundreds were very good, and many were special. But only a few are program-changers—the kind of players people will look back on perhaps one hundred years from now and still recognize for their prowess on the field. Of those, thirty-four have been honored as first-team All-American players, and even more have earned some other All-American recognition. Only six players, however, are two-time All-American players: end Von Morgan (1953, 1954), wide receiver Johnny Perkins (1975, 1976), defensive back Danieal Manning (2004, 2005), offensive lineman Nathan Young (2006, 2007), running back Bernard Scott (2007, 2008), and offensive lineman

Tony Washington (2008, 2009). In 2008, Scott won the Harlon Hill Trophy as the top player in NCAA Division II football after finishing as the runner-up for the award in 2007. The Wildcats have also had other award winners at the Division II level in Sam Collins (2008 Gene Upshaw Award as the top lineman and 2008 Dave Rimington Award as the top center) and Matt Webber (2011 Rimington Award).

More than fifty have played in the National Football League, and many others have plied their trade in various other professional leagues, including the Canadian Football League. Only one Wildcat through 2017 has been part of a Super Bowl championship team as a player, and that was kick returner Cle Montgomery, who was part of the Los Angeles Raiders team that won Super Bowl XVIII in January 1984 in Tampa, Florida, with a 38–9 win over the Washington Redskins.

Von Morgan was a three-sport standout at ACU, earning first-team All-American honors in football in 1953, while also playing basketball and competing in track and field.

However, several other Wildcats have been part of teams that have played in the Super Bowl: quarterback Clint Longley (Dallas Cowboys, 1975), running back Wilbert Montgomery (Philadelphia Eagles, 1980), offensive lineman Dan Remsberg (Denver Broncos, 1987), Danieal Manning (Chicago Bears, 2006), and wide receiver Taylor Gabriel (Atlanta Falcons, 2016). Wilbert Montgomery has been part of three other Super Bowls as an assistant coach, winning titles with the St. Louis Rams (1999) and Baltimore Ravens (2012) and losing with the Rams in 2001.

Behind the scenes, 1978 ACU graduate and twelve-time Emmy Award-winning producer Lance Barrow has called all the programming shots for CBS Sports on four occasions: Super Bowl XLI in 2007 when

Manning was a rookie with the Bears; Super Bowl XLIV in January 2010 when New Orleans won the title while a record 106.5 million viewers watched; Super Bowl XLVII in New Orleans in February 2013 when Baltimore (with Wilbert Montgomery as the running backs coach) beat San Francisco; and for the final time in February 2016 when Peyton Manning won his final game, leading the Broncos to a win over Carolina in Super Bowl 50.

While many Wildcats have earned places in various halls of fames around the country, only one—running back Wilbert Montgomery—has found a spot in the College Football Hall of Fame. He was inducted in August 1996 in a class that also included NFL Hall of Famers Walter Payton (Jackson State), Terry Bradshaw (Louisiana Tech), and Buck Buchanan (Grambling), as well as Heisman Trophy winner Charles White (USC).

The ACU football record book is dotted with the great names in the program's history, dating all the way back to the all-decade team of the 1920s that included players like Leslie Cranfill, future head coach Vic Payne, Theo Powell, and Dalton Hill. In the 1930s, "Goober" Keyes, Thurmon "Tugboat" Jones, "Squib" Carruthers, future head coach Garvin Beauchamp, and Red Stromquist were the standouts, while in the 1940s, Buster Dixon, V. T. Smith, Dick "Moose" Stovall, Alton Green, E. J. "Tiny" Moore, and Pete Ragus starred. The 1950s were loaded with talent from Ted Sitton to Paul Goad,

Morgan was drafted by the Philadelphia Eagles in 1954, but declined the Eagles' offer, choosing instead to attend dental school.

Jimmy Hirth to Jerry Mullins, Bob Bailey to Sonny Cleere, future head coach Les Wheeler to another future head coach in Wally Bullington, Johnny Phillips to Ray Hansen, Stanely Staples to Von Morgan, and two-sport standout Robert McLeod to Don Smith.

In the 1960s, players like Jim Lindsey, Dennis Hagaman, Mike Love, Pat Holder, Bill Lockey, Ronnie Vinson, Wayne Walton, and Bob Keyes dominated on the offensive side of the ball, while Larry Cox, Mike Capshaw, Jack Kiser, Bernard "The Beast" Erickson, Tommy Young, and Buddy Rawls held down the defense. In the 1970s, ACU won two NAIA Division I national championships (1973 and 1977) with a slew of stars ranging from quarterbacks Clint Longley, Jim Reese, and John Mayes to receivers Johnny Perkins, Cle Montgomery, running backs Kelly Kent and Wilbert Montgomery to tight end Greg Stirman, and offensive linemen like Mike Layfield, Bob Harmon, Don Harrison, and Greg Feasel. Defensively, the standouts were Chip Martin, Mike Lively, Chuck Lawson, Ray Nunez, Reuben Mason, Chuck Sitton, Glenn Labhart, and Mike Belew.

The 1980s were an up-and-down period in program history featuring quarterbacks Loyal Proffitt and Rex Lamberti, running backs Anthony Thomas and Gerald Todd, receivers Arthur Culpepper, Quinton Smith, and Steve Thomas, and offensive linemen like John Layfield, Richard Van Druten, Dan Remsberg, Travis Wells, and

John Layfield, a first-team selection to ACU's All-Century Team as an offensive tackle, is celebrated worldwide as one of the stars of World Wrestling Entertainment (WWE). Layfield won 24 championships, including a reign as WWE champion.

Eddie DeShong. Defensively, Bill Clayton, Kenny Davidson, Richard Flores, Dan Niederhofer, Mike Funderburg, Steve Freeman, Mark Wilson, and Jasper Davis controlled opposing offenses.

In the 1990s, players like receivers Angel Alvarez and Sean Grady, tight end Chris Thomsen, offensive linemen Keith Wagner, Brandon Avants, and Victor Diaz starred on offense while the defense was led by Junior Filikitonga, James Henderson, Richard Wooten, Victor Randolph, Ryan Boozer, Jody Brown, Jay Jones, John Douglass, Victor Burke, Justin Lucas, and Keith Graham.

Offense took over in the twenty-first century as players like Billy Malone, Mitchell Gale, Bernard Scott, Daryl Richardson, Eric Polk, Darrell Cantu-Harkless,

In just two seasons, Knox established himself as one of the great wide receivers in program history. He became the all-time ACU leader in touchdown receptions and advanced to a career with the Chicago Bears.

Johnny Knox, Jerale Badon, Clyde Gates, Gabriel, Darian Hogg, Ben Gibbs, Justin Andrews, Chris Conklin, Emery Dudensing, and Kendrick Holloway helped their offenses put up huge numbers. They couldn't have done it without the help of offensive linemen like Britt Lively, Matt Raesner, Cody Savage, Nathan Young, Tony Washington, Sam Collins, Joseph Thompson, Royland Tubbs, Trevis Turner, Josh Perez, and Neil Tivis. Defensively, the likes of Clayton Farrell, Aston Whiteside, Donald Moore, Mike Jones, Marvin Jones, Ryan Boozer, Cody Stutts, Fred Thompson, Kevin Washington, Courtney Lane, Danieal Manning, Kendrick Walker, Eric Edwards, Mike Kern, Dawon Gentry, Darien Williams, Alex Harbison, Craig Harris, Tony Harp, Nick Richardson, Angel Lopez, Justin Stewart, Justin Stephens, and Sam Denmark made big play after big play. And placekickers Eben Nelson, Matt Adams, Morgan Lineberry, and Nik Grau rewrote the ACU record books during their terrific careers.

In 2005, just as ACU was beginning to celebrate the university's one-hundredth year, a panel of sports information directors and former head coaches selected the university's all-time team, and it included many of the names listed above. Beauchamp and Bullington were voted as the co-head coaches, while Wilbert Montgomery was voted the all-time offensive MVP and Bennett the all-time defensive MVP. Only one active player—Manning, who was entering his final season as a Wildcat—was selected to the team. The team was selected before many of the great players from the last fourteen years ever suited up for the Wildcats, which would make for an interesting vote if another team were to be selected sometime in the next five to ten years. More great players will suit up for the Wildcats in the next one hundred years, especially now that the Wildcats have moved to NCAA Division I athletics, and that will impact how future generations look back on the first all-century team. But nothing can lessen the impact that the players in the first near-one hundred years of ACU football have had on the program.

⁓

The Bennett name has been associated with Abilene Christian University since the 1920s when the gymnasium on the university's second campus was named after the Bennett family. Bennett Gym is where the Wildcats played basketball from the late 1920s until 1968 when Moody Coliseum opened its doors, leaving Bennett as the university's intramural home for almost fifty years. But in 2014, the gym was repurposed and renovated into space for the university's engineering students as part of the Vision in Action campaign, which saw the university renovate or build three new science facilities on campus as well as the new on-campus football and track and field/soccer stadiums. One of the people most excited to see the gym repurposed was Chip Bennett,

whose athletic legacy at ACU had nothing to do with the gym named for his family, but rather for the destruction he doled out on the football field from 1966 to 1968. "I'm very thankful the university has taken a building that had outlived its usefulness and turned it into something that will be a benefit to an entirely new generation of students," he said.

A walk-on from Denver City, Texas, Bennett didn't even play football at ACU as a freshman in 1965, instead joining the team as a nonscholarship player in spring 1966. It didn't take defensive assistant coach James Lyda very long to discover the Wildcats had a special player on their hands. "I started out at defensive end and Coach Lyda liked how I played," Bennett said. "He told some of the other coaches, 'This kid is making the tackle on this side

Chip Bennett still has 4 of the top 5 single-game tackle totals in ACU history, including the top two: 27 against Howard Payne and 26 against East Texas State, both in 1968.

Lloyd Jones

and on the next play he's making the tackle on the other side of the field.' He told them to put me at middle linebacker and just let me go to the ball." And for the next four seasons, that's exactly what he did. From 1966 to 1969, Bennett racked up 374 tackles, which was the school record when he left ACU and is currently fourth on the all-time list. Bennett also has the two best single-season tackle totals in program history (184 in 1968 and 161 in 1969), and he owns four of the five top single-game tackle totals in program history, with his 27-tackle game against Howard Payne in 1968 setting the standard. All of that begs the question of how a walk-on from West Texas becomes the all-time leading tackler in school history and the defensive MVP on the program's all-century team.

"I guess it was just my personality," Bennett said. "Whatever I do, I do it wide open. It doesn't make any difference what it is, I'm going do it with everything I've got and that's the way I played middle linebacker. I got a lot of that philosophy from watching a guy named Dean Bagley, who was a couple of years older than I was when I was playing at ACU. He just went for the ball with reckless abandon. You wanted to know where Dean was at all times because if you weren't watching for him, he was going to hurt you. I told myself that's how I wanted to play, and from that point on that's how I played. I went wide open on every play." Bennett was drafted in the third round of the 1970 NFL draft by the Cincinnati Bengals, and he played for three seasons before retiring. He had suffered knee injuries in each of his three seasons, and when he retired, he moved back to the family ranch in Yoakum County and ran it for forty-five years, before retiring with his wife, Darla, in Abilene.

Danieal Manning was an All-American safety in each of his three seasons at ACU and was the Chicago Bears' first pick in the 2006 NFL Draft. He started in the Super Bowl game against Indianapolis in 2007.

Gerald Ewing

Danieal Manning was never supposed to end up playing college football at ACU. A highly recruited defensive back at Corsicana High School, Manning signed with the University of Nebraska with the intent to become the next great Cornhusker defender. But Manning never played for the Cornhuskers for academic reasons and returned to Corsicana. He stayed away from football for one season (2001) before enrolling at ACU in January 2002, knowing he would have to sit out the 2002 season as well. "My best friend, Kendrick Walker—we called him Boss— was headed to ACU, and he told me that an assistant coach at ACU was going to call me about going to Abilene, and when he did, that was the first time I ever talked to Colby Carthel," Manning said. "We didn't talk about football, and that's what I liked about talking to Colby. He didn't recruit me more than three days, and I was on my way to Abilene."

Despite playing on a smaller stage at the NCAA Division II level, Manning found a home at ACU. A twelve-time All-American selection, Manning left school after his junior season in 2005 to enter the NFL draft. However, he did so with a thankful heart for what he found at ACU. "The journey I had to get to ACU was all a part of God's plan, and I know that now," he said. "I took some classes at Nebraska that were so big that you never got to know anyone. At ACU, I knew the professors and everyone on the campus cared about me. ACU was a real place, and its impact on my life can't be overstated. ACU changed my life." After declaring for the NFL draft in December 2005, the Chicago Bears made him their first selection in the 2006 NFL draft (second round, 42nd overall pick), and he became a stalwart in the Bears' secondary over the next five seasons. He started in the Super Bowl in his rookie season, and even though the Bears lost to the Indianapolis Colts, Manning's season was one of many highlights for the Bears in 2006. He went on to play for the

Cle Montgomery was an All-American wide receiver in 1977 and is still the only Wildcat to win a Super Bowl as a player, earning his ring as a kick return specialist with the 1983 Los Angeles Raiders.

Bears until 2010 and then played the final four seasons of his NFL career with the Houston Texans, whom he helped reach the playoffs in 2011 and 2012.

But seemingly none of those things mean more to Manning than the four years he spent in Abilene. So much so that in January 2017 he moved back to Abilene and re-enrolled at ACU to work on finishing his undergraduate degree. "I was baptized at University Church of Christ," Manning said. "I met my wife at ACU. Both of my boys were born in Abilene. A lot of great things happened in my life because of ACU."

———

Cle Montgomery was determined that he wasn't going to follow his brother's footsteps from Greenville, Mississippi, to Abilene, Texas. It didn't matter that Wilbert

More than forty years after he played his final game, Johnny Perkins still ranks fourth in receiving yards and eighth in touchdown catches in ACU history.

Montgomery had found tremendous success in a 1973 freshman season that ended with an NAIA Division I national championship. Cle thought he was bound for greener pastures. "I had no intention of going to Abilene," Cle Montgomery said. "We had made a pact to either go to Oklahoma or Nebraska because they were running the wishbone offense similar to what we ran in high school. Nebraska was after me because I could return kicks, play wide receiver, and carry the ball out of the backfield like Johnny Rodgers. And OU wanted me to do those things like Greg Pruitt had done." However, after the entire recruiting saga involving Wilbert Montgomery, ACU, Jackson State, and others, Cle's tune changed about where he would go to school. Actually, it was a two-week visit to Wilbert in Abilene during Christmas 1973 that helped seal the deal.

"Dick Felts came to Greenville and brought me and Wilbert back to Abilene for Christmas, and I fell in love with that family, and I ended up meeting Tommy Morris and his family and Rip Ripley and his family and many other great people," Cle said. "Racial tension in Mississippi in the early 1970s was running pretty high, but I met great people in Abilene. It got to a point where I thought Abilene might be where I needed to be, although I was still leaning toward OU. When I got back home from the Christmas break, I told my mother I was still going to go to Oklahoma. But she wanted me to go Abilene with Wilbert, and when she started crying, I

couldn't say no to her, and that's how I ended up at ACU."

It turned out to be a great decision for both parties. Cle Montgomery turned into one of the greatest offensive threats in program history. He is ninth all-time in all-purpose yards with 3,307, and his senior season in 1977 still ranks as one of the best ever by an ACU wide receiver. That year, he caught 57 passes for 1,168 yards and 10 touchdowns and was the last 1,000-yard receiver until Jerale Badon in 2007. As a freshman in 1974, he ran for 547 yards in place of his older brother, who fought through various leg injuries in his final three seasons as a Wildcat. He was an honorable mention All-American in 1977 and a two-time first-team all-Lone Star Conference selection. "The decision to go to ACU is one of the wisest I've ever made because I had the chance to meet great people who influenced my life," Cle said. "I had never been around people like the ones I met in Abilene who were willing to share, and they taught me a lot about life. Had I gone to OU or Nebraska, I know I wouldn't have become the person I've become."

When Johnny Perkins passed away in April 2007 at the relatively young age of fifty-four, his former quarterback at ACU couldn't talk enough about the man who rarely spoke much himself. "He was the perfect combination of personality, disposition, and friend," said former ACU quarterback Jim Reese. "I never found anything negative about Johnny Perkins, and that's hard to say about a lot of people." Perkins was a three-year letterman at ACU and played wide receiver for the New York Giants in the NFL for eight years. He is still the highest draft choice (32nd player overall) in ACU football history after his second-round selection by the Giants in the 1977 NFL draft.

Perkins finished his career in 1976, helping ACU to a 9–2 finish and a win over Harding University in the Shrine Bowl in Pasadena, Texas. Perkins—who teamed with fellow wide receiver Cle Montgomery and quarterback Jim Reese to form one of the most lethal passing games in college football—is 4th in ACU history in receiving yards (2,529 yards), 6th in touchdown catches (22), and 11th in receptions (116). "Johnny was the best wide receiver I'd ever seen when he got here," Reese said. "He was so much fun to throw the ball to because he caught absolutely everything. I never remember him dropping a ball. The other thing I remember about him is that we never got angry at each other, no matter what happened during a game."

Perkins joined the Wildcat football program in 1974 after one season at Ranger Junior College, where he played after a standout career at Granbury High School. Bullington echoed Reese's comments about Perkins' ability. "Johnny had great hands and outstanding speed," said Bullington. "The thing about Johnny was that he was deceptive because he was tall and smooth. The cornerbacks he faced

wouldn't give him the cushion he should have gotten, and he was able to run right by them. Consequently, we threw him the deep ball quite often, and more often than not he caught the ball." Perkins, in fact, had 5 touchdown catches of at least 71 yards in his All-American career, including catches of 88 yards against East Texas State in 1975, 84 yards against Cameron in 1976, and 82 yards against Texas A&I in 1975. The 88-yard catch against ETSU was part of a day that saw him catch 8 passes for 217 yards and 2 scores in a 20–18 loss to the Lions. That 217-yard day is still the fifth-best single-game total in ACU history. And it was in the biggest games, Reese recalled, where Perkins was at his best.

In a 1975 game against rival Howard Payne, Perkins caught 10 passes for 185 yards and 3 scores. And on October 23,

Johnny Perkins was selected thirty-second overall (second round) by the New York Giants in the 1977 NFL Draft, the highest draft choice in ACU history.

Lloyd Jones

1976, when Reese threw for a still-standing ACU record 564 yards against Angelo State, Perkins caught 5 passes for 147 yards and 1 score. "Nothing ever rattled him," Reese said. "We could be in the middle of a real tight game, and he would have the same attitude as he had in practice. He was just such a happy-go-lucky guy in everyday life, and that carried over to the field. I think that kept us all loose." And that's what Bullington remembers most about Perkins. "He just made the locker room better," Bullington said. "He got along so well with his teammates, and he was a great team player. The things he did on the field put the spotlight on him, but he never put those things above the team and the accomplishments of the team."

Johnny Perkins was a star player for the Wildcats from 1974 to 1976, earning first-team All-American honors in 1975 and 1976.

Milton Taylor

Aside from the Montgomery brothers, one of the greatest sibling duos to ever play for the Wildcats were the Feasels, Greg and Grant, both of whom were All-American offensive linemen and both of whom went on to play in the NFL.

Greg came to Abilene first, by way of Barstow, California, where he had never played high school football. However, after two junior college seasons, he was recruited to ACU by Bullington and Don Smith. "When I think about Coach Bullington, I think of a father figure, but also a man with great intensity," Greg Feasel said. "Don Smith had great enthusiasm, and Ted Sitton was an offensive mastermind. I also played for [offensive line coach] Don Harrison, and he was a great student of the game. He helped me to understand it wasn't just about ability, but other facets of your game took you to the next level."

Greg became one of the most dominant offensive linemen in ACU football history, earning unanimous first-team all-Lone Star Conference selection in 1979, the same season he was NAIA all-District IV and honorable mention Associated Press college division All-American. He was also a team captain in 1979. Following his senior season, he was selected to play in the annual Blue-Gray All-Star game. As a sophomore in 1977, he played on the NAIA Division I national championship team. Greg played professionally from 1983 to 1987, and his career covered stints with the Green Bay Packers and San Diego Chargers of the NFL

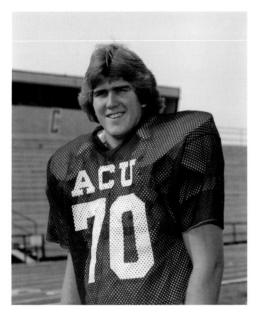

Colts in 1983 and started for Seattle in the 1987 AFC playoffs, and also competed for the team in the 1988 playoffs. He played every offensive snap of the 1989 season for the Seahawks, proving to be one of the most durable players in the league.

As a Wildcat, Grant was chosen first-team All-American in 1982 by both the Associated Press and American Football Coaches Association. He was also voted second-team Academic All-American, team captain, All-Lone Star Conference, Academic All-Conference, LSC Offensive Lineman of the Year, and was a member of the All-LSC and All-ACU teams for the decade of the 1980s. He became all of that from a skinny kid who showed up at ACU barely weighing 200 pounds. "He was tall and lanky when he showed up at ACU," Bullington recalled. "But he worked hard in the weight room and became, in my opinion, maybe the best offensive lineman we've ever had here."

Upon his retirement from the NFL following the 1993 season, Grant, along with his brother Greg, spoke of their abiding appreciation for ACU at a retirement dinner for Grant in the Dallas-Fort Worth Metroplex. "Grant and I are what we are today because of what we learned from the people in this room," Greg said to a room full of ACU supporters at the Fort Worth Club on August 23, 1994. "We learned to exceed standards, see past problems for solutions, and to have respect for God's creation. Grant and I were blessed to have attended and played at ACU." Grant

Greg Feasel was an NAIA first-team All-American in 1979 and played professionally from 1983 to 1987. He currently serves as executive vice president and chief operating officer for the MLB's Colorado Rockies Baseball Club.

and the Denver Gold in the United States Football League. After his football career, he moved into marketing and sales, eventually working his way up to Coca-Cola's division director of sales and marketing for the state of Colorado. He joined the Colorado Rockies' organization in January 1996 as the vice president of sales and marketing, and is now the team's executive vice president and chief operating officer. "ACU was a great training ground for me," Greg said. "The class sizes were such that you knew the teachers were invested in your life and they would straighten you out if you weren't doing the right things."

Grant Feasel played at ACU from 1979 to 1982 and then went on to an eleven-year career in the NFL with the Baltimore Colts (1983), Minnesota Vikings (1984–1986), and Seattle Seahawks (1987–1993). He was a sixth-round draft choice of the

One of the greatest athletes in ACU history, Robert McLeod was an All-American receiver in football, and in basketball he was an NCAA All-Southwest Region selection who set the ACU career scoring record.

have since been broken as the passing game became more and more a part of ACU's offensive focus. McLeod was drafted by the Chicago Bears of the NFL and the Houston Oilers of the AFL in 1961, and he chose the Oilers, helping lead them to an AFL championship in his rookie season. McLeod would go on to play six seasons with the Oilers, retiring after the 1966 season. Despite all his football accolades and his career in the sport at the professional level, McLeod told the *Abilene Reporter-News* in 1992 that basketball was his favorite sport. He was a dominant player on the floor for the Wildcats, rewriting the ACU record book by the time his career came to an end after the 1960–1961 season. His records at the time included the most points (43) and rebounds (23) in one game, best season rebound average (13.6), career points (1,607), and rebounds (1,237). Through the 2017–2018 season, he is still ACU's all-time leading rebounder and 6th-leading scorer, almost sixty years after he played his last game.

echoed those sentiments when it was his turn to speak. "I'm nobody special," said the longtime NFL offensive lineman, who passed away July 15, 2012. "I can give you a list of names as long as my arm of people who have been helped by ACU. It's an unbelievable place."

One of the greatest two-sport stars in ACU athletics history was Robert McLeod, who dominated on both the basketball floor and the football field. A 1989 inductee into the ACU Sports Hall of Fame, McLeod was an All-American wide receiver who set the ACU career record for receptions, and in basketball he was NCAA All-Southwest Region and set the ACU career scoring record that has since been broken.

While competing from 1957 to 1960 in football for ACU, he set records for receptions in a game, season, and career, as well as career receiving yards and touchdown receptions in a game. All those records

ACU wasn't his first choice of college after he completed a stellar multisport career at Merkel High School. He had basketball offers from Kansas, Marquette, and the University of Texas. He signed with Texas, but shortly after arriving on the Forty Acres, he was informed by football coach Darrell Royal that he could play both football and basketball his first year, but then would have to choose one or the other. That didn't sound like something McLeod could abide by, and he left Austin for Abilene. "I made my decision right then," McLeod told the *Reporter-News*. "I packed my bags and went to ACU where I knew I could play both sports." That turned out to be a fortuitous decision for both McLeod and ACU. During his junior season at ACU, he finished his football season on a Saturday, worked out once with the basketball team, and then left with the squad for a three-game swing through Middle America. Three days after the football season ended, he scored 22 points against Texas Wesleyan and also played well against both St. Louis and Marquette.

Multisport athletes have always been a part of ACU athletics history—Theo Powell got it started, and it goes all the way through several who competed in football and track and field or football and basketball or track and field and basketball—but not many, if any, compare to McLeod's accomplishments during his one-of-a-kind ACU career.

Over the years, ACU has found great players all over the country. From the prairies of West Texas to the big city of Dallas, they've come to Abilene. From California and Colorado, from Austin to San Antonio to Houston, they've made their way to the Big Country. But in the late 2000s, no city in America had more of an impact on the Wildcats' success than did Vernon, Texas, a small city of a little more than ten thousand residents near the Texas-Oklahoma state line.

It really started in 1993 when TCU graduate transfer Chris Thomsen, who called Vernon home, showed up to play tight end with his final year of eligibility and then hung around for a few years as first a graduate assistant, assistant coach, and then offensive coordinator. In those later years, he brought to ACU his brother-in-law and fellow Vernon native, Ken Collums, to work with quarterbacks. When Thomsen returned to ACU as the head coach in 2005, he brought Collums back with him as the offensive coordinator of some of the most dynamic offenses in NCAA Division II history, and certainly in ACU history. After Thomsen left to become a Football Bowl Subdivision (FBS) assistant coach following the 2011 season, Collums served as the ACU head coach from 2012 to 2016. Those two men recruited hundreds of players during their years at ACU, but few made as big an impact as did four players—all related—that they plucked from Vernon. The first was running back Bernard Scott, who arrived in

In just two seasons, Bernard Scott established himself as one of the great players in ACU football history, rushing for a school-record 4,321 yards and becoming the Wildcats' all-time leader in all-purpose yards.

Gerald Ewing

Abilene in the summer of 2007 after one season at Central Arkansas (2004) and another at Blinn College (2006).

All Scott did in two seasons at ACU was become the program's all-time leader in rushing yards (4,321), all-purpose yards (5,712), and points scored (438), and finish second in total touchdowns (73) behind Wilbert Montgomery (76). He's also ACU's all-time leader in 100-yard rushing games with 23 in 24 career games, and as noted earlier, he set the school record for all-purpose yards in a game with 409 in a remarkable performance in ACU's 52–35 win at West Texas A&M on October 18, 2008. And Scott's performance in ACU's 93–68 playoff win over the Buffs on November 22, 2008—7 total touchdowns and 292 rushing yards—is the stuff

of legend. But Scott wasn't a slam dunk to attend ACU, despite the fact that his relationship with Thomsen went all the way back to the days when Thomsen was friends with his father, Daryl Richardson Sr., and his uncle, Floyd Richardson.

ACU had two running backs, Taber Minner and Chauncy Campbell, who had put together fine 2006 seasons, and coming out of Blinn in 2006 after his lone junior college season, Scott questioned whether he would have a chance to break into the ACU starting lineup. The answer was yes, and he never left it. "After he left Central Arkansas [following the 2004] season, he sat out the 2005 season and went home to Vernon," Thomsen said. "I saw him during the Christmas break when I went home and asked him if he still wanted to play and

Bernard Scott won the Harlon Hill Trophy in 2008 as the top player in NCAA Division II football, one year after finishing as the runner-up for the award.

Gerald Ewing

he said he did. We placed him at Blinn and he had a great year, leading the nation in rushing and winning the national championship. But we had to sell him on the idea of coming to ACU. Thankfully he did, because he turned out to be the playmaker at running back that we needed."

When Scott showed up in the summer of 2007, he brought with him his cousin, who had enrolled at ACU with the intent of playing basketball. But Clyde Gates didn't have what the Wildcat coaches were looking for on the basketball court, so he decided on a whim to try out for football. "I really thought we'd give him some pads and let him go out there and he'd quit after the first week," Thomsen said. "I wasn't going to let him play, but Bernard talked me into it. It didn't take very long to see that we had something special. You can't coach that kind of speed, and we had to figure out ways to get him involved in the offense." Gates was more of a threat on jet sweeps and reverses his first couple of seasons while he honed his craft as a wide receiver. But he ended up posting a school-record thirteen 100-yard receiving games, and he's now fourth in career receptions (158), third in career receiving yards (2,885), and tied for second in career touchdown receptions (27). His senior season of 2010 when he caught 66 passes for 1,182 yards and 13 touchdowns is one of the finest in ACU history.

Also making the trek from Vernon to ACU in the summer of 2007 was a two-way player from Vernon whom Thomsen wasn't even sure about offering a scholarship to until late in the recruiting process. Aston Whiteside was a starter at both fullback and defensive end at Vernon, but whenever Thomsen would see him play, he had expended so much energy on the offensive side of the ball that he wasn't nearly as impressive on the defensive side. But Jason Johns, the ACU defensive coordinator at that time, kept hounding Thomsen, telling him about the competitor that Whiteside was and that he would be a player for the Wildcats. Good thing for Thomsen that he listened to Johns. The Wildcats wound up signing Whiteside and, after redshirting in 2007, he went on to become Lone Star Conference Freshman of the Year (2008) and a three-time league Defensive Lineman of the Year (2008, 2010, 2011). "One of the things that sold me on finally giving him a full scholarship was that the people at Vernon High School—administrators and teachers—raved about him," Thomsen said. "They talked about his character and his work ethic, and that made it click for me. He's a great kid who turned into a great player."

One of Thomsen's regrets about his ACU tenure is not burning Whiteside's redshirt in 2007 and allowing him to play. By the end of that season, ACU's depleted defense was on the field way too much because the offense was scoring with such ease, putting a thin defensive unit in bad spots all season. It came to a head in the second-round NCAA Division II playoff loss at Chadron State when the Wildcats lost a 49–20 fourth-quarter lead and eventually lost to the Eagles, 76–73, in triple overtime. "Looking back, I should have played him in 2007 because we just had a hard time defensively at the end of the season with our depth," Thomsen said. "If I had it to do over again, I would have played him. We might have won the Chadron game if he had played because he would have made some plays in the fourth quarter to keep the game under control."

Just as Scott was leaving after the 2008 season, another connection to Vernon showed up, although in a bit of a roundabout way. Daryl Richardson—Scott's brother—lived with their father, Daryl Sr., in Jacksonville, Florida, and was one of the top running backs in Florida out of Sandalwood High School. But he didn't qualify academically for NCAA Division I programs, so he went to Cisco College because it was close to his family—brother Bernard and first cousins Clyde and Aston. He got his academic priorities in order at Cisco and played well enough to earn a look at several schools around the country. However, he settled on ACU because of the ties to his family and to Thomsen and Collums.

Richardson went on to have a terrific, if understated, ACU career. He was never a first-team all-Lone Star Conference performer, but he finished fifth on the all-time rushing list (2,303 yards), seventh in carries (453), third in rushing touchdowns (34), fifth in scoring (228 points), third in touchdowns (38), and eleventh in all-purpose yards (3,082). "Daryl's career was a bit underrated for two reasons: he was banged up some and that cost him some games, and his numbers weren't quite as gaudy as some of the guys who came before him," Thomsen said. "That probably hurt some other guys, too, like Charcandrick West and Taylor Gabriel. But all of those guys put together great careers."

And the reason, Thomsen said, that they put together those careers is because of a competitive streak that ran through each of them. "They all loved to play and compete," Thomsen said. "They all loved the game, and they all needed the game to get somewhere in life and achieve some of the things they set out to achieve. Three of the four graduated from ACU, and they all played in the NFL. Football and ACU gave them the tools they needed to make a better life for themselves."

THE GREATEST MOMENTS

by Lance Fleming, Dr. Charles Marler,
James Norman, and Garner Roberts

In the long history of ACU football, trying to narrow down the greatest games and moments into just a select few proves difficult. So that's why this chapter will focus on all the greatest games and moments in capsule form. In 2005–2006 when ACU celebrated its centennial, the sports information office was tasked with coming up with the greatest moments in ACU athletics history, and that's where this list of greatest football moments originated. The top five moments are ranked in order, and then the rest of the moments are ranked in chronological order. Enjoy the look back through the history of ACU football.

1 **August 17, 1996**—Former Wildcat All-American running back Wilbert Montgomery receives the highest honor of his career when he is inducted into the College Football Hall of Fame in South Bend, Indiana.

Steve Butman

Wilbert Montgomery is inducted into the College Football Hall of Fame in 1996.

2 **October 16, 1976**—Ove Johansson kicks a still-standing world-record field goal (69 yards) and Wilbert Montgomery becomes the leading touchdown scorer in college football history with his 67th career score in ACU's 17–0 homecoming win over East Texas State.

3 **November 22, 2008**—ACU beats West Texas A&M, 93–68, in a second-round NCAA Division II playoff game at Shotwell Stadium that became the greatest offensive performance in NCAA and

Gerald Ewing

ACU wide receiver Clyde Gates makes a leaping catch during the Wildcats' 93–68 win over West Texas A&M during an NCAA Division II playoff game in 2008.

▲

Former ACU quarterback Jim Lindsey visits with ACU President Dr. John C. Stevens prior to a game in the early 1970s.

▶▶

Lone Star Conference history. Coverage of the game is featured on SI.com, ESPN.com, and ESPN, as well as in newspapers around the world.

4 **October 24, 1970**—Quarterback Jim Lindsey registers Abilene Christian's first 400-yard passing game in an epic 28–23 loss to top-ranked Arkansas State at Shotwell Stadium. Lindsey completes 33 of 63 passes for 414 yards and 3 scores for the nationally ranked Wildcats. The game attracts national attention, including coverage in Sports Illustrated. Lindsey, who still ranks second in Southland Conference history in career passing yards (8,521) and fourth in career total offense (8,359), is the Wildcats' all-time leader in both categories.

A 1970 first-team all-American and three-time all-SLC quarterback, he had twelve career 300-yard passing games and two career 400-yard passing games. He is still the ACU and Southland Conference all-time leader in career completions (642)

and attempts (1,237), even though ACC dropped out of the SLC after the 1972–1973 athletic year.

5 **December 2, 1950**—Perhaps the most celebrated football team in ACC history completes its magical 11–0 season with a 13–7 win over Gustavus Adolphus in the Refrigerator Bowl in Evansville, Indiana. The Singing Christians of Head Coach Garvin Beauchamp are the only team in the United States that season to finish unbeaten and untied, and it is still the only ACC football team to accomplish the feat. Future ACC head coaches Les Wheeler, Wally Bullington, and Ted Sitton star on the team that also features Alton Green, E. J. "Tiny" Moore, Bill Ayres, Ray Hansen, Don Smith, Jerry Mullins, Stanley Staples, Harry House, Pete Ragus, Bob Bailey, and Bailey Woods.

The Other Top Moments in Chronological Order

October 18, 1919—In their first intercollegiate football game, the Wildcats defeat Midland College, 40–0, in Midland. A brief three-paragraph account of the game in the *Abilene Morning Reporter-News* lists fourteen players who accompanied Coach S. Vernon McCasland to the game but gives no details of scoring.

November 11, 1929—In its fifth annual Armistice Day game, Abilene Christian defeats Texas Tech, 7–3, for the third straight year. About six hundred fans

Wide receiver Stanley Staples was voted an honorable mention All-American in 1952.

gather in Sewell Auditorium where ACC President Batsell Baxter arranges for a play-by-play telegraph of the game from Lubbock. Garland "Goober" Keyes catches a 74-yard touchdown pass from Harrell Cheves in the fourth quarter to give ACC the upset win.

November 25, 1933—In the final game of the season, before a crowd of five thousand—the largest to see Abilene Christian play in six years—Bert Ezzell boots a field goal in a 3–0 win over McMurry to give Coach A. B. Morris's team a final record of 5–3–2.

November 23, 1946—In the first season for official NCAA college division football statistics, ACC has two national leaders as Buster Dixon wins the total offense title with 960 yards, and teammate V. T. Smith Jr. is the national rushing leader with 733. ACC earns a share of the Texas

V. T. Smith Jr. is one of the greatest running backs in program history, and he went on to win an NFL championship with the 1951 Los Angeles Rams.

Conference title and invites golfer Byron Nelson to speak at its postseason banquet.

September 20, 1947—Halfback V. T. Smith Jr. returns his first two kickoffs of the season for touchdowns in a 19–13 win over Southwest Texas State in Abilene. That gives him three straight kickoffs for touchdowns following a 90-yard run with his final return of the 1946 season.

October 7, 1950—E. J. "Tiny" Moore, a five foot ten, 265-pound lineman, blocks Southwestern's PAT in the first quarter to preserve a 7–6 Wildcat win in Georgetown in the closest game of the season for the only undefeated, untied team in school history (11–0). Bill Ayres scores ACC's only points in the game with a 40-yard

interception return, and also kicks the game-winning PAT.

January 18, 1951—Halfback Bailey Woods, the MVP of the Refrigerator Bowl, is the first Wildcat taken in the NFL draft when he is chosen in the fourteenth round (168th pick) by the Chicago Bears. Woods gained 103 yards and scored 1 touchdown in the bowl game win over Gustavus Adolphus.

October 11, 1953—Leondus Fry, Gene Boyd, and Tommy Morris score touchdowns in Abilene Christian's 20–7 win in Tallahassee, Florida, over a Florida State team that includes future actor Burt Reynolds, then a freshman halfback.

September 18, 1954—The Wildcats score 41 points in a remarkable fourth-quarter rally to beat East Texas State in a 41–19 win in the season opener. The Wildcats trail 13–0 going to the fourth quarter but score 6 touchdowns at Fair Park Stadium in Abilene to snap the Lions' 31-game winning streak.

November 14, 1959—Robert McLeod catches four passes for 111 yards and 2 touchdowns to lead ACC to a 28–22 win at Texas-El Paso. His 53-yard TD catch in the third quarter begins the Wildcats' comeback from a 22–6 deficit, and his 11-yard TD catch with 3:50 to play proves to be the game-winning score.

October 6, 1962—ACC whips the No. 1 team in the Associated Press small-college poll, Fresno State, 26–14, in San Angelo to break the Bulldogs' 13-game winning streak. Owen Morrison runs for 138 yards and scores 3 times to help Head Coach Les Wheeler celebrate a happy birthday.

December 30, 1963—After leading the nationally ranked Wildcats on defense during an 8–1 season, senior linebacker Jack Griggs becomes the school's first student-athlete to win Academic All-American honors. Since Griggs's award, Abilene Christian has had more than fifty athletes earn Academic All-American honors in 12 sports.

September 28, 1968—Linebacker Chip Bennett collects a single-game record 27 tackles in the Wildcats' 50–49 win over Howard Payne. ACC wins with 28 seconds to play when Jim Lindsey connects with Bill Lockey for a 15-yard touchdown pass and Bob Bearden kicks the PAT.

September 8, 1973—Quarterback Clint Longley throws for a school-record 6 touchdowns, and freshman running back Wilbert Montgomery scores a touchdown on a 39-yard pass the first time he touches the football in a 56–46 road loss to Arkansas State.

October 6, 1973—Wilbert Montgomery runs for a university- and Lone Star Conference-record 6 touchdowns in a 57–50 win over Stephen F. Austin State University at Shotwell Stadium.

December 8, 1973—Head Coach Wally Bullington's team wins the first of two NAIA Division I national football championships with a 42–14 win over Elon College in the Champion Bowl in Shreveport, Louisiana. During the season, the Wildcats outscored opponents 466–206, and the defense had a string of 11 straight shutout quarters. The team set 16 Wildcat records, 9 of which still stand.

October 30, 1976—On a rain-soaked Shotwell Stadium turf, senior quarterback Jim Reese posts the greatest passing day in Lone Star Conference and Abilene Christian history, throwing for 564 yards in a win over Angelo State. Reese—sixth on ACU's career passing chart with 5,946 yards—completes 26 of 39 passes for 564 yards and 2 scores.

November 6, 1976—In the final game of his collegiate career, Wilbert Montgomery rushes for 99 yards and 1 touchdown on

Freshman quarterback Clint Longley drops back to throw in the Wildcats' season-opening win over McMurry.

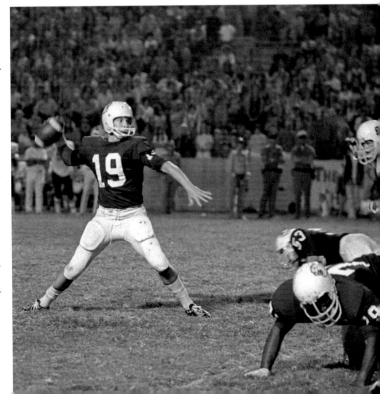

Gerald Ewing

just 6 carries—all in the first half—to lead ACU to a 42–0 win over Cameron. He finishes his career with college division records for career touchdowns (70) and touchdowns in a regular season (31 in 1973) and sets the ACU record for most career points with 422.

October 8, 1977—In front of a crowd of 18,500 fans—at the time the largest crowd to ever witness a Lone Star Conference football game—No. 1-ranked Texas A&I rallies at home for 25 fourth-quarter points to force a 25–25 tie against No. 2 Abilene Christian. The Wildcats lead 25–0 early in the fourth quarter only to see the Javelinas roar back for the tying points late in the contest. The only consolation for Coach Dewitt Jones's team is that the tie snaps Kingsville's 42-game winning streak and

sets the stage for ACU's run to the NAIA Division I national championship.

December 10, 1977—Coach Dewitt Jones's Wildcats ride the passing of John Mayes and the running of Kelly Kent to a 24–7 win over Southwestern Oklahoma in the Apple Bowl in Seattle's Kingdome to claim the school's second NAIA Division I national football title. The Wildcats finish 11–1–1, rebounding from a 0–1–1 LSC start to win the national title.

December 11, 1997—In New York, the Associated Press names defensive lineman Junior Filikitonga and defensive back Victor Burke first-team college division All-American in football. It's the only time the Wildcats have had two first-team All-American selections in football in the same season.

October 30, 2004—ACU beats No. 2 Texas A&M-Kingsville, 17–10, in Kingsville for the Wildcats' first win over the Javelinas since 1983. The win marks ACU's second road win of the season over a top-10 opponent (31–14 win in September at No. 7 Tarleton State). ACU safety Danieal Manning—later named to six All-American teams—knocks down a fourth-down pass in the end zone late in the game to preserve ACU's lead.

April 29, 2005—The Chicago Bears make ACU defensive back Danieal Manning their 2nd-round selection in the NFL draft (42nd pick overall). Manning goes on to start all nineteen games in 2006 for the Bears, who advanced to play the Indianapolis Colts in Super Bowl XLI in February 2007. Manning played five seasons for the Bears before signing a free-agent contract with the Houston Texans prior to the 2011 season.

October 19, 2006—In their national television debut, the ACU Wildcats whip West Texas A&M, 49–33, in Canyon behind sophomore quarterback Billy Malone's school-record 6 touchdown passes. The Wildcats fall behind 15–0 early in the game before Malone took over. John Brock caught 3 touchdown passes, including a 67-yarder in the first quarter and the game-clinching 84-yarder in the fourth quarter. The Wildcats would go on to finish the season 8–3 under Chris Thomsen, the second-year head coach, and qualify for the NCAA Division II playoffs for the first time in their history. ACU's season came to a close on November 18 in Canyon with a 30–27 overtime loss to West Texas A&M.

November 17, 2007—The ACU Wildcats beat Mesa State (Colorado), 56–12, in the first NCAA Division II home playoff game in their football history. The win is the final one of the season for the Wildcats, who finish 10–3 for their first 10-win season since the 1977 NAIA Division I national championship team went 11–1–1. During the season, the Wildcats knocked off NCAA Division I-AA foe Texas State, 45–27, in San Marcos, and scored at least 50 points seven times as they led NCAA Division II football in points per game.

The Wildcats used 6 touchdowns from junior running back Bernard Scott to take a heart-stopping 70–63 win over Tarleton State on October 27, and then forged a thrilling second-half comeback to knock off Midwestern State, 42–41, in the regular-season finale and earn a spot in the national playoffs for a second straight season. ACU's season came to a crushing end November 24 when they lost to Chadron State (Nebraska), 76–73, in triple-overtime. The Wildcats had a 49–20 fourth-quarter lead but weren't able to hold it, despite Scott's 303 yards rushing and 6 touchdowns. He finished the season with 2,165 rushing yards and 35 rushing touchdowns (39 overall) and was second in voting for the Harlon Hill Trophy, given annually to the top football player in NCAA Division II. Chadron State's star running back, Danny Woodhead, would win the second of his consecutive Harlon Hill Trophies the next month, narrowly edging out Scott for the award.

December 12, 2008—Running back Bernard Scott caps his remarkable two-year ACU career by becoming the first Wildcat to win the Harlon Hill Trophy,

Running back Bernard Scott runs for 178 yards and 4 scores in ACU's 42–41 win over Midwestern State in the 2007 regular-season finale, a victory that pushed ACU into the NCAA Division II playoffs for the second straight season.

Gerald Ewing

Gerald Ewing

Center Sam Collins prepares to snap the ball in ACU's 2008 season-opening win over Northwest Missouri State. Collins won the Gene Upshaw Award in 2008 as the top lineman in NCAA Division II.

given annually to the top football player in NCAA Division II. Scott beat out a pair of record-setting quarterbacks in Central Washington's Mike Reilly and North Alabama's A. J. Milwee. Scott has a 168-point margin of victory in the voting with 253 points, the third-highest point total in the history of the award. In just two seasons as a Wildcat, Scott ran for 4,321 yards to become ACU's all-time career rushing leader. He topped the 2,000-yard mark twice, becoming the only player in Lone Star Conference history to put together multiple 2,000-yard rushing seasons. His 63 rushing touchdowns are second in ACU history, and his 73 total touchdowns are second in ACU and LSC history. In 2008, he rushed for 2,156 yards (second in LSC and ACU single-season history behind his 2,165 yards in 2007) and 28 touchdowns and caught 47 passes for 826 yards and another 6 touchdowns. He led NCAA Division II in points per game (17) and all-purpose yards (256.8) and was second in

rushing, averaging 179.7 yards per game. He led his team to an 11–1 record, the Wildcats' first outright LSC championship since 1973, ACU's highest-ever NCAA Division II national ranking (No. 2), and to the quarterfinal round of the playoffs. Scott averaged 8.4 yards per carry and rushed for more than 200 yards in four of the Wildcats' final six games of 2008 and ran for at least 100 yards in his last 17 games dating back to the 2007 season. He was at his best in big games, helping ACU to an 8–3 record against top-25 opponents over the last two seasons. In those eleven games, he rushed for 2,277 yards (207.0 per game), scored 38 rushing touchdowns, and caught 4 touchdown passes for 631 receiving yards (57.4 per game). He made his case for the year's Harlon Hill Trophy in two wins against West Texas A&M in which he shredded the Buffaloes' defense, combining to rush for 572 yards and 7 touchdowns on 46 carries and catch 10 passes for 202 yards and 2 scores. Scott touched the ball 56 times in those two games for 774 yards and 9 touchdowns, averaging 13.8 yards from scrimmage every time he touched the ball. His 6 rushing touchdowns, 7 total touchdowns, and 42 total points in the playoff win were NCAA Division II playoff, NCAA Division II, LSC, and ACU single-game records.

January 7, 2009—Senior center Sam Collins wins the Gene Upshaw Award from the Manheim (Pennsylvania) Touchdown Club as the top lineman in NCAA Division II. As a senior in 2008, Collins was selected first-team Daktronics All-American and second-team Associated Press Little All-American.

April 26, 2009—For the first time since 1983, the ACU Wildcats have multiple players chosen in the same NFL draft as Johnny Knox is selected in the fifth round by the Chicago Bears and Bernard Scott goes one round later to the Cincinnati Bengals.

August 27, 2009—In the first nationally televised football game at Shotwell Stadium, the No. 5 ACU Wildcats open the season with a 19–14 win over No. 2 Northwest Missouri State in a battle of NCAA Division II football heavyweights. Arthur Johnson returns a fumble 42 yards for a touchdown late in the first quarter and Clark Harrell throws a 24-yard touchdown pass to Ben Gibbs late in the second quarter to help ACU to a 16–0 halftime lead. In a defensive battle, the Wildcats hold the Bearcats to just 230 yards of offense and get the season started on the right foot.

September 12, 2009—In ACU's first game at the venerable Cotton Bowl, the Wildcats need only a few extra seconds to knock off Texas A&M-Commerce. Drew Cuffee's interception and ensuing 85-yard return for a touchdown on the first play of overtime give the No. 2 Wildcats a 20–14 win over the Lions on a rainy day in Dallas.

October 12, 2009—For the first time during their tenure in NCAA Division II, the Wildcats become the No. 1-ranked team in the nation, according to the American Football Coaches Association poll. Two days earlier, No. 2-ranked ACU improved to 7–0 on the season with a 38–24 win over Angelo State. ACU went on to make the national playoffs for a fourth straight season, beating Midwestern State, 24–21, in the first round before falling to Northwest Missouri State, 35–10, in the second round to finish 9–4 on the season.

November 6, 2010—In one of the greatest games ever against their biggest rival, the No. 2 ACU Wildcats score 35 second-half points—including 21 in the fourth

Gerald Ewing

All-American defensive end Aston Whiteside sacks Texas A&M-Commerce quarterback Adam Farkes during the Wildcats' 20–14 overtime win over the Lions at the Cotton Bowl.

Jeremy Enlow

quarter—while rallying to beat No. 14 West Texas A&M, 41–34, at Kimbrough Stadium in Canyon. Junior Daryl Richardson, who ran for 98 yards, scores 3 second-half touchdowns, including a 7-yarder with 4:51 to play to tie the game at 34–34 and then a 23-yarder with one minute to play to give ACU a 41–34 lead. The following week, the Wildcats whip Southwestern Oklahoma State, 47–17, to cap their first 11–0 regular season and win a second Lone Star Conference title in three seasons. ACU's season comes to an end November 27 with a 55–41 loss to Central Missouri in the second round of the national playoffs at Shotwell Stadium. That game marked the final contest for wide receiver Edmond "Clyde" Gates, who earned first-team All-American honors with 66 catches for 1,182 yards and 13 touchdowns and became the Miami Dolphins' fourth-round draft choice in April 2011. Sophomore quarterback Mitchell Gale was one of nine national finalists for the Harlon Hill Trophy and earned All-American honors after throwing for 3,595 yards and 38 touchdowns against just 3 interceptions.

September 17, 2011—ACU plays its first football game in the AT&T Stadium in Arlington in front of a Lone Star Conference-record crowd of 24,837 in the inaugural Lone Star Football Festival. North Alabama snaps the Wildcats' twelve-game regular-season winning streak with a 23–17 win, the first of only three losses in 2012 as ACU advances to the NCAA Division II playoffs for the sixth straight

Jeremy Enlow

in touchdown passes (97) behind the 114 thrown by Billy Malone from 2005 to 2008. Gale's effort and finishing number of 12,109 yards made ACU just the fourth program in NCAA football history to have consecutive starting quarterbacks throw for at least 12,000 yards, joining Hawaii, Louisiana Tech, and Houston in the category.

August 31, 2013—In ACU's first game as an NCAA Division I independent Football Championship Subdivision (FCS) program, the Wildcats blasted Concordia (Alabama), 84–6, at Shotwell Stadium. Senior quarterback John David Baker completed 17 of 20 passes for 322 yards and an ACU single-game record 7 touchdowns. Senior Darian Hogg had 10 catches for 208 yards and 2 scores. Baker would go on to author one of the greatest seasons ever by an ACU quarterback as he completed 247 of 369 passes for 3,376 yards and 35 touchdowns, while throwing just 5 interceptions. He also ran for 5 touchdowns and was responsible for a school-record 40 touchdowns. He also

Wide receiver Taylor Gabriel—second in ACU history for catches, receiving yards, and receiving touchdowns—turns up the field against North Alabama in the Wildcats' 23–17 loss to the Lions at AT&T Stadium.

◄◄

In his first career start, quarterback John David Baker set an ACU single-game record with seven touchdown passes in the Wildcats' 84–6 win over Concordia College (Alabama) on August 31, 2013.

▼

season. Along the way, the Wildcats knock off rival West Texas A&M, 28–18, and then rally on the road to beat Texas A&M-Kingsville, 42–34. In the first round of the playoffs (November 19 in Topeka, Kansas), the Wildcats drop a heartbreaking 52–49 decision to Washburn to finish 8–3. Mitchell Gale, a junior, totals 506 yards and 4 touchdowns in the loss, becoming only the second ACU quarterback to throw for at least 500 yards in a game (joining record-holder Jim Reese, who had 564 against Angelo State in 1976).

November 10, 2012—Senior quarterback Mitchell Gale finishes his career by completing 25 of 36 passes for 408 yards and 2 touchdowns, leading the Wildcats to a 24–12 win over Incarnate Word in San Antonio. Gale's 408-yard effort helped him finish his career with 12,109 passing yards, which still stands as both the ACU and Lone Star Conference record. Gale is also ACU's all-time leader in completions (931) and attempts (1,513) and is second

Jeremy Enlow

had plenty of help as current NFL standouts Taylor Gabriel and Charcandrick West were on the field at wide receiver and running back, respectively. Gabriel finished the season with 73 catches for 1,060 yards and 10 touchdowns receiving, while West ran for 906 yards and 14 touchdowns while adding 32 catches for 443 yards and a pair of touchdowns. Hogg had a terrific season with 48 catches for 747 yards and 6 touchdowns, while Darrell Cantu-Harkless finished his fantastic career with 376 yards and 5 touchdowns on the ground and another 484 yards and 4 touchdowns receiving. Defensively, standouts like Angel Lopez, Justin Stewart, Thor Woerner, Justin Stephens, and Nick Richardson led a defense that limited opponents to less than 400 yards of offense per game. Richardson had 11 sacks, one of the top single-season totals in ACU history.

Running back Charcandrick West runs for some of his 102 yards in the Wildcats' narrow 34–29 loss to New Mexico State in 2013, ACU's first game against an NCAA Division I opponent since 1980.

October 26, 2013—The Wildcats dropped a 34–29 decision at New Mexico State, but it wasn't for a lack of offense. The Wildcats put up 574 yards against the NCAA Division I Football Bowl Subdivision (FBS) Aggies, and ACU led 22–21 going to the fourth quarter. NMSU, though, scored 13 fourth-quarter points and pushed its lead to 34–22 with 2:32 to play before ACU put together a drive that ended when Charcandrick West scored on a 5-yard pass from John David Baker with 19 seconds to play. ACU recovered the onside kick but was penalized after the recovery. After another penalty on ACU's first offensive play pushed the ball back to its own 21-yard line with time left for just one more play, the Wildcats had no other choice but to heave it deep. On the game's final play, Baker rolled out to his right and heaved the ball as far as he could. Monte Green-Avery caught a tipped ball in traffic, spun around, and was about to be dragged down around the 20-yard line when he flipped the ball to Gabriel, who had open field in front of him. The senior from Mesquite, who set the ACU single-game record with 15 catches for a career-high 188 yards, sprinted down the sideline for what looked like would be a game-winning touchdown that would rival "The Play" by Cal in its 1982 win over Stanford. But just as it appeared that Gabriel would score, he was knocked out of bounds by Trashaun Nixon at the 6-yard line, leaving the Wildcats just short of a finish that would have gone down as the greatest in program history.

Jeremy Enlow

Jeremy Enlow

February 14, 2014—ACU President Dr. Phil Schubert and then-Director of Athletics Jared Mosley announced a $30 million gift to the university by Mark and April Anthony, with $15 million designated toward construction of an on-campus football stadium, which would become Anthony Field at Wildcat Stadium when it opened in 2017.

August 27, 2014—Playing in the city where he was born, sophomore quarterback Parker McKenzie, making his first career start, lit up Atlanta's Georgia Dome in the Wildcats' first game as a member of the Southland Conference since 1972. McKenzie completed 30 of 40 passes for 403 yards and 4 touchdowns and gave ACU a 9-point lead in the fourth quarter before Georgia State rallied to win, capping the victory on a 26-yard field goal by Wil Litz as time expired. Still, it was an amazing debut for McKenzie, who had played sparingly as the backup in 2013. He would go on to throw for 3,084 yards and 22 touchdowns, leading ACU to a 6–6 finish in its first season back in the Southland.

September 13, 2014—Just two weeks after narrowly losing to FBS member Georgia State, the Wildcats pulled off a stunning upset when they knocked off FBS member Troy (Alabama), 38–35, the program's first win over an FBS program since beginning its transition to NCAA Division I status. In fact, prior to the game, the last time the Wildcats had beaten a team that was at the time of the game playing at the highest level of college football and was currently an FBS member was November 14, 1959, when the Wildcats went to El Paso and knocked off UTEP, 28–22, at the Sun Bowl. The Wildcats twice rallied from 14-point deficits in the game (21–7 in the first half and 28–14 in the third quarter) before finally taking the lead at 31–28 on a 27-yard field goal by Nick Grau with 6:10 to play. Third-string running back Adrian Duncan—pressed into service because of injuries to starter De'Andre Brown and backup Herschel Sims—iced the game with 1:17 to play with a 9-yard touchdown run to make it 38–28. Troy would score a late touchdown, but ACU recovered the onside kick and celebrated the milestone victory.

November 5, 2016—Quarterback Dallas Sealey threw for 304 yards and scored the go-ahead touchdown on a 1-yard run midway through the fourth quarter to lead ACU to a 25–22 win over Northwestern State in the Wildcats' final game ever at

Offensive lineman Chance Rieken hugs Head Coach Collums after the Wildcats beat Troy, Alabama, 38–35, on September 13, 2014.

Mark and April Anthony (third and fourth from left) cut the ribbon on Anthony Field at Wildcat Stadium during the first game at the Wildcats' on-campus home on September 16, 2017. They were joined on the field by (left to right) Jodey Arrington, Lee De León, Dr. Phil Schubert, Anthony Williams, Barry Packer, and Stan Lambert.

Shotwell Stadium, their home of fifty-seven full seasons. Sealey completed 29 of 45 passes and led his team in rushing with 52 yards, helping ACU outscore NSU 23–9 after managing just 2 points in the first quarter on a rare defensive 2-point conversion.

September 16, 2017—ACU inaugurates the first on-campus football stadium since World War II, Anthony Field at Wildcat Stadium, with a spectacular 24–3 win over Houston Baptist. ACU's defense limited HBU to just 129 yards of offense in the victory, which came in front of a sellout crowd of 12,000 fans. ACU, which played several miles from campus at Shotwell Stadium for fifty-seven full seasons, opened the scoring when De'Andre Brown scampered 5 yards for a touchdown in the first quarter. HBU countered with a 54-yard field goal by Alex Chadwick. Wildcat quarterback Dallas Sealey tossed a 33-yard scoring pass to Carl Whitley with 38 seconds left in the first half and Nik Grau added a 23-yard field goal at the start of the fourth quarter. Luke Anthony wrapped up ACU's scoring with a 17-yard TD throw to Josh Fink with 2:03 left in the game.

This list of the greatest moments in ACU football history was compiled by ACU sports information directors Dr. Charlie Marler (1958–1963), James Norman (1963–1973), Garner Roberts (1973–1998), and Lance Fleming (1998–present).

REMEMBERING SHOTWELL

A ll four stories in this chapter were published previously in November 2016 on the *ACU Today* blog as the Wildcats closed out their fifty-eight-year stay at Shotwell Stadium. Each of the authors—Grant Boone, Garner Roberts, Ron Hadfield, and Lance Fleming—were on hand for many of the greatest moments in the history of the stadium that served as ACU's home from 1959 to 2016.

So Long Shotwell:
Mud, Sweat, and Tears

by Grant Boone

There is nothing special about Shotwell Stadium. Never has been. It's a pair of parallel concrete seating structures in a barren patch of a nondescript landscape. But the men who have played and coached football there for Abilene Christian University and the magic they've made? That is another story entirely. ACU's fifty-seven-year history at Shotwell began with a delay of game. After using Fair Park as their home field for a dozen years after World War II, the Wildcats were scheduled to host Lamar University (then called Lamar Tech) on October 3, 1959, at the new facility originally known as Public Schools Stadium. But a downpour that Saturday soaked the city and the stadium's natural grass surface. So to keep the new sod from being trampled under the heavier foot of college-sized players, the game was moved to the old digs at Fair Park where the Wildcats lost to Lamar, 8–7, on what *Optimist* reporter Royce Caldwell called "a sea of mud."

Jeremy Enlow

Grant Boone—the voice of the Wildcats since 2007—calls the action from the home radio booth at Shotwell Stadium during the team's final home game at the stadium on November 5, 2016.

Three straight road games followed on the 1959 schedule, pushing the Wildcats' debut at Shotwell back to a rather oxymoronic homecoming date with Trinity University as alumni came home to a place they had never been. Playing what lineman and punter Thurman Neill called "good ole southern football" ("We punted, played it rugged on defense, and watched for a break," Neill said afterward), ACU turned back Trinity, 13–12, getting its tenure at Shotwell off on the right foot. Or feet, specifically those of Neill, who dropped two punts inside the Tigers' 10-yard line and recovered a fumble in the end zone for a touchdown, and Bill Locke, who scored the other touchdown on a 7-yard run and whose extra point kick provided the winning margin. ACU found its new home turf to its liking in those early years, going 17–6 at home from 1959 through 1964, including a perfect 5–0 record in 1963 when the Wildcats won their last eight games of the season. The overall win streak stretched to 10 into the second game of 1964 with a 17–11 victory over Texas A&M University-Commerce that saw running back Dennis "The Menace" Hagaman scurry around a soggy Shotwell for a season-high 126 yards, highlighted by a 50-yard touchdown burst and a 32-yard gallop on fourth down to help seal the deal.

That 1964 season was the first football campaign for the brand-new Southland Conference, which ACU cofounded after seven years as an independent. The Wildcats' first Southland game at Shotwell was a 21–7 loss to Arkansas State University that also was noteworthy for the number of passing yards the home team accrued that day: zero. Six years later to the day, All-American ACU quarterback Jim Lindsey would set a conference record with 414 passing yards and earn a write-up in *Sports Illustrated*. For a town famously and historically dry—in more ways than one—the skies above Shotwell seemed frequently open when the Wildcats were there. In addition to the aforementioned deluges and drizzles, there was the game on October 30, 1976, that *Abilene Reporter-News* reporter Art Lawler described as a mud pile. Jim Reese was in hog heaven as he threw for what remains an ACU-best 564 yards in a 26–0 rout of Angelo State University. Incredibly, Reese needed just 26 completions to reach that record total as Gary Stirman, Johnny Perkins, and Wilbert Montgomery each had more than 100 receiving yards. But that wasn't the most memorable game ACU ever played at Shotwell. In fact, it wasn't even the most memorable that *month*. The one right before it, a 17–0 homecoming decision over Texas A&M-Commerce, featured not one, but two record-setting performances. Late in the first quarter, Ove Johansson kicked a 69-yard field goal, which 40 years later is still the longest in football history. In the second quarter, Montgomery passed Walter Payton as college football's all-time touchdown leader.

The Purple and White's head coach at the time, Wally Bullington, lost his first

An aerial view of Shotwell Stadium during an Abilene Christian College game in 1961.

game patrolling Shotwell's sidelines but not many more. A lineman and punter on the Wildcats' undefeated team in 1950, Bullington took over the program in 1968 and brought with him his former teammate Ted Sitton as offensive coordinator. Together, they ushered the modern passing game into this corner of the college football world where teams generally ascribed to the old adage that only three things can happen when you throw the football, and two of them are bad. Riding the rocket right arms of Lindsey, Clint Longley, and Reese, Bullington won more games at Shotwell (35) than any other ACU

head coach, including a perfect 6–0 home mark in 1973 when the Wildcats joined the Lone Star Conference and won the NAIA national championship. Bullington will put a headset back on to help me call ACU's final game ever at Shotwell this Saturday against Northwestern State University, the school he beat in his first game as the Wildcats' coach. In the spirit of ACU's great track and field teams, Bullington passed the baton in 1977 to another former Wildcat player, Dewitt Jones. After going 11–2 at Shotwell as a tight end, Jones' record in two seasons as head coach was 12–1. It included a 35–7 playoff victory over the

The Wildcats' defense awaits the Angelo State offense in front of a capacity crowd at the 2002 Homecoming game.

Gerald Ewing

University of Wisconsin-Stevens Point on December 3, 1977, that sent the Wildcats on to the NAIA national championship game in Seattle, which they won. Sitton took over for Jones, and Wildcat quarterbacks continued to sling it around Shotwell as ACU and the Lone Star Conference moved from the NAIA ranks to NCAA Division II. Under Sitton's tutelage, Loyal Proffitt was the LSC's Freshman of the Year in 1981 and a four-year starter. And on October 29, 1983, at Shotwell, he completed an ACU-record 35 passes and threw for 466 yards and three touchdowns in a 24–10 win over Stephen F. Austin State University, perhaps proving a Proffitt isn't *always* without honor in his own hometown.

Odessa native Rex Lamberti took the reins of the ACU offense in 1985, and the Permian High School product brought his own brand of mojo to Shotwell Stadium, off and on, for nearly a decade. In his first two seasons as a starter, Lamberti threw 56 touchdown passes, a then-team record 32 of them coming in 1986. Proving you can go home again, Lamberti was coaxed out of retirement in 1993 by first-year head coach and former Wildcat player Dr. Bob Strader. At the age of twenty-seven,, Lamberti led ACU to its first winning season since his last year in 1986 and earned All-American honors by tossing 28 more touchdowns to finish as the program's all-time leader. Eight of Lamberti's scoring strikes in 1993 were caught by twenty-four-year-old tight end Chris Thomsen, another jurassic classic Strader excavated that year. Thomsen had played three years at TCU then a couple of seasons in the Oakland A's minor league system before returning to football at ACU and, like Lamberti, being named All-American. He stuck around Abilene as an assistant coach under Strader and Jack Kiser from 1994 to 1999 and, after assistant positions at Wichita Falls High School and the University of Central Arkansas, Thomsen was named ACU head coach in 2005. Like Bullington with Sitton nearly forty years before, Thomsen brought with him a secret weapon and quarterback guru in brother-in-law and UCA offensive coordinator Ken Collums. The pair would turn Shotwell Stadium artificial turf into a virtual video game screen. In 2007, the Wildcats led the nation in scoring with 49.2 points per game and were second in yards per game. In 2008, they were tops in both categories and produced the first unbeaten regular season since

1950, capping it at Shotwell with a 47–17 rout of Midwestern State University.

What happened next remains nearly impossible to describe almost a decade later. A month after ACU whipped West Texas A&M University, 52–35, on the road, the archrivals met again November 22 at Shotwell in a second-round play-off game. With more than a half dozen future pros on the field in what looked like a small-college NFL combine, ACU scored 13 touchdowns in 15 possessions and won, 93–68, obliterating most every scoring record in NCAA history and even outscoring the Wildcat men's basketball team, which needed two overtimes later that evening to reach 90 points in a loss. Billy Malone threw touchdown passes to six different receivers, leaving Shotwell as ACU's all-time leader in touchdown passes with 114. Under Thomsen and Collums, the Wildcats' final seven seasons in NCAA Division II produced six playoff appearances and one pro after another, including Danieal Manning, Bernard Scott, Johnny

Jeremy Enlow

Players and their families linger on the field after ACU's 25–22 win over Northwestern State in the Wildcats' final game at Shotwell Stadium.

ACU running backs De'Andre Brown (left), Tracy James (center), and Adrian Duncan (right) offer a pre-game prayer before the Wildcats' final game at Shotwell Stadium.

▲

Garner Roberts, former ACU sports information director, climbs the steps to the Shotwell Stadium press box for the final time, after working more than 250 games at the stadium.

▶▶

Knox, Clyde Gates, Daryl Richardson, Charcandrick West, Aston Whiteside, Taylor Gabriel, and Mitchell Gale, who ended his ACU career as the school's and the Lone Star Conference's all-time leading passer with 12,109 yards. Collums took over for Thomsen in 2012 and, facing hurdles no Wildcat sprinter—much less head football coach—had ever seen, continued to churn out record-setting performances and quality young men.

In 2013, ACU began its four-year transition to Division I FCS (football championship subdivision, formerly I-AA) with a bang, pummeling Concordia (Alabama) College at Shotwell, 84–6, as John David Baker fired a program-best 7 touchdown passes in his first career start. They say home is where the heart is. And while Shotwell hasn't been much to look at or even remotely whispered to passersby or guests that it is the home of the Wildcats,

it is for better or worse where 12 ACU head coaches, scores of assistants, and hundreds of players have left their hearts. For that reason alone, a small piece of our hearts, along with a huge chunk of our history, will always be there.

So Long Shotwell: The Greatest Show in Town

by Garner Roberts

Saturday night, October 24, 1970, music legends Chet Atkins, Floyd Cramer, and Boots Randolph performed at Taylor County Coliseum. Likely, it was an entertaining concert (I don't know because I wasn't there), but the biggest show in town that night was across the street. That's where the top-ranked Arkansas State University Indians invaded P. E. Shotwell Stadium to battle the nationally ranked Abilene Christian College Wildcats in a

Southland Conference showdown with national implications. ("They'd never schedule that concert to conflict with a high school game," James Norman, the Wildcats' director of sports information that season, told a reporter from New York.) From my seat in the press box at Shotwell, where I was for forty-nine of the Wildcats' fifty-seven full seasons there, it was the GOAT (greatest of all time)—the greatest Wildcat football game ever at Shotwell. Raise your hand if you were there, along with *Sports Illustrated* and 11,999 other college football fans.

Coach Bennie Ellender's Indians (their mascot now is Red Wolves) came to town with the latest two Southland championship trophies. They were undefeated at 5–0, ranked No. 1 in the NCAA college division (before the days of Divisions II and III) by the Associated Press, and ranked No. 2 in the UPI coaches poll, which had the University of Tampa—coming off a victory over the University of Miami Hurricanes—ranked No. 1. Coach Wally Bullington's Wildcats were 5–1 (having lost their season opener to Howard Payne before taking 5 straight wins in Bullington's third season) and rated No. 8 by UPI and No. 12 by AP. Seven players now in the ACU Sports Hall of Fame were on Bullington's roster that night. (And three more hall of famers were on the sideline coaching, including quarterback guru Ted Sitton.) *Sport Illustrated* reporter Skip Myslenski and photographer Jerry Cabluck spent two days in Abilene to contribute to *SI* columnist Pat

Putnam's article on college division football in the upcoming November 2 issue of the magazine.

Record-setting quarterback Jim Lindsey—and his talented set of receivers featuring Ronnie Vinson and Pat Holder—led the Wildcats. He was nearing the end of his Wildcat career as college football's all-time passing leader and the cause of no small amount of anxiety on the Indian sideline that night. Before the game, Arkansas State assistant coach Bill Davidson told Myslenski, "They can't drink, they can't smoke, they can't dance. Why did they stop there? Why didn't they put in a rule against quarterbacks?" Fortunately, there was nothing in the student handbook prohibiting quarterbacks. Unfortunately, the Indians prevailed 28–23 in this intense battle—called "one of the hardest fought games ever seen at Shotwell Stadium" by *Abilene Reporter-News* sportswriter Steve Oakey. The outcome was always in doubt, and virtually every play was as intense as each pitch in a 1–0 World Series game. That night, Lindsey recorded Abilene Christian's first

Chip Marcum takes the field at Shotwell Stadium before ACU's 1970 game against Arkansas State.

400-yard passing game by throwing for 414 yards and 3 touchdowns (all to the "incomparable" Vinson), but Arkansas State never trailed, and the Wildcats' fourth quarter comeback came up 5 points short. Lindsey led his team on an 81-yard scoring drive that ended with 5:05 to play to pull within five, but a final drive that started at 1:55 was unsuccessful after a third-down QB sack. "This was one of our best games ever," Bullington told the *Reporter-News* after the game. "I'm extremely proud of our football team. They kept their poise under pressure."

Putnam, writing in "They Don't Play No Mullets Down There" in the next issue of *Sports Illustrated*, said, "Go down to Abilene, Texas, sometime and catch Jim Lindsey, the nation's all-time total offense

leader. Not small college, not big college, but all college . . . . Lindsey is a God-fearing riverboat gambler, and you don't find that kind everywhere. He is a reverent man in a reverent school—Abilene Christian—but he tends to forget the Sermon on the Mount when he goes into battle, like Saturday night as he passed for three touchdowns against the percentage players of Arkansas State, the AP's very top small school, No. 1 in the NCAA division." The November 2 issue included Cabluck's classic photograph of the surfer-blond-haired Lindsey spinning a football. "This guy's the greatest," Cabluck said that weekend of Lindsey. "You don't have to worry about good 'pix' of him." Ellender, a hall of famer at Arkansas State who died in 2011, called Lindsey "the best quarterback

ACU and McMurry renew their cross-town rivalry in 1971 at Shotwell Stadium in a game the Wildcats won, 53–20.

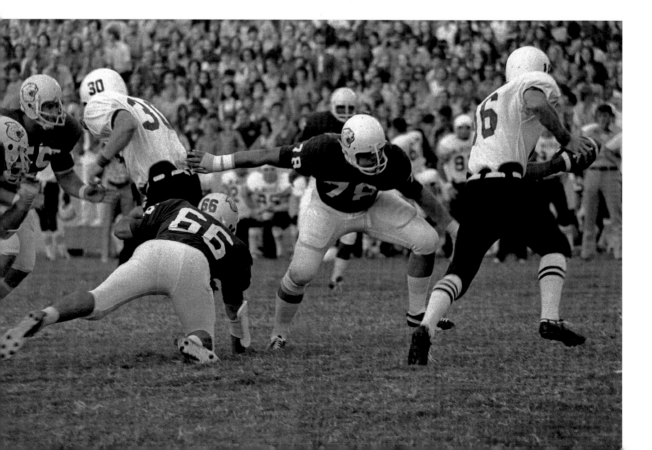

I've faced." Ellender added, "He could have easily ducked his head and left the field, but he sought me out, held his head high, and offered congratulations. It was a tribute to the outstanding young man Jim Lindsey is." The Indians finished 11–0 (capped by a win in the Pecan Bowl in Arlington) and were ranked No. 1 in the final polls to earn the 1970 national championship (before the NCAA instituted a playoff system), and Ellender left after the season to become head coach at his alma mater, Tulane University.

Sitton, Lindsey's quarterback coach who died in 2016 at the age of eighty-four, said the Sweeny, Texas, native had "everything a coach looks for in a quarterback. I wish I could say I taught Jim all he knew, but really he taught me all I know about throwing the football."

Lindsey's career ended two weeks later at Shotwell Stadium when he suffered a broken left collarbone early in the fourth quarter of a 21–7 win over the University of Texas-Arlington. With two games still to play, and an average of 300.8 passing yards per game, he would likely have been the first collegiate quarterback to throw for 9,000 yards in his career if he had been able to finish the season. The 1970 Wildcats finished 9–2 (after 8–2 in 1969), and Lindsey was 21–9–1 in his three seasons.

I've spent forty-nine seasons in Shotwell's venerable press box (and a few more games in earlier years in the stands); the first Shotwell game I remember was the 1960 homecoming game I attended with

Quarterback Jim Lindsey drops back to pass in the Wildcats' 1970 home game against Arkansas State.

my dad and uncle against the University of Southern Mississippi. Twenty-five years as director of sports information and twenty-one as a member of the highly acclaimed ACU "stat crew" after three on *The Optimist* staff. Wow! That's a lot of barbecue sandwiches! That string of Wildcat games at Shotwell Stadium that started on Halloween in 1959 with a one-point homecoming victory over Trinity came to an end Saturday, November 5, 2016, against Northwestern State University in another Southland contest. A few Wildcats returned to cheer for their alma mater one final time at Shotwell. One who I'm sure was there in spirit was Lindsey, another GOAT—the best quarterback ever at Abilene Christian. He threw for 8,521 yards and 61 touchdowns for the Purple and White. Yes, he was a reverent man

Quarterback Jim Lindsey (right) still ranks in the top 10 in ACU history in passing yards, total offensive yards, completions, attempts and touchdown passes.

how they're going to break me in two, and I just have to put it out of my mind and go back to the huddle." Lindsey, who died September 9, 1998, at the age of forty-nine, told Myslenski, "I feel God gave me all that I have. *And I know he can take it back at any time.* I just feel grateful for what's happening to me."

So Long Shotwell: A View from the Sidelines

by Ron Hadfield

I was not born around these parts, and have no natural affinity for P. E. Shotwell Stadium, whose namesake was Prince Elmer Shotwell, also known as "Pete," a Texas football-coaching legend.

Shotwell looks like other mostly concrete high school gridiron venues I have seen before in Texas. It also has a certain charm about it, and some engineering features not everyone has seen, like a restroom with a strategically placed window down the hall in the press box, allowing 99.9 percent privacy as well as a fine view of the game below. Say what? It's hard to explain, but one need not worry about answering the call of nature and missing a play. I am one of the fortunate fellows invited to help staff the press box at home ACU football games, a privileged view of the action I don't take for granted. It's not really a box and not everyone present is a member of the press, but there is no cheering in this upper room, at least in the professional press boxes at Shotwell run

who made an impression on Myslenski (and everyone else he met), who reported to his editors in New York, "Despite constant requests not to, Lindsey insisted on calling me 'Sir' during our whole talk. For real." Myslenski said Lindsey had "the confidence of a bluff poker player."

"Sure I'm confident," Lindsey told him the day before the game. "It's the only way to be. I don't think that's being conceited. It's just a fact. If you're scared, you're whipped before you start. Then there's no sense going out at all. I love being a leader. It's the only thing. It's all I've ever known, ever." (Lindsey played quarterback on all of his football teams since the eighth grade.) A daily reader of the Bible, Lindsey added in his conversation with Myslenski, "I like to read about Christ. They criticized him, spit on him, beat on him, did everything to him, and he kept cool. It just proves you can't lose your temper. Guys try to badmouth me, call me dirty names, tell me through the years by ACU sports media icons Lance Fleming and his Hall of Fame predecessor, Garner Roberts, who help keep the statistics team running smoothly and media guests happy.

The Shotwell press box has no central air-conditioning nor heat, so there are several games each season when we experience some combination of spring, summer, fall, and winter, depending on the wind direction. That makes it a great place to get a snoot full of mountain cedar, the most pristine puffs of West Texas pollen one can inhale at those lofty heights each fall. It also is a fine place to have your ankles chewed on by mosquitoes with stingers long enough to penetrate two layers of socks. But I'm not complaining. The fellowship and swapped stories are priceless, and the food, which serves as our compensation (mostly barbecue with some chicken fajitas thrown in for good measure), is mighty tasty. Oh, and there are those purple thumbprint cookies as they are called in these parts.

I was spoiled by a couple of seasons of writing about some really fine college football when I first transferred to ACU as a junior in fall 1976. That was the last Wildcat team with Wally Bullington as head coach, and he had a stable of good-enough-to-play-on-Sunday talent on his roster: Wilbert and Cle Montgomery, Johnny Perkins, Ove Johansson, and Chuck Sitton. They finished 9–2 and runner-up that season to mighty Texas A&I University, that era's football-playing

Babylonians of the Lone Star Conference. The Wildcats advanced to play in the Shrine Bowl in Pasadena (Texas, not California—rats) before Wilbert, Johnny, Ove, and others headed to NFL training camps the next summer. How good was the football? A&I was the only LSC team with more annual potential pro talent than ACU, and only one team other than the Javelinas or Wildcats won the NAIA Division I national title from 1973 to 1979. ACU ended A&I's 42-game winning streak with a disputed 25–25 tie in 1977, and both programs had amazing pedigrees of producing pros—better than many universities much larger and more well known. As sports editor of *The Optimist* in 1976–1977 and editor the next two years, I liked to stand on the home sideline for a closer view of the action and an insight to help

Willie the Wildcat and a young fan catch the action at ACU's last game at Shotwell Stadium.

Jeremy Enlow

write the game story. It proved a great angle to catch these memories:

Johansson's world-record 69-yard field goal on October 16, 1976, which still stands as the best a mortal has ever kicked in game competition. I had experience as a fan with long-distance field goals, having watched my hometown Detroit Lions fall to the awful New Orleans Saints in 1969 on a last-second 63-yarder by Tom Dempsey, who was born with half a foot and only one hand. He booted that NFL record kick (six yards longer than the previous, which made it that much more shocking) wearing a special-made high-top shoe, sort of like a club or mallet into which he laced up his half-foot. Pro Bowl tackle Alex Karras of Detroit promised he would walk home to Michigan if the Lions lost to the lowly Saints in the road game. He didn't, of course, but I have a soft spot in my heart for teams deflated by such mighty feet. East Texas State players trudged off the field after Johansson's kick, hands on hips and heads bowed while the Wildcats celebrated at midfield and the crowd went wild. They may as well have loaded onto their bus and headed back to Commerce, knowing ACU only needed to reach its 41-yard line to be in scoring position, effectively the largest "red zone" known in the sport. They and their collective psyche were toast.

Wilbert Montgomery's last collegiate season offered fleeting glimpses of the immense talent he possessed to run with a football. One opposing coach described his team's effort to tackle number 28 as "old men trying to catch a jackrabbit." Wilbert broke Walter Payton's career college touchdown scoring record the same day as Johansson's field goal in 1976, yet it took him three seasons to double the amazing 36 TDs he scored in 1973 as a freshman on ACU's national championship team. Targeted by defenses on every play, he suffered a deep thigh bruise in a game in Wichita Falls with Cameron University on November 6, 1976. He recovered after his senior season, was drafted in the NFL's fifth round, and went on to a record-breaking career with the Philadelphia Eagles, and induction into the College Football Hall of Fame the same year (1996) as fellow Mississippian Payton. Montgomery was still hobbled by that thigh injury and did not play in the 1976 season-ending Shrine Bowl against Harding University, likely an answer to a lot of pregame prayers among the Bison brethren in Searcy, Arkansas. The Wilbert-less Wildcats still beat ACU's sister school handily and haven't had a rematch since.

A cold 1976 night in late October, I watched quarterback Jim Reese throw for what is still a school-record 564 yards in a 26–0 win over Angelo State University. It had rained heavily that week in Abilene, and what was left of the brown Bermuda grass in Shotwell was skimpy at best. It was a muddy quagmire in places, and I still have no idea how any of Reese's receivers maintained enough traction to run routes. But they did, and perhaps were the only fellows on the field that night who knew in advance where they were headed.

I saw a Cameron University player leave the bench to trip Wildcat halfback Alex Davis as he was running free down the visiting team's sideline September 24, 1977, in Shotwell. The player, a drink in one hand and his helmet in another, stepped onto the field, stuck out his leg, and felled Davis in clear view of one of the officials. They awarded Davis a 52-yard touchdown, and ACU continued its 46–13 dismantling of the visiting Aggies.

Kelly Kent, the aw-shucks, country-boy sophomore fullback of the 1977 national championship team, suffered an embarrassing moment in a home game one afternoon in Shotwell. Running with the ball toward the south end zone in front of his team's bench, a would-be tackler reached for anything he could to stop the Cisco Kid, as *Abilene Reporter-News* sportswriting legend Bill Hart referred to Kent. The opponent came up with mostly air and a handful of the elastic waistband of Kelly's athletic supporter. Undaunted, Kent continued downfield while that key piece of equipment unraveled for yards behind him. Once the play was over, Kent headed to the locker room with a trainer to look for replacement gear. The laughter from his teammates continued for most of the game.

Later that season, Kent ran for 200 yards in ACU's national semifinal win over the University of Wisconsin-Stevens Point in Shotwell. The visitors from up north had a first-team All-American quarterback, Reed Giordana, who had thrown for 10,000 yards and 74 touchdowns in his career. The poor fellow spent a good bit of the afternoon on his back, counting clouds after a sack or knock-down by Wildcat defenders like Ruben Mason, Ray Nunez, Harold Nutall, Glenn Labhart, and others. Kent was named Offensive MVP of that game and the Apple Bowl, which followed. Not a fan of air travel, he kept his mind off things by reading his Bible from his back row plane seat on the long return flight to Abilene. A little more than a year later, he died suddenly of a heart attack at the age of twenty-one.

The Wildcats won the national championship in 1977 with an 11–1–1 record, their tie taking place in Kingsville to No. 1-ranked Texas A&I and their only loss occurring at homecoming in Shotwell the following week to longtime nemesis Angelo State. Dewitt Jones, the first-year ACU head coach, righted the ship and led the Wildcats to the Apple Bowl and their title in the Kingdome in Seattle, Washington. I was on the sideline and it was a superb roller coaster ride of a season.

The food is always better in the press box, but the on-the-field view will always be a fascinating angle from which to follow a game and gain the insights few fans get to see. I enjoyed the vista. Many seasons have passed since the Wildcats' heady days of the mid- to late-1970s when they were a small-college powerhouse. NCAA Division I and FCS are creating some growing pains for ACU football, but pro scouts still know to stop in Abilene each year for a look at the next Charcandrick West, Taylor Gabriel, Daryl Richardson, Bernard Scott, Clyde Gates, Mitchell Gale, Aston Whiteside, Tony Washington, and others.

However, the sideline is no longer a place for a sportswriter who is pushing sixty (and pushing it really hard), with tight hamstrings, slowing reflexes, and a distracting iPhone in his pocket. A fellow down there on Saturday without his head on a swivel could wake up in Hendrick Medical Center on Monday, or perhaps not at all.

I'll take my spot for a media-row view in the last game in Shotwell this Saturday, and like my similar-age teammates there, look forward to an upstairs seat in Wildcat Stadium next September. It will have carpet, central air and heat, a loo without a view, and other amenities beyond anything experienced at the venerable stadium on East South 11th Street we've shared with local high schools since Eisenhower was president. I'm convinced there are more memories to make, records to set, wins to describe, trophies to hoist. So make me a brisket and sausage sandwich, pour some sweet tea, log in to the wifi, and let's get the 2017 edition of an on-campus, home-sweet-home football show on the road. See ya, Shotwell. I'll leave my can of bug spray on the counter and the bathroom window open, conveniences only a sportswriter in West Texas might appreciate.

So Long Shotwell: A Son of Abilene's Reflections

by Lance Fleming

For a son of Abilene, P. E. Shotwell Stadium has always held a special place in my heart. It was never the best. It was never the biggest. It certainly didn't boast many of the most modern amenities. But it was our stadium. It's where we went on Friday nights to watch the Eagles or Cougars and then on Saturday to watch the Wildcats. I don't remember the first time I saw a game in the stadium, but I remember a lot of the games I watched in the fifty-eight-year-old venue.

I remember as a boy of seven years old being in the stadium on October 16, 1976, when Ove Johansson kicked a world-record 69-yard field goal and Wilbert Montgomery broke college football's all-time rushing touchdown record with the 67th score of his remarkable ACU career. Of course, instead of watching the game, I was undoubtedly playing one of the many games of "touch football" being contested on one of the berms on the north or south

ACU sports information directors (left to right) Lance Fleming, Dr. Charles Marler, and Garner Roberts pose together in the press box before ACU's final game at Shotwell Stadium on November 5, 2016.

Jeremy Enlow

end of the stadium. So I can say I was "at" the game when those two things happened, but I can't say I remember "seeing" either one of those plays. I remember just about one month later watching Abilene High play Abilene Cooper as the teams slogged through a 14–0 Cougar win in a driving snowstorm that had already piled several inches of snow on the field by the time the game started. I was there in 1977 when the Wildcats beat the University of Wisconsin-Stevens Point in the NAIA Division I semifinals to earn a bid to the Apple Bowl in Seattle, Washington, where they beat Southwestern Oklahoma State University to win the national championship. I remember the night in 1981 when the Eagles snapped Cooper's fifteen-year winning streak, thanks in large part to the "Pekowski Special," a guard-around play that helped the Eagles get off to a fast start and an early lead they never relinquished in a 17–7 win that freed the north side of town from the bonds of that divisive spell the Cougars held over the Eagles.

I remember watching my favorite college team—the ACU Wildcats—win big game after big game at the stadium, all in front of huge crowds on bright, sunny days that seemed to last forever. I remember Kelly Kent and Chuck Sitton. Jim Reese and John Mayes. Wilbert and Cle. Anthony Thomas and Boo Jones. Kurt Freytag and Mike Funderburg. Mark Wilson and Bob Shipley. Loyal Proffitt and Rex Lamberti. Mark Jackson and Arthur Culpepper. Dan Remsberg, John Layfield, and Dan

The Big Purple plays its halftime show before a packed house at the 1977 Homecoming game at Shotwell Stadium.

Niederhofer. Greg and Grant Feasel, and so many others. I remember the coaches who prowled those sidelines on Saturdays and ate almost daily at my father's barbecue restaurants, first The Smoke Pit on Highway 351 (where the Allsup's is now, just west of the Coca-Cola plant), and later at Danny's Bar-B-Q in the old gas station on Ambler Avenue in front of the now-defunct Bill Agnew's Superette. I would see those men in his restaurant when I was there either after school or working there

Jeremy Enlow

ACU fans cheer on the Wildcats during a second-half come-back that resulted in a 25–22 win over Northwestern State.

in the summer. Men like Wally Bullington and Dewitt Jones. Ted Sitton and Don Smith. Jack Kiser and Dr. Bob Strader. Don Harrison and Jerry Wilson. Those players and coaches are part of the memories of my youth, and many of those memories occurred in the confines of Shotwell Stadium.

I was fortunate enough to work for the *Abilene Reporter-News* for ten years from 1987 to 1997, and for the last five of those I was a full-time sportswriter covering Abilene High and Cooper athletics. That meant that most Friday nights, I was either at Shotwell Stadium or one of the other venues in West Texas where the only thing hotter than the hot chocolate was the head coach's seat after a loss. I was fortunate to cover several great

games in Shotwell—including Cooper's first home playoff victory in decades—as well as players like Dominic Rhodes, John Lackey, Ahmad Brooks, and Justin Snow, to name just a few from the Abilene ISD. There were great players from other teams as well, like Roy Williams from Odessa Permian, Cedric Benson from Midland Lee, and many others. I was there in 1993 when Cooper hosted Permian on a night when the temperature plummeted about forty degrees thirty minutes before kick-off, turning a brisk fall evening into a frigid winter night. The wind—howling out of the north at about forty miles per hour—actually blew a PAT attempt back onto the field of play in the Panthers' narrow win over Cooper. That night in the press box—which has never been outfitted with heating or air-conditioning and still only has one restroom for men and women to share—the sleet, wind, and cold weather combined to keep the windows of the press box fogged over so badly that we could barely see the field. So who spent the game wiping the windows in the press box so we could see the field? Legendary former Brownwood head coach Gordon Wood, because why wouldn't he?

I was hired at ACU in August 1998 as the new sports information director after the great Garner Roberts resigned as SID after twenty-five years in the role. As an ACU journalism student from 1987 to 1992, I had covered plenty of ACU football games for *The Optimist*, and I still believe Garner thought I was more trouble than I was worth as a student. Thank goodness he took pity on me when I got the job here and showed me the ropes. It took about two years before I felt like I was approaching knowing what I was doing. Some would probably still question, even after twenty-plus years on the job, if I know what I'm doing. There have been many great games and great players roll through Shotwell during my tenure in ACU athletics, some that won't soon be forgotten. The 2002 Wildcats won a share of the Lone Star Conference South Division title out of nowhere under the direction of then-head coach Gary Gaines. Then Chris Thomsen rolled

back into town in January 2005 and the program changed completely. With offensive coordinator Ken Collums calling the plays, quarterback Billy Malone at the controls, and a plethora of big-play players at their disposal, the Wildcats let loose the fury of a here-to-fore unseen offensive attack on the Lone Star Conference. Games where the Wildcats posted as many as 50 points were commonplace with the likes of Bernard Scott, Jerale Badon, Johnny Knox, Mitchell Gale, Clyde Gates, Taylor Gabriel, Daryl Richardson, Darrell Cantu-Harkless, and others roaming the field for the Wildcats. No one will ever forget the November day in 2008 when the Wildcats put up 93 points in a 93–68 win over West Texas A&M University in the NCAA Division II playoffs, a game that still stands the test of time as, arguably, the greatest in ACU history.

On a personal note, I'll not soon forget two days in the life of Shotwell, the first coming on Saturday, November 27, 2010, when the Wildcats hosted the University of Central Missouri in the second round

Wildcats (left to right) Joseph Thompson, offensive linemen Royland Tubbs, and tight end Trey Simeone lead the team onto the field for the 2009 season-opener at Shotwell Stadium against Northwest Missouri State.

Gerald Ewing

of the NCAA Division II playoffs. Just five days before, my then-eight-year-old son, Rex Fleming, had been diagnosed with a golf-ball size brain tumor and was going to be undergoing surgery the next week to remove what we would later learn was a cancerous tumor. I couldn't stand sitting at home, so I made my way out to the stadium where I found my comfort zone for about three hours. I hadn't been at the office at all during the week after we learned of Rex's condition, so my trusty assistant at the time, Phillip Dowden, along with Garner Roberts and Ron Hadfield, ran the press box for me that day. I stood on the sidelines, not able to muster the courage to be in the press box or stands and answer the hundreds of questions about Rex I knew were headed my way. But one moment I

didn't expect nearly sent me scurrying for the nearest private location I could find for a long, quiet cry. As he walked onto the field, my friend Chris Thomsen walked over to me, wrapped me in a tight bear hug, said a few words, and walked away with tears streaming down his face. We lost that day to the Mules, 55–41, but for the only time in my ACU career, I couldn't have cared less.

The second day was November 3, 2012, when Collums—who had become ACU's head coach in December 2011 after Thomsen left for an assistant coaching job at Arizona State University—asked Rex to be in the pregame locker room, call the coin flip, call the first play, and stand on the sidelines with him for as long as he wanted during ACU's final home game of

ACU captains (left to right) Parker McKenzie, Nik Grau, Austin Kilcullen, and Hayden Brodowsky watch the coin flip before the Wildcats' final game at Shotwell Stadium.

Jeremy Enlow

The Shotwell Stadium press box crew from the final game at the stadium on November 5, 2016—Seth Wilson, Keith Benfer, Chris Macaluso, Joey Roberts, Garner Roberts, David Catalina, Ron Hadfield, Grant Boone, Dr. Charlie Marler, and Lance Fleming.

Jeremy Enlow

the season against the University of West Alabama. Rex's play call of choice—the deep ball—went for a 33-yard completion from Gale to Gabriel on the first play of the game, and the Wildcats went on to a 22–16 overtime win. That turned out to be the last game of any type Rex ever attended. Five days later, he suffered a seizure that put him into hospice care and, twenty-two days after helping coach the Wildcats to the win over the Tigers, Rex went home, cured forever of cancer.

I greatly anticipate the first game at Wildcat Stadium and can't wait to see my team run out onto the field of a beautiful new facility that will be the best in the Southland Conference and one of the best at the FCS level. We'll have plenty of amenities, including heating and air-conditioning, and more than one restroom in the press box. But the memories I leave at Shotwell aren't negative. I spent a good portion of my youth there watching thousands of young men play a game we love and numerous great men I'm blessed to call friends coach those games. So as I leave Shotwell Saturday night, I'll take a look at the berms on each end and remember the good times and great friendships forged on those grassy hills. I'll also take a look over at the fairgrounds, close my eyes, and see the lights of the West Texas Fair and Rodeo twinkling again, just like they've done during every September home game most of my life.

I'll take a look at the scoreboard on the north end of the stadium and remember seeing the numbers "93" and "68" on the

The view from the north parking lot at Shotwell Stadium as ACU closes out its fifty-eight-year run at the stadium on November 5, 2016.

board and wishing we could have scored 100 against the Buffs. I'll take a look down the sideline and think about the great men and players who have roamed the home sideline for the past fifty-seven seasons, and I'll ask them to make sure their ghosts make the drive north on Judge Ely Boulevard and take up residence at our new digs. Then I'll squint really hard and see if I can still see my boy Rex down on the sideline or running around under the stands with his friends—Jaden Bullington, Nathan Watts, Connor Mullins, and others—playing their own games of touch football. And, finally, I'll take one last look around the place, hopefully feel a cool early November breeze against my face, and thank the old yard for being such a good home.

Farewell, Shotwell.

Jeremy Enlow

REVIVAL AND BEYOND

Chris Thomsen still remembers what some of his friends in the coaching profession told him back in December 2004 when he was a candidate for the head coaching position at ACU. The ACU job, they told him, was a coach killer. It was a dead-end job. It was, by all accounts, an impossible situation. He was told to run as fast and as far away from ACU as he possibly could because the Wildcats would never win big again. He heard all that and

Gerald Ewing

took the job anyway and was introduced on January 21, 2005, as the eighteenth head coach in program history.

Standing inside the Teague Center that day where Thomsen was introduced, no one had any idea that he was about to lead a renaissance of ACU football that would produce championship teams again, mold boys into men, take the university to the edge of NCAA Division I athletics, and provide the momentum needed to build the $50 million stadium that now stands on the north end of campus. ACU football was in store for a revival, and it would lead to the longest period of sustained success in program history.

After the great players of the 1970s and 1980s finished their eligibility and moved on from ACU, the program fell on some hard times. In the fifteen seasons spanning the years from 1987 to 2001, the ACU program enjoyed only three winning seasons and one other when it finished .500.

Head Coach Chris Thomsen watches the action on the field at Shotwell Stadium on November 22, 2008.

A lack of facilities, funding, and resources hampered the program, which went through five head coaches in those seasons: John Payne (26–34–2 from 1985 to 1990), Ronnie Peacock (4–15 from 1991 to 1992), Dr. Bob Strader (14–17 from 1993 to 1995), Jack Kiser (21–20 from 1996 to 1999), and Gary Gaines (21–30 from 2000 to 2004, although the Wildcats were 17–13 in his final three seasons). As the director of athletics, Cecil Eager hired Peacock and then moved past him after two down seasons and brought Strader in to try to revive the program. He did in 1993 with the help of quarterback Rex Lamberti, who returned after a seven-year absence to play

Linebacker Ryan Boozer left ACU as its all-time leading tackler and held that record until linebacker Sam Denmark broke it in 2017.

his final season, leading the Wildcats to a 7–3 record.

And it was Director of Athletics Stan Lambert who plucked Gaines from his job as the head coach at San Angelo Central to take over the program prior to the 2000 season. Gaines—who served two stints as the head coach at Odessa Permian High School and was one of the central figures in Buzz Bissinger's 1990 best seller, *Friday Night Lights*—was the head coach at Abilene High School for a couple of seasons (1994–1995) before heading south to San Angelo, where he was the Bobcats' head coach from 1996 to 1999. Before he arrived at Abilene High, the Eagles hadn't made the Class 5A state playoffs since 1959. But he laid the groundwork for a program that Steve Warren made into a perennial playoff contender and one that captured the Class 5A Division II state championship in 2009. After his first two seasons with the Wildcats, he and his coaching staff began to turn the tide of the Wildcats' program as they tied Texas A&M-Kingsville for the Lone Star Conference South Division title in 2002, finishing 6–4 overall and 5–1 in the LSC South before posting another 6–4 record in 2003.

That season, a redshirt freshman defensive back named Danieal Manning burst onto the scene with a combination of speed and playmaking ability that has only been seen in a few ACU athletes in the program's history. As Houston Oilers Coach Bum Phillips once said of Earl Campbell: "He might not be in a class by himself, but

Gerald Ewing

it don't take long to call the roll." The same can still be said of Manning, along with the likes of Wilbert Montgomery, Johnny Perkins, Bernard Scott, Johnny Knox, and Taylor Gabriel. There were other standouts for Gaines, as players like defensive linemen Clayton Farrell, Barrett Allen, Joe Edwards, and Devian Mims, linebackers Ryan Boozer and Shawn Taylor, running backs Eric Polk, Richard Whitaker, and Rashon Myles, offensive linemen Britt Lively and Blake Lewis, quarterback Colby Freeman, and defensive backs Dawon Gentry and Kendrick Walker helped lead a resurgence of ACU football.

Perhaps the biggest win of the Gaines era was his last as the head coach when, on the night of October 30, 2004, the Wildcats—banged up and playing without four injured starters and more than twice as many key backups—went to Kingsville and beat the No. 2 Javelinas, 17–10, to snap a twenty-year losing streak to Kingsville. Myles ran for 134 of his 148 yards in the second half of the game, and Doug Barnett had an end zone interception, and Manning posted a fourth-down pass breakup in the end zone near the end of the game as the Wildcats beat the Javelinas for the first time since a 38–24 win in 1983. But a little more than two months later, Gaines stepped away from ACU to become the director of athletics for the Ector County Independent School District in Odessa.

"I certainly enjoyed my five years at ACU," Gaines said. "We had a lot of fun, and I had the opportunity to coach some great kids and had a great staff to work with. I certainly enjoyed watching some of those young guys grow and develop, and that's always gratifying as a coach." That set then-Director of Athletics Jared Mosley off on a coaching search that had to be quick because National Signing Day was less than one month away when Gaines made his announcement. Mosley quickly set his sights on a former ACU player-turned-assistant coach, who left after the 1999 season to enter private business before getting back into coaching, first at Wichita Falls High School and then at the University of Central Arkansas, where he was the offensive line coach. "When you think back to the team that was already in place when Coach Gaines left, there was some talent there, maybe even a significant amount of talent," said Mosley, who left ACU in 2014 and is now the associate vice president and chief operating officer in the athletics department at the University of North Texas. "Chris was at the top of our list of candidates from the beginning because I remembered when he was at ACU the first time and I was a student-athlete that you would hear guys talking about him in the dorm and you could just hear how much respect and love they had for him."

Two weeks after Gaines announced his resignation, Thomsen was being introduced to the ACU community as its next head coach. "I believed the guys we had returning would buy into him and his system, and the culture he was going to instill was something that we needed," Mosley said of Thomsen. "We needed a really strong leader for the program, and we got that and more. His ability to recruit was the other selling point. He's always had the ability to identify and go out and get quality players and then get them to buy into what he's about. This was a program that was starting to make strides. I thought we could continue to build a program, but I don't think I ever imagined it would happen as quickly as it did, nor did I expect the success to sustain itself for as long as it has. I don't know that anyone could have predicted that." What transpired in a little less than ten years would forever change the course of ACU athletics.

—

The biggest and most important sales pitch that Thomsen had to make in January 2005 wasn't to a recruit, although they were important. First, he set his sights on the man he believed would help turn the program in the right direction: his brother-in-law, Ken Collums. Thomsen and Collums became friends in Vernon, Texas, when Thomsen moved there as a seventh-grader after his mother, Linda Nelson, remarried and his stepfather moved the family from San Antonio. It was while living in Vernon that Thomsen became acquainted with and comfortable in either a rural or urban setting. "When my biological father [Steve Thomsen] was alive, we lived in a multicultural neighborhood before I later moved to a farm," said Thomsen, who left ACU after the 2011 season and is now the offensive line coach at TCU, where he earned his undergraduate degree. "Because of that background, I feel comfortable in a lot of different environments, and that's helped me reach kids from all different backgrounds."

As young boys and then young college football players (Thomsen at TCU and Collums at Central Arkansas) and then young coaches together at ACU in the late 1990s, Thomsen and Collums dreamed of one day running a college football program that would focus on not just wins and losses on the field, but in the spiritual sense as well. They both liked to say that ACU offered "the most unique college football experience in the country" because of the emphasis that they each placed on "manhood." It got serious a couple of years into Thomsen's tenure when he took his team out of two-a-days in August and took them to a Promise Keepers retreat for a couple of days before returning to workouts in preparation for the upcoming season. No other college football program in the country would do that, but ACU continued to do it through the end of Collums's run as Thomsen's successor in 2016. "When we were both assistants at ACU [in the late 1990s], Ken and I would talk a lot about giving kids the chance to grow as men and using the game of football as the vehicle by which they would do it," said Thomsen, who is married to Collums's sister, LeAnn. "We ended up, after going through some detours along the way, being at a place in ACU where you could do it freely."

"I believe God put a vision in both of us through different experiences," Thomsen said. "Part of mine was that I had played at TCU and had seen college football in a different light and wanted to do it differently. Ken really helped me with the vision of being intentional with players in terms of teaching them about God and using the game to reach them for Jesus. When I got the job, I was overwhelmed with the logistical part of being a head coach. That first year, he really kept on pushing the 'manhood' aspect of the program. Then when I got a little more comfortable, we were able to carry out that vision." Collums, who would go on to become the Wildcats' head coach for five seasons from 2012 to 2016, said the program's mission was always bigger than wins and losses. "I always told

Gerald Ewing

Thomsen led the Wildcats to undefeated regular seasons in 2008 and 2010, the only head coach in ACU history to accomplish such a feat.

Gerald Ewing

ACU had one of the best offensive lines in NCAA Division II football in 2007, featuring (left to right) 2008 first-team All-American Joseph Thompson and Matt Raesner at tackle, Cody Savage at guard, 2008 first-team All-American and Gene Upshaw Award winner Sam Collins at center, and two-time first-team All-American Nathan Young at guard.

▲

guys when we recruited them that we were going to play football at a high level, and that we were going to make them better people before they left ACU," he said. "We wanted to create a movement of men who would change their families for generations to come by leaving behind their old ways and learning how to become real men, real husbands, and real fathers." One of the keys to making the whole thing work the way that both Thomsen and Collums desired came in the form of a redshirt freshman offensive lineman from

inner-city Dallas who was ready to leave just as Thomsen was getting started.

Joseph Thompson served a redshirt season in 2004 and met with Thomsen shortly after he got the job in January 2005, mainly to tell Thomsen that he was ready to leave for somewhere, actually anywhere, else. The culture shock of moving from Dallas (Lincoln High School) to Abilene was, at times, more than he could handle. And he told Thomsen that in their first meeting. "I struggled to make friends early on because of the cultural differences, and, more than anything, I started to dislike white people," Thompson said. "I believed I had done a lot to try and make friends and it wasn't being reciprocated, so I had my mind on leaving."

And so he met with his new head coach with every intention of getting out of Abilene as quickly as possible. "I had a grand plan and told [Thomsen] that I thought he was a great guy, but I didn't like white people and I was leaving ACU," Thompson said. "But then he spent time with me meeting me one-on-one and

Jeremy Enlow

Wide receiver Taylor Gabriel is second in ACU history in catches, receiving yards, and touchdown receptions. He is now in his fourth season in the NFL after having signed with the Chicago Bears prior to the 2018 season.

▶

trying to reach me. He spent time with me throughout the spring and summer, but it took about six months before I realized he was different. He was real, and I got to know as much about him as he got to know about me. The thing that really made me trust him was that he wasn't dismissive of the things I was complaining about. He began to help me work through those issues." And while those off-field issues were never squelched to the degree that Thompson would have liked, they definitely got better. And because of his background and willingness to change and adapt to different cultures, he became a leader in the Wildcats' locker room, along with players like Cody Stutts, Sam Collins, Jerale Badon, Kendrick Holloway, Nathan Young, Eric Edwards, Bryson Lewis, and later Mitchell Gale, Taylor Gabriel, Kevin Washington, and many others. The common denominator for each of those men was that they were all terrific players, lending credibility to their voices when they spoke up.

"The impact I think I was able to have was that I was able to operate in both worlds," said Thompson, who is now working with the Fellowship of Christian Athletes and is the athletics chaplain at the University of Houston. "I think I fit somewhat of the mold of someone who was trying to grow into a man and what it meant to follow Christ. Some guys started following that as we began to hang out and bond off the field, and that transferred onto the field." Thomsen said the January 2005 meeting between the two of them set the tone for the program and for the life that Thompson has gone on to lead.

"When he told me that he was going to transfer to North Texas, I asked him

Left tackle Joseph Thompson (center) was a second-team NCAA Division II All-American selection in 2008 and a key part of Head Coach Thomsen's plan to rebuild the culture inside the Wildcats' locker room.

the main problem and he told me that he didn't feel comfortable either culturally or racially," Thomsen said. "I told him that maybe God had sent him to ACU to help change all of that, to help make it a place more welcoming in a multicultural world. God used that to really change his mind about ACU and what his mission and purpose in life was going to be. That guy bridged a lot of barriers with a lot of people while he was at ACU, and he's still doing it today. He already knew the Lord when he got to ACU, and he has wonderful parents. God used each of us to impact the other. He was a tremendous leader and catalyst for change in our football program. He and Sam Collins were best friends, and Sam was another huge catalyst for us. Those are special people in my life."

Collins is now a high school football coach at his alma mater, Denton Ryan High School, after starting every game the Wildcats played from 2005 to 2008 and then serving as an assistant coach for the Wildcats from 2009 to 2013. After a rocky start with Thomsen, Collins became one of the new head coach's most important high school signees in February 2005. "I was about to commit to Central Arkansas when Coach Thomsen was there, but then he left and I got a call from UCA telling me my scholarship had been pulled," Collins said. "I got a call from Coach Thomsen about a week later, and he wanted me to go to Abilene and play for him at ACU. But I didn't want to play at ACU." But an old Wildcat who was coaching at UCA at

the time, Adrian Eaglin, told Collins to take Thomsen up on his offer and play in Abilene. "Coach Eaglin told me that Coach Thomsen was one of the best men he knew and that if I had the chance to play for him, I shouldn't pass it up. I ended up going to Abilene on a visit and fell in love with it. I could tell immediately there was something different about ACU and about what Coach Thomsen and Coach Collums were trying to put together. Everything that Coach Eaglin told me about Coach Thomsen and Coach Collums was exactly right. I could tell right away those two guys were going to invest in me as a man first and as a football player second."

Thomsen was able to understand some of what his players had seen growing up because he had grown up in his own tough circumstances. When he was ten years old, his parents divorced after his mother spent years putting up with a husband who had graduated from the University of Texas and had a lucrative sales job in Sealy only to throw it all away on drugs and alcohol. "My dad had a good job and let substance abuse—mainly alcohol—ruin him," Thomsen said. "My mom had to divorce him, and we had to move on. I saw that play out firsthand, so I know how destructive that is for families. That's a big part of why there was so much intentional teaching about what it is to be a man and how to identify the meaning of being a real man.

"Our goal was to win championships on the field, give those guys an opportunity to graduate, and give them a clear

Gerald Ewing

Head Coach Chris Thomsen waits to lead the Wildcats onto the field before a game at Shotwell Stadium.

and compelling definition of what a man is that they could carry with them for the rest of their lives," he said. "I still go back to the standards we talked about, even today, when I don't think I'm being the husband or the man I should be each day."

The culture that Thomsen and Collums created in the football program even rubbed off on other programs within the athletics department. "The impact those guys had on the football program in particular and the department as a whole was phenomenal," Mosley said. "It really kind of propelled a lot of our other coaches to think more intentionally about how they were going to build a culture in their own programs, what they were going to focus on, and what they were striving for each season." As things were starting to turn in

the right direction off the field, the pace quickly picked up on the field as well. It was hastened by the arrival of a pair of players in 2007 who would lay waste to the ACU record book.

The 2005 season was the definition of "up-and-down season." The Wildcats let a couple of games get away from them they should have won, won a couple they shouldn't have, beat two nationally ranked teams in Tarleton State and Texas A&M-Kingsville near the end of the season, and eventually settled in at 4–6 on the season. Quarterback Billy Malone and offensive coordinator Collums had an off-season heart-to-heart talk that eventually led to Malone becoming the program's first 12,000-yard career passer, and Danieal

Gerald Ewing

Award-winning center Sam Collins takes the field before a 2007 game at Shotwell Stadium.

Manning left school early to enter the 2006 NFL draft, where he was the 42nd pick overall by Chicago—the Bears' first selection.

And then 2006 rolled around.

Thomsen had his mind set on making the Wildcats winners again, and it started in January 2006 with 6:00 A.M. workouts four mornings every week when school resumed. "I vividly remember walking out one morning and saying, 'I hope fifty of you quit today,'" he said. "We weren't easy on them. I remember screaming at Billy [Malone] to just quit and take the easy way out while he was doing up-downs in the snow. Then there was Jerale Badon, who was a little bit crazy. He was the type who loved it even more the harder we made it. Cody Stutts was the same way. Mike Kern. Tony Harp. Travis Carpenter. Cody Savage.

Matt Raesner. Caleb Stone. We had some tough players on that team. That team wasn't as talented as some we would have later, but it might have been our most mentally tough team."

Badon—the heart and soul of the 2006 and 2007 teams—had played for Gaines in 2004 after a stellar career at Abilene High School, but blossomed under Thomsen and Collums. "When Coach Thomsen first arrived, he made believers out of everyone," Badon said. "We all believed we would be winners, and that process started on those cold January and February mornings. We would show up and sit on that frozen ground and our pants would be soaking wet, along with our socks and underwear. But those mornings ultimately built the toughness that we all wanted but didn't know how to get. Those mornings built our minds and our bodies, but they also gave us something to draw on during the season when things got tough; we could all look back on those moments and pull through because nothing we were facing on the field was worse than some of those 6:00 A.M. workouts."

Collins remembers those mornings as laying the groundwork not only for the 2006 season, but also for the next seven or eight that followed. "We worked out on the 'frozen tundra' of old Elmer Gray Stadium," Collins said, "and Coach Thomsen and Coach Collums made sure there was discipline and accountability for everyone. The thing that made everything work was we had a great group of leaders on that team.

Guys like Cody Stutts and Jerale Badon and Travis Carpenter, just to name a few. We had good players, but those guys gave that 2006 team a mentality that we could fight in close games and win them. The whole team rallied around those guys."

ACU won its season opener at home against Central Oklahoma, and then won again at nationally ranked Southeastern Oklahoma State, beating the Savage Storm, 51–14. That set the tone for a run that saw ACU open the season 6–0 and return to the NCAA Division II national rankings for the first time since October 1997. Then came the game that put ACU football back on the map and turned the tide of the program: October 19 in Canyon, Texas, against No. 4 West Texas A&M. The No. 20-ranked Wildcats were supposed to be a mere speed bump in the Buffaloes' road to the Lone Star Conference championship,

and that's how it started with WT jumping out to a 15–0 first-quarter lead. But Malone threw a then-school record 6 touchdown passes—three of them to John Brock, who had four catches for 160 yards—as ACU rallied to a 49–33 win in front of a national television audience and a huge throng of ACU fans who made the drive from Abilene. "There was a lot of talk coming out of Canyon about how we were 6–0, but hadn't played anybody," Thomsen said. "We honestly didn't know how good we were, either, but we knew we were about to find out. After we won the game, we all realized that it was possible that this was a playoff team."

The game that clinched a playoff berth came on November 4 in Kingsville, where many Wildcat seasons had gone to die. Taking on an uncharacteristically poor Kingsville team (it would finish winless

Wide receiver Jerale Badon—the heart and soul of the 2004–2007 Wildcats—is ACU's all-time leader in receptions and receiving yards. He is also tied for eighth in career touchdown receptions.

Gerald Ewing

in conference play), the Wildcats found themselves in a battle going to the fourth quarter, tied 31–31. ACU took a 38–31 lead with 6:38 left in the game on a Taber Minner 1-yard touchdown run, only to see the Javelinas tie the game at 38–38 with 1:03 to play on a 6-yard touchdown pass. That's when Malone, Badon, and the right leg of Matt Adams rode to the Wildcats' rescue. After two completions to Chris Morris and one to Minner moved the ball to the ACU 40-yard line, Badon, who had left the game in the first half with an injured left knee and remained on the bench icing the knee

Placekicker Matt Adams is the Wildcats' all-time leading scorer among kickers as well as the career leader in PATs and PAT attempts.

throughout the second half, limped back onto the field and settled into his position in the left slot. He caught a quick slant from Malone and began half-limping, half-running down the middle of the field as the game clock ticked under 10 seconds. He finally began to veer toward the far sideline, finally collapsing out of bounds at the Kingsville 8-yard line with three seconds left on the clock. It was the play that typified the player and the Wildcats' season all in one 10-second burst. Adams banged home a 25-yard field goal at the buzzer and the Wildcats had their eighth win of the season, securing a spot in the NCAA Division II playoffs for the first time ever. But the season would come to a crushing end two weeks later when ACU gave up a 27–12 fourth-quarter lead in Canyon and lost to WT, 30–27, in overtime when a game-tying field goal attempt by Adams was blocked by Wildcat-turned-Buffalo Don Hooks, sending the Wildcats into the off-season. "We knew that with Billy in place for two more seasons we were set at quarterback," Thomsen said. "But we just didn't have a game-breaker at wide receiver, and we had to get some speed. We had to get faster and more athletic all over the field, and, fortunately, we were able to do that."

Just as the Vernon connection brought Thomsen and Collums to Abilene, in the summer of 2007, it also brought Bernard Scott, Clyde Gates, and Aston Whiteside to town. And while he didn't get to Abilene via Vernon, Johnny Knox got there like he

Jeremy Enlow

did everything else—very quickly. Four of the greatest playmakers in ACU history hit the campus at about the same time, and while Whiteside would redshirt as a defensive end in 2007, the coaches knew they had something special just waiting to be unleashed on unsuspecting offenses in 2008. What they were really looking forward to, however, was putting Scott and Knox into the lineup. They didn't really know about Gates until the first time they saw him run. He showed up with Scott (his cousin) and Whiteside (another cousin) in 2007 and was trying on a helmet when Thomsen strolled by the equipment room and did a double take as he saw Gates in person for the first time since he was a young man in Vernon. He asked him what he was doing, and Gates told him he thought he'd try out for the football team, despite having never played high school football. "Were you planning on telling me?" Thomsen asked, before eventually agreeing to the tryout. It was a good move on his part. Gates was a whirling dervish of long hair and long legs, but he was also one of the fastest men to ever wear the Purple and White. His only competition on those teams was Knox, who blistered cornerbacks from Canyon to Kingsville and all parts in between in his two seasons as a Wildcat.

Then there was the incomparable Scott, who had a troubled past but put it all behind him when he transferred to ACU from Blinn College, where he had helped his team to a national championship in

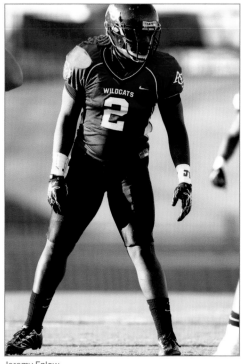

Jeremy Enlow

Defensive end Aston Whiteside finished his career with 31.5 career sacks and is regarded as one of the best pass rushers in ACU history.

2006. He would leave ACU after two seasons that saw him rush for a school-record 4,321 yards, score a school-record 438 points, become the program's all-time leader in all-purpose yards (5,712), and win the Harlon Hill Trophy in 2008 as the top player in NCAA Division II football, one year after he finished as the runner-up for the award to Chadron State (Nebraska) running back Danny Woodhead. "Bernard and Johnny were obviously big-time difference-makers," Thomsen said, "and then Clyde just kind of unknowingly popped onto the scene and that gave us even more punch."

Knox was a Thomsen kind of player: always had a smile on his face, didn't care if he caught one ball or ten as long as his team won, and worked extremely hard

Jeremy Enlow

One of the fastest players to ever play for the Wildcats, wide receiver Clyde Gates was selected in the fourth round of the 2011 NFL Draft by the Miami Dolphins.

every play. Scott was simply a breathtaking runner and pass-catcher, and both went on to be selected in the 2009 NFL draft, Knox by the Bears and Scott by the Bengals. "I tried to be a leader by example; it was the only thing I ever knew," Knox said. "I practiced hard every day and I played hard because I wanted the younger guys to see that and know that was the only way to get better and contribute to a winning program. I didn't really care who got the credit as long as we won games.

"I understood that when we had a guy like Bernard in the backfield, he was going to be the guy to get the ball in a lot of crunch-time situations," he said. "If he got the ball, I was going to be blocking hard down the field to try to spring him for some extra yards, and I knew he would do the same to help Billy deliver the ball when we had a pass play called."

The playmaking ability of Scott and Knox didn't take long to notice, even for Collins, who spent most of his career with those two players never seeing their exploits, mainly because he was too busy snapping the ball and then protecting Malone from oncoming pass-rushers. "We kind of got the ball rolling in 2006, and then we added dynamic playmakers in 2007, and that took it to another level," Collins said. "When you add dynamic players with a great quarterback, then you have a chance to have some great teams."

With the talent that was now running around the practice field, sometimes day-to-day workouts were tougher than the actual games themselves, something Scott quickly noticed. "That was a big part of why we were so successful," he said. "Everybody practiced so hard that when we got into games, it was almost easier than the week of practice. Coach Collums wouldn't let us settle for mediocrity, even in practice. So if that meant he had to get in somebody's face or throw a hat around, that's what he was going to do." After a stumble to start the 2007 season at Central Oklahoma, ACU's offense clicked into high gear. The Wildcats battered NCAA Division I Football Championship Subdivision (FCS) member Texas State, 45–27, in the second game and then proceeded to bomb the next five opponents on the schedule, never scoring fewer than 41 points in those five games and rolling to a 6–1 record. West Texas A&M ruined the party on homecoming with a 41–31 win as Scott was limited because of an injury, but ACU then reeled off three wins in their final three games—including 70 points in a wild 70–63 win at Tarleton State the week after the loss to WT—to secure a 9–2 regular season and a second straight bid to the NCAA Division II playoffs. The Wildcats secured the playoff berth with a 42–41 road win at Midwestern State in Wichita Falls in the regular-season finale when they rallied from a 17-point second-half deficit to beat the Mustangs, who had a last-play Hail Mary into the end zone broken up by the ACU defense. ACU topped Mesa State (Colorado), 56–12, in the first round, setting up a showdown against Woodhead and Chadron State the next week in northwestern Nebraska. The Wildcats dominated the game for three quarters, carrying a 49–20 lead into the fourth quarter only to be outscored 36–7 in an incredible fourth-quarter display by the Eagles, who got the game to overtime tied at 56–56. Chadron eventually won the game, 76–73, in triple-overtime, cementing the most heartbreaking loss of the Thomsen era.

ACU rebounded in 2008 to run the table in the regular season, including a come-from-behind win at perennial powerhouse Northwest Missouri State in the season opener that saw ACU rally from a 21–7 first-quarter deficit to win going away, 44–27.

Those two teams would meet again in the second round of the playoffs, and November 22, 2008, turned out to be the wildest game in ACU football history. The Wildcats won the game, 93–68, on a day when both offenses—featuring NFL-level talent across the board—were clicking at peak efficiency, leaving the defenses powerless to stop them. Scott was the decisive factor in the game, scoring a school-record 7 touchdowns as the teams shredded the NCAA, Lone Star Conference, ACU, and West Texas A&M record books. The Wildcats and Buffs combined to set forty-four NCAA, NCAA Division II, NCAA Division II playoff, conference, and school records in the Wildcats' amazing win. A crowd of 11,797 fans watched ACU tally a school-record 810 yards of offense and score touchdowns on 13 of 15 possessions. Scott ran for 292 yards and 6 touchdowns and had another 61 yards and 1 touchdown receiving. Malone completed 16 of 25 passes for 383 yards and 6 touchdowns, and Knox caught 5 passes for 125 yards. West Texas A&M's 68 points were the result of 721 yards of offense: 595 yards of passing and 7 touchdowns for quarterback Keith Null (NCAA playoff, LSC, and WT single-game records) and 14 catches for 323 yards and 5 touchdowns for wide receiver Charly Martin.

The only negative part of the game for the Wildcats came at the end when Null, with his team trailing 93–61, hit Martin with a 52-yard touchdown pass with just three seconds to play. That meant the Wildcats would get the ball one more time on a kickoff return with a chance to

Bernard Scott breaks loose for one of his record-setting 7 touchdowns in ACU's 93–68 win over Division II rival West Texas A&M.

put triple digits on the scoreboard. And the fans at Shotwell Stadium knew it, too, as the student section began chanting "We want 100! We want 100!" Gates and fellow receiver Marcus Franklin tried to give them 100 as they lateraled the ball a couple of times in an attempt to score another touchdown.

When the game finally ended with the ball at the ACU 47-yard line, the Buffs were in no mood to shake hands, instead engaging the Wildcats in a postgame shoving match at midfield because of what happened on the kickoff return, as well as what had just taken place over the previous four hours of play. "I haven't seen anything like that game before that or since," Thomsen said. "What gets lost is that Don [Carthel] started onside kicking in the second half, and we recovered every one of them and had great field position. Once that started happening, it just snowballed on them. As

Gerald Ewing

Jeremy Enlow

far as the end of the game, I wouldn't have been proud of one hundred points. But it never should have gotten to that point. WT had the ball and could have run out the clock, but they decided to throw it deep and that made our guys angry. The kick-off return was not a designed or called play, but it was perceived to have been by their players and coaches. That's not what we were about as a program."

ACU broke in a new quarterback, Gale, in 2009 and finished 9–4, returning to the playoffs again, reaching No. 1 in the nation for the first time ever at the NCAA Division II level, and winning a road playoff game for the first time in program history with a 24–21 first-round win at Midwestern State. But the season ended with a disappointing 35–10 loss at Northwest Missouri State in the second round of the playoffs. The Wildcats were perfect in 2010, at least in the regular season, as Gale had a magical season, throwing for 38 touchdowns against just 3 interceptions as ACU finished 11–0 in the regular season for the first time in program history. Gates led a fantastic receiving

crew that included Kendrick Johnson, Raymond Radway, and Gabriel, finishing the season with 66 catches for 1,182 yards and 13 touchdown catches. ACU's potent running game was led by the trio of Darrell Cantu-Harkless, Daryl Richardson (Scott's younger brother and a terrific player in his own right), and Charcandrick West, who combined for 1,406 rushing yards and 15 touchdowns. But another disappointing playoff loss in the first round—this time a 55–41 home loss to Central Missouri in the second round—brought a sudden end to the ACU season.

The 2011 campaign got off to a good start as ACU was 5–1 going into a late-season showdown at Midwestern State. But the Mustangs had their way with the Wildcats on October 22, whipping ACU, 70–28, in the team's worst loss of the Thomsen era. But another playoff trip awaited at the end of the regular season, and it resulted in another disappointing ending as the Wildcats dropped a 52–49 decision

Jeremy Enlow

Running back Daryl Richardson put together one the quietest great careers of any player in ACU history, as he ranks in the top ten in career carries, rushing yards, and rushing touchdowns.

▲

Running back Charcandrick West was one of the most electrifying players in ACU history and ranks fourth in career rushing touchdowns and eighth in career points.

▶▶

at Washburn in a game that saw Gale become only the second ACU quarterback in history to throw for at least 500 yards in a game—joining record-holder Jim Reese, who still holds the school record with 564 yards in a 1976 win over Angelo State—finishing the game with 506 yards and 4 touchdowns in a valiant performance.

Less than one month after the season-ending loss, Thomsen was gone, leaving ACU for a job as an assistant coach at Arizona State, where he would spend about two months before moving back to Texas to be the offensive line coach at Texas Tech. He spent one season (2012) at Texas Tech, even leading the Red Raiders to a Texas Bowl win over Minnesota as the interim head coach after Tommy Tuberville abruptly left the program, only to return to Arizona State where he would spend four seasons (2013–2016)

before moving back to the Big 12 and his alma mater in early 2017 as the offensive line coach at TCU. "I still believe I was fortunate to have spent seven seasons as the head coach at ACU," Thomsen said. "Those were amazing years, and we had a great run. I'll be forever grateful to Jared and [then-ACU president] Dr. Royce Money for giving me the opportunity to be a head coach on the collegiate level. ACU is an exceptional university, and I'll always have great memories of my time there." Just one week after Thomsen announced he was leaving, Mosley announced Collums as the nineteenth head football coach in ACU history, and the winning continued. But changes were looming. Changes that would lead to a pair of announcements that had been long-awaited by ACU fans for a number of years.

CHANGE IS GONNA COME

A few hundred people watched intently as Southland Conference Commissioner Tom Burnett stood on a press conference stage in the Hunter Welcome Center lobby on August 25, 2012, turned to ACU President Dr. Phil Schubert, and extended an invitation two

Jeremy Enlow

years in the making. With trustees, administrators, staff, coaches, current and former student-athletes, alumni, and fans peering down from the walkway above and assembled in front of them, Schubert shook Burnett's hand, thanked him, and provided the answer everyone was gathered to hear: the Wildcats were headed back to the Southland and on to NCAA Division I, returning to the athletics league it had helped create more than fifty years prior. The move aligned ACU's academic vision with some of the top universities in the nation and brought the entire athletics program to the NCAA Division I level for the first time.

Not long after taking office as ACU's eleventh president in June 2010, Schubert made a request of Mosley. "I told Jared I needed him to help me gain a good, strong perspective about the dynamics of intercollegiate athletics and whether or not we were properly positioned in NCAA Division II," Schubert said. "I'd heard

ACU President Dr. Phil Schubert speaks to the crowd as Southland Conference commissioner Tom Burnett looks on, shortly after Schubert accepted Burnett's invitation for ACU to rejoin the Southland Conference in 2013.

people say we should be Division III or Division I or remain Division II forever. But I wanted a complete study of the question and to be able to assemble the kind of perspectives and information that would lead us to a conclusion we could reach with confidence." The assessment took seven months—April through November 2010—and evaluation another three. The development of a transition plan, including an intense focus on its financial aspects, then continued for more than eighteen months. Concurrently, the Southland found itself exploring expansion while looking to replace three members it was losing to the Western Athletic Conference.

The answers Schubert received from Mosley were complex and took time to analyze, but they led the board of trustees in late August 2012 to make a historic decision in the life of ACU. With $4.3 million in first-year "transition funding" secured from a small group of alumni and other donors, the board voted August 24 to accept an official invitation to rejoin the Southland and move ACU into a new era as a full member of NCAA Division I, beginning July 1, 2013. The vote ended forty years of membership in the LSC (ACU left at the end of the 2012–2013 academic year) and returned ACU to a league it helped form in 1963. However, the decision didn't come without untold hours of research, many meetings, and campus-wide forums, and the input of trustees, administrators, faculty, staff, and coaches. Schubert's acceptance of the Southland Conference invitation on behalf of ACU was an affirmative answer to more than a question about the future of Wildcat athletics. The board's vision for ACU is not wrapped up in winning national championships or how many football players it can send to the National Football League. While athletics will remain a vitally important part of the ACU landscape, the move was made more for academic reasons, and while some might scoff at that notion, a look at the facts reveals the university had little choice but to reach that conclusion.

According to the report Mosley prepared for Schubert and the board, ACU's Division II student-athletes were less academically prepared and less likely to graduate from ACU when compared to the general student population. The average ACU ACT score of student-athletes at the time was 22.3, compared to 24.2 for their classmates. During the five years previous to the move to Division I athletics, the first-year retention of student-athletes averaged 67 percent, while nonathletes averaged almost 75 percent. During those five years, the disparity was as much as 15 percent (59 percent to 76 percent). According to *U.S. News and World Report* rankings, the average SAT score for all students in LSC-affiliated universities was nearly 100 points below the average of students at ACU. As ACU's academic requirements for admission and expectations for retention performance continued to rise, those gaps would likely have

Jeremy Enlow

widened without a philosophical change or a move to Division I.

"By far, the most significant issue of the move was academic alignment," Schubert said. "The standards for academic eligibility at the Division I level are significantly different than in Division II, and they align much more closely with our broader academic aspirations. We were in a situation at the Division II level where we were trying to pull both ends of a rubber band, so to speak. We wanted to remain highly competitive, but had found it increasingly difficult to do so in an environment that stretched us in the wrong direction in regard to the academic standards we'd like to maintain [at ACU]." Certainly the move to Division I athletics was spurred on by the success of the football program, as well as sustained excellence in track and field, baseball, women's basketball, and success in the relatively young softball (started in 1997) and women's soccer (started in 2007) programs.

But for Mosley, it all goes back to what was going on in the football program. "There's no question that had we not gotten football off the ground, I don't think we could have gotten the momentum we needed to make a move to Division I athletics," he said. "And I honestly don't believe we would have had the momentum we needed to get facility upgrades like what has taken place since before and after I left ACU. When you get football going at the level we did for a long period of time, it opens people's eyes to the possibilities. You eliminate the excuses we might have heard had we not been so successful. Excuses like 'We can't afford it,' or 'We can't make it at Division I.' I think what those guys [Thomsen and Collums] did from start to finish laid the groundwork and really created the momentum that got people excited about ACU football again and believing we could compete on a level with the big boys of intercollegiate athletics."

Not long after the move to Division I athletics became a reality, a buzz about an on-campus football stadium began to move through the university. And on February 14, 2014, Schubert stood in front of the campus community at daily chapel and announced $55 million in donations to the university to kick off the Vision in Action initiative, which would change the face of the ACU campus in a way not seen for more than fifty years through five capital projects. Three facilities were for ACU's science programs, and two were

Jared Mosley—ACU's seventh director of athletics—hired Chris Thomsen as the head football coach in 2005, a move that eventually helped ACU land an on-campus football stadium and push the athletics program to NCAA Division I affiliation.

ACU alumni Mark and April Anthony were the lead donors in making the Wildcats' on-campus stadium a reality with their $25 million commitment.

▶

Former Director of Athletics Lee De León speaks to the crowd during the ground-breaking ceremony for Anthony Field at Wildcat Stadium in February 2016.

▶▶

for athletics, highlighted by the addition of a new on-campus football stadium where the legendary Elmer Gray Stadium once stood. ACU alumni Mark and April Anthony made a $30 million commitment to ACU to help with campus facilities and College of Business Administration endowments, $15 million of which was earmarked for Wildcat Stadium. They eventually increased the amount of their stadium gift to $25 million. "I was a student-athlete, so I know the importance of athletics on campus, as well as high standards for the academic side," said Mark Anthony, who played on the Wildcat golf team. His wife, April, was a member of the university's Board of Trustees before becoming the first woman in ACU history to chair the board when she was elected to the post in February 2018. "This is going to bring the alumni, current students, and faculty all together in a first-class facility of which everyone will be proud," said Mark. The Anthony gift was the single largest in

ACU history, but they were carrying on the long-standing tradition of giving to athletics set forth by the many generous donors who had come before them.

"I credit Chris [Thomsen] a lot because by the end of his second year, we were able to get a couple of architecture firms to draw up some possible plans for a stadium," Mosley said. "We weren't trying to raise money, but just trying to create some excitement and give people a glimpse at what we could have. It took a number of years to push that vision to the point where the Anthonys came on board to get it done. And then for the Anthonys and Onsteads and Halberts to all come together at the same time with the largest influx of capital in ACU's one hundred-plus years was an amazing blessing. As excited as people are today, it'll be fun to look back fifteen

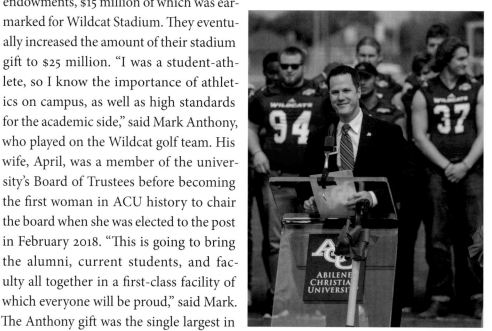

Steve Butman

Steve Butman

or twenty years from now and see exactly what the impact will have been. There have been a lot of people who have dreamed about that stadium for a number of years, so it's really exciting to see that dream is now a reality."

Mosley stepped down as the director of athletics in October 2014 to become the CEO of the Texas Sports Hall of Fame, and he was replaced by Lee De León, who was announced as ACU's eighth director of athletics in November of that same year. He quickly got up to speed on the stadium project and began courting new donors for various improvements throughout the athletics program. The Halbert family donated $3 million in October 2016 to name the press box tower at the new stadium the "Chuck Sitton Tower" in memory of David's best friend. And the Wessel family donated $2.85 million in February 2017 for the naming rights to the video

scoreboard on the north end of the stadium. "Being fortunate enough to help with the building of Wildcat Stadium has been the greatest honor and privilege of my professional career," said De León, who resigned his post in May 2018 to accept a job in the athletics department at Purdue University. "I might work another thirty years and never experience such an exciting and fulfilling, yet challenging, process. I've been so blessed to have been at ACU during this transformative time. A new football stadium—especially an on-campus stadium—is a once-in-a-generation opportunity. This is going to inject pride, passion, and school spirit into the campus unlike anything this university has experienced in many years. Athletics has the unique ability to unify a diverse campus community, and our hope is that Anthony Field at Wildcat Stadium will create an incredible culture of Wildcat pride."

Wildcat Stadium, Anthony Field, and Chuck Sitton Tower under construction in December 2016.

The transition from NCAA Division II affiliation to Division I athletics was tough on the football program, although there were highlights, like the program's win over Troy (Alabama) in September 2014, its first over an FBS program since 1959, as well as numerous national television appearances. There was also the 2014 season—ACU's first playing a Southland Conference schedule—when the Wildcats finished 6–6 overall and 4–4 in league play with wins over Central Arkansas and Stephen F. Austin. But the record slipped to 3–8 in 2015 and then 2–9 in 2016, and De León decided to relieve Collums of his duties as head coach after five seasons and a record of 24–32. A little more than one month after releasing Collums from his contract, ACU sent ripples through the world of college football when it announced that it had hired the winningest coach (by winning percentage)

in all of college football in Adam Dorrel of NCAA Division II powerhouse Northwest Missouri State.

Dorrel left his alma mater after six seasons where he led the Bearcats to an incredible 76–8 record (90.5 winning percentage), back-to-back NCAA Division II national championships (2015–2016), a thirty-game winning streak to end his tenure there, and three national championships overall with the other title coming in 2013. "I wanted the challenge of taking

Jeremy Enlow

ACU announced Adam Dorrel as the twentieth head coach in program history in December 2016, just two days after his team at Northwest Missouri State won back-to-back NCAA Division II national championships.

▶▶

ACU Wildcats greet their fans after they beat Houston Baptist, 24–3, in the first game ever played on Anthony Field.

▶

Kim Leeson

Kim Leeson

the formula we had used at Northwest Missouri and put it in place here and see if we could do the same things at a place that hasn't had the success it wanted over the last few seasons," Dorrel said.

When the first on-campus home football game in more than fifty years had come to an end on the evening of September 16, 2017, De León spotted Schubert on the turf at the new Anthony Field at Wildcat Stadium and wrapped him in a bear hug. "We did it!" De León exclaimed through his own tears and above the roar of the sellout crowd of 12,000 fans, whose celebration had suddenly turned a football game into a block party. "We did it!" They certainly had. What they and an army of people across the ACU campus, along with partners at HKS Architects and HOAR Construction, had done was successfully bring Wildcat football back to a permanent on-campus venue for the first time since 1942, and for the first home contest since a 1958 game against Howard Payne was played at Elmer Gray Stadium. But even with three years of planning and thought given to the grand opening, no one could have been prepared for the night they experienced. From Wildcat Country tailgating, to the Wildcat Walk by the players, to the stadium, to the postgame fireworks show, the debut of Wildcat Stadium surpassed even the loftiest of expectations.

The unforgettable night, more than three years in the making after Dr. Schubert announced April and Mark Anthony's historic gift, came to an end with Dorrel presenting the Anthonys, Schubert, and De

Many of the fans who attended the first game in the new Wildcat Stadium stayed for the spectacular post-game fireworks.

An aerial view of Anthony Field at Wildcat Stadium just a few days before the stadium opened.

León each with a game ball in recognition of the win and their leadership in getting the stadium built. "We had an unbeliev-able atmosphere out there," Dorrel said after the game. "I've been fortunate in my years of college coaching to have been in some big venues and big games: national championship games and coaching over-seas with Team USA. But that night ranks right up there with some of the very best memories I've had of being on the foot-ball field. It was a special night because so many people put so much hard work into it. This is a milestone win for our program." After being presented with his game ball, Schubert briefly addressed the team, saying, "This is a new era in Wildcat football. Every day from today on is part of a different era."

The feeling of turning the page from one era to the next—Shotwell Stadium to Anthony Field at Wildcat Stadium—was palpable on the field, in the stands, and in Chuck Sitton Tower, the gleaming five-story structure that houses a club level, loge seats, luxury suites, and a press level. No longer will the Wildcats have to share a stadium with the Abilene Independent School District where "Eagles" and "Cougars" are in the north and south end zones, respectively. No longer will stu-dents have to leave campus to go to home football games. No longer will the Wildcats have to take a bus—or in some cases, their own vehicles—to games. In the stands, the 9,000 seats (plus 2,500 on the north berm and 500 in the tower) provide a cozy home field advantage as compared to the spread-out seats at Shotwell Stadium, where even a decent crowd of 10,000 fans could make the stadium seem empty. And the press level in Chuck Sitton Tower features a men's and women's restroom (Shotwell had one unisex restroom), as well as heating and air-conditioning and an elevator, none of which have ever made an appearance at Shotwell's press box.

But it wasn't just inside the stadium that was different. Outside, there was tailgating in the mall area of campus and a Wildcat Walk that escorted the players and coaches through thousands of fans from theMcGlothlin Campus Center to their locker room to get ready for the game. "This is ours," De León told thousands of people during his tenure. "We don't have to share it with anyone. This is a game-changer for the ACU football program, and I believe we'll look back on this night as a monumental one in the history of ACU football."

The Wildcats finished the 2017 campaign at 2–9 (2–7 in the Southland Conference), but there was excitement generated by the home-opening victory, a 45–20 road win at Incarnate Word, a tough 13–7 loss to No. 22 McNeese, and a 44–35 loss to No. 4 Sam Houston State in the regular-season home finale in a game that saw the Wildcats rally from down 31–7 in the third quarter to ahead 35–31 with 5:37 left in the game. And senior middle linebacker Sam Denmark capped his career by surpassing Ryan Boozer as the program's all-time leading tackler, breaking the record in the game against Sam Houston State.

Fans enjoy the view and visiting with friends during the Wildcats' first game at Anthony Field.

There is still work to be done to get the program where Dorrel wants it—at the top of the Southland Conference, competing for league titles and playoff berths, but the challenge is new and exciting for ACU athletics, ACU football, and Dorrel and his coaching staff. How they all answer that challenge will be the next great story to be told in the history of Wildcat football.

So here's to the next revival of the ACU football program.

Three cheers for the Purple and White!

Jeremy Enlow

ACU offensive lineman Jon Crisp (left), deep snapper Andrew Toothman (center), and linebacker Quincy Dunn (right) kneel to pray before the Wildcats take on Sam Houston State on November 11, 2017.

EPILOGUE

by Grant Boone

It happened again this spring, as it has each year since I returned to the radio booth to call ACU football in 2008—alumni messaging me asking if any Wildcats might be taken in the NFL Draft. Fair question. Since 2006, five ACU players have been drafted—as high as the second round, the forty-second selection overall (safety Danieal Manning, by the Chicago Bears in 2006); and as low as the penultimate pick (running back Daryl Richardson, by the then-St. Louis Rams in 2012)—and another half dozen were signed to free agent contracts.

In 2009, in fact, ACU had more players drafted (two—wide receiver Johnny Knox in the fifth round by the Bears and running back Bernard Scott in the sixth round by the Cincinnati Bengals) than noted professional football factories Notre Dame University and the University of Miami (one each). And those players have gone on in many cases to enjoy great success in the NFL. Manning started as a rookie in the Bears' Super Bowl loss to the Indianapolis Colts. Knox was named to the Pro Bowl team as a rookie, and in his first year, Scott led the league in average yards per kick return. Wideout Taylor Gabriel (Atlanta Falcons) and running back Charcandrick West (Kansas City Chiefs) went from undrafted free agents to the NFL playoffs. Gabriel was brilliant (3 catches, 76 yards) on football's biggest stage in 2017 as his Falcons fell in an instant classic, overtime thriller to the New England Patriots in Super Bowl LI. Many of this group's ACU teammates have thrived on the frigid gridirons north of the border in the Canadian Football League. The list includes the Wildcats' all-time passing leader Mitchell Gale, defensive end Aston Whiteside, offensive lineman Tony Washington, and defensive back Major Culbert.

These latter-day stars have followed in the footsteps, almost literally, of Wildcat legends like V. T. Smith Jr., Robert McLeod,

Jim Lindsey, Wilbert and Cle Montgomery, Johnny Perkins, Grant and Greg Feasel, Dan Remsberg, and others whose professional careers were launched from their days in Purple and White. There have been other small schools through the decades with championship pedigrees and a track record of producing NFL-caliber players. ACU's former Lone Star Conference rival Texas A&M-Kingsville University in the 1970s and Mississippi Valley State University in the 1980s, to name two. But no FCS, Division II, or Division III institution—certainly none this size or character as both private and overtly Christ-centered—has made an impact like Abilene Christian since 2005 when Chris Thomsen became head coach and Ken Collums offensive coordinator. The brothers-in-law revived a once-proud program with an unapologetically bold approach, on and off the field. On, Thomsen turned Collums loose to orchestrate an offense that led the nation in points and yards per game. Their magnum opus, a 93–68 obliteration of ACU, West Texas A&M University, Lone Star Conference, and NCAA record books.

Right away, Thomsen and Collums made clear their ultimate purpose: building men. Which is why they carved out two days from training camp each August—in the world of college football with a limited number of practices allowed, days are currency—to take their teams on what they called the Manhood Retreats, bringing in speakers and creating discussions around the concept of God creating them to be good husbands, fathers, and citizens. Thomsen and Collums were simply building upon the foundation laid by many of their predecessors. The *Prickly Pear* in 1935 noted Coach A. B. Morris and Assistant Sammy Bryan "tried to teach their players to play clean, hard football, to win if they can do so fairly, if they can not win to take their lickings without complaining." Beginning in 1968 and for each of his nine years as ACU head coach, Wally Bullington brought in motivational speaker Ron Willingham each week during the season to present to the team his internationally renowned leadership training.

It is that off-the-field touch that has ultimately connected Wildcat players through the decades to something more significant than a final score. That doesn't mean that the track record has been perfect or that every player was impacted in the same way. It does mean that football at ACU has always been more about what happens in a heart than a huddle. The fulcrum on which the Abilene Christian football experience pivots is Bullington. A player on the undefeated team in 1950 and national champion as head coach and director of athletics, Bullington has been an active participant in and eyewitness to the greatness of Wildcat football across the generations. In 20 13, he voiced the audio introduction to ACU football radio broadcasts. It reads as a manifesto to the Wildcat Way.

Hello, my name is Wally Bullington, and I want to tell you what ACU football is.

It's two-a-day practices in three-digit heat.

It's poodle skirts, pep rallies, and perfect seasons.

It's the school song and three cheers for the purple and white.

It's a long line of great coaches. From A. B. to C. T., Tonto and Beech, and Dewitt to D-I.

It's lone stars like Vitamin T and Tiny.

Sitton and Smitty.

Lindsey, Longley, and Lamberti.

Wilbert and Cleotha. Wolfie and Shark.

Danieal and Jerale. Billy and Bernard.

Mitch, T. G., and Clyde—and Whiteside from the blind side.

It's a couple of Chips, two Johnnys, and a pair of Darrells.

It's Ove Johansson from the other side of the 50 and a 69-yard world record field goal.

It's 93 to 68. It's playoff runs and national titles.

It's little kids and big purple.

It's go deep and P4X.

It's Fair Park, Shotwell, and comin' home to Wildcat Stadium.

It's old friends and a new era.

It's arrivin' as a boy and learnin' what it means to be a man.

I'm Wally Bullington, and this is ACU football.

ACU FOOTBALL STATISTICS

Year	Head Coach	Conference	Overall			Conference		
			W	L	T	W	L	T
1919	Vernon McCasland	independent	2	2	0	0	0	0
1920	Sewell Jones	independent	4	0	1	0	0	0
1921	Russell Lewis	independent	2	5	0	0	0	0
1922	Victor Payne	independent	6	2	0	0	0	0
1923	Victor Payne	independent	6	1	0	0	0	0
1924	A. B. Morris	TIAA	3	4	2	1	3	1
1925	A. B. Morris	TIAA	2	5	2	2	1	1
1926	A. B. Morris	TIAA	4	4	0	2	3	0
1927	A. B. Morris	TIAA	6	1	1	4	1	1
1928	A. B. Morris	TIAA	5	4	0	4	4	0
1929	A. B. Morris	TIAA	6	1	1	3	1	1
1930	A. B. Morris	TIAA	2	7	1	2	2	1
1931	A. B. Morris	TIAA	4	5	0	4	2	0
1932	A. B. Morris	TIAA	2	6	1	1	5	1
1933	A. B. Morris	Texas	5	3	2	3	1	2
1934	A. B. Morris	Texas	1	7	2	1	5	2
1935	A. B. Morris	Texas	1	6	3	1	5	1
1936	A. B. Morris	Texas	1	7	1	1	5	1
1937	A. B. Morris	Texas	0	9	0	0	7	0
1938	A. B. Morris	Texas	6	2	1	5	1	1
1939	A. B. Morris	Texas	6	2	1	6	1	0
		Texas Conference co-champions						
1940	A. B. Morris	Texas	7	2	0	5	1	0
		Texas Conference tri-champions						
1941	A. B. Morris	Texas	6	3	0	5	0	0
1942	Tonto Coleman	Texas	6	2	0	3	1	0
	(No team fielded from 1943–1945 because of World War II)							
1946	Tonto Coleman	Texas	8	1	1	5	0	1
1947	Tonto Coleman	Texas	6	3	0	2	2	0
1948	Tonto Coleman	Texas	5	3	1	3	1	1
		Texas Conference co-champions						
1949	Tonto Coleman	Texas	3	6	0	1	4	0

Year	Head Coach	Conference	Overall W	L	T	Conference W	L	T
1950	Garvin Beauchamp	Texas	11	0	0	5	0	0
		Texas Conference champions						
		Refrigerator Bowl champions						
1951	Garvin Beauchamp	Texas	6	4	0	4	1	0
		Texas Conference champions						
1952	Garvin Beauchamp	Texas	6	3	1	4	1	0
		Texas Conference champions						
1953	Garvin Beauchamp	Texas	7	3	0	3	1	0
		Texas Conference champions						
1954	Garvin Beauchamp	independent	6	3	1	0	0	0
1955	Garvin Beauchamp	Gulf Coast	3	5	2	2	2	0
		Gulf Coast Conference co-champions						
1956	N. L. Nicholson	Gulf Coast	4	6	0	1	2	1
1957	N. L. Nicholson	independent	5	3	1	0	0	0
1958	N. L. Nicholson	independent	5	5	0	0	0	0
1959	N. L. Nicholson	independent	5	5	0	0	0	0
1960	N. L. Nicholson	independent	5	5	0	0	0	0
1961	N. L. Nicholson	independent	4	6	0	0	0	0
1962	Les Wheeler	independent	6	4	0	0	0	0
1963	Les Wheeler	independent	8	1	0	0	0	0
1964	Les Wheeler	Southland	5	5	0	1	3	0
1965	Les Wheeler	Southland	4	5	0	2	2	0
1966	Les Wheeler	Southland	4	6	0	0	4	0
1967	Les Wheeler	Southland	3	6	0	0	4	0
1968	Wally Bullington	Southland	4	5	1	1	2	1
1969	Wally Bullington	Southland	8	2	0	2	2	0
1970	Wally Bullington	Southland	9	2	0	3	1	0
1971	Wally Bullington	Southland	5	5	0	1	4	0
1972	Wally Bullington	Southland	3	8	0	1	4	0
1973	Wally Bullington	Lone Star	11	1	0	9	0	0
		Lone Star Conference champions						
		NAIA Division I national champions						
1974	Wally Bullington	Lone Star	7	4	0	6	3	0
1975	Wally Bullington	Lone Star	6	3	1	5	3	0
1976	Wally Bullington	Lone Star	9	2	0	5	2	0
		Shrine Bowl champions						
1977	Dewitt Jones	Lone Star	11	1	1	5	1	1
		Lone Star Conference champions						
		NAIA Division I national champions						
1978	Dewitt Jones	Lone Star	7	3	0	5	2	0
1979	Ted Sitton	Lone Star	7	4	0	5	1	1
1980	Ted Sitton	Lone Star	2	8	0	1	6	0
1981	Ted Sitton	Lone Star	8	2	0	5	2	0
1982	Ted Sitton	Lone Star	6	4	1	4	3	0
1983	Ted Sitton	Lone Star	7	3	0	4	3	0
1984	Ted Sitton	Lone Star	3	7	0	2	2	0
1985	John Payne	Lone Star	5	4	2	2	3	0
1986	John Payne	Lone Star	7	3	0	4	2	0

Year	Head Coach	Conference	Overall W	L	T	Conference W	L	T
1987	John Payne	Lone Star	5	6	0	2	3	0
1988	John Payne	Lone Star	3	7	0	3	4	0
1989	John Payne	Lone Star	5	5	0	5	2	0
1990	John Payne	Lone Star	1	9	0	1	6	0
1991	Ronnie Peacock	Lone Star	1	9	0	1	5	0
1992	Ronnie Peacock	Lone Star	3	6	0	2	4	0
1993	Dr. Bob Strader	Lone Star	7	3	0	3	2	0
1994	Dr. Bob Strader	Lone Star	3	7	0	0	5	0
1995	Dr. Bob Strader	Lone Star	4	7	0	2	5	0
1996	Jack Kiser	Lone Star	6	4	0	4	3	0
1997	Jack Kiser	Lone Star	7	4	0	5	4	0
1998	Jack Kiser	Lone Star	4	6	0	3	6	0
1999	Jack Kiser	Lone Star	4	6	0	4	5	0
2000	Gary Gaines	Lone Star	1	9	0	1	7	0
2001	Gary Gaines	Lone Star	3	8	0	3	6	0
2002	Gary Gaines	Lone Star	6	4	0	6	2	0
		Lone Star Conference South Division champions						
2003	Gary Gaines	Lone Star	6	4	0	5	3	0
2004	Gary Gaines	Lone Star	5	5	0	5	4	0
2005	Chris Thomsen	Lone Star	4	6	0	4	5	0
2006	Chris Thomsen	Lone Star	8	3	0	7	2	0
		First round of NCAA Division II playoffs						
* 2007	Chris Thomsen	Lone Star	0	3	0	0	1	0
		Second round of NCAA Division II playoffs						
2008	Chris Thomsen	Lone Star	11	1	0	9	0	0
		Lone Star Conference champions						
		Quarterfinals of NCAA Division II playoffs						
2009	Chris Thomsen	Lone Star	9	4	0	6	3	0
		Second round of NCAA Division II playoffs						
2010	Chris Thomsen	Lone Star	11	1	0	10	0	0
		Lone Star Conference champions						
		Second round of NCAA Division II playoffs						
2011	Chris Thomsen	Lone Star	8	3	0	7	1	0
		First round of NCAA Division II playoffs						
2012	Ken Collums	Lone Star	7	4	0	4	4	0
2013	Ken Collums	independent	6	5	0	0	0	0
2014	Ken Collums	Southland	6	6	0	4	4	0
2015	Ken Collums	Southland	3	8	0	3	6	0
2016	Ken Collums	Southland	2	9	0	2	7	0
2017	Adam Dorrel	Southland	2	9	0	2	7	0
Totals			488	420	32	267	246	18

*Ten wins from season (including 8 in Lone Star Conference play) vacated because of NCAA violations.

All-Time Conference Records

	W	L	T	Pct.
Texas	57	42	8	.570
Lone Star	162	128	2	.560
TIAA	23	22	6	.510
Gulf Coast	3	4	1	.438
Southland	22	50	2	.311
TOTAL	267	246	18	.520

ACU Head Football Coaches

Name	Seasons	Years	W	L	T	Pct.
Sewell Jones	1	1920	4	0	1	.900
Dewitt Jones	2	1977–1978	18	4	1	.804
Victor Payne	2	1922–1923	12	3	0	.800
*Chris Thomsen	7	2005–2011	51	21	0	.708
Garvin Beauchamp	6	1950–1955	39	18	4	.672
Wally Bullington	9	1968–1976	62	32	2	.656
Tonto Coleman	5	1942, 1946–1949	28	15	2	.644
Ted Sitton	6	1979–1984	33	28	1	.540
Les Wheeler	6	1962–1967	30	27	0	.526
Jack Kiser	4	1996–1999	21	20	0	.512
Vernon McCasland	1	1919	2	2	0	.500
N. L. Nicholson	6	1956–1961	28	30	1	.483
A. B. Morris	18	1924–1941	67	78	18	.469
Dr. Bob Strader	3	1993–1995	14	17	0	.452
John Payne	6	1985–1990	26	34	2	.435
Ken Collums	4	2012–2016	24	32	0	.429
Gary Gaines	5	2000–2004	21	30	0	.412
Russell Lewis	1	1921	2	5	0	.286
Ronnie Peacock	2	1991–1992	4	15	0	.211
Adam Dorrel	1	2017	2	9	0	.182
TOTALS	96	1919–2017	488	420	32	.536

* Ten wins from 2007 season vacated from both Thomsen's individual record and school's all-time record because of NCAA violations.

ACU Championship Teams

Year	Championships
1939	Texas Conference co-champions
1940	Texas Conference tri-champions
1948	Texas Conference co-champions
1950	Texas Conference champions
	Refrigerator Bowl champions
1951	Texas Conference tri-champions
1952	Texas Conference champions
1953	Texas Conference champions
1955	Gulf Coast Conference co-champions
1973	Lone Star Conference champions
	NAIA Division I national champions
1976	Shrine Bowl champions
1977	Lone Star Conference champions
	NAIA Division I national champions
2002	Lone Star Conference South Division co-champions
2008	Lone Star Conference champions
	Lone Star Conference South Division champions
2010	Lone Star Conference champions
	Lone Star Conference South Division champions

ACU Wildcats in All-Star Games

AFCA All-America Game, *Lubbock, Texas*
- 1974   Richard Williams, WR
- 1977   Chuck Sitton, DB

Senior Bowl, *Mobile, Alabama*
- 1977   Johnny Perkins, WR
- 2011   Edmond Gates, WR

Valero Cactus Bowl, *Kingsville, Texas*
- 2002   Brad Raphelt, P
- 2004   Colby Freeman, QB; Britt Lively, OT
- 2005   Dawon Gentry, DB
- 2006   Clayton Farrell, DE
- 2008   Jerale Badon, WR; Chris Johnson, TE; Nathan Young, OG
- 2009   Jonathan Ferguson, WR; Joseph Thompson, OT
- 2010   Tony Harp, DB; Major Culbert, DB
- 2011   Trevis Turner, OL

Blue Gray Game, *Montgomery, Alabama*
- 1976   Johnny Perkins, WR
- 1979   Greg Feasel, OL

Shrine North-South Game, *Miami, Florida*
- 1970   Jim Lindsey, QB

East-West Shrine Game, *San Antonio, Texas*
- 2006   Danieal Manning, DB

Texas vs. The Nation Game, *El Paso, Texas*
- 2009   Bernard Scott, RB; Johnny Knox, WR
- 2013   Mitchell Gale, QB; Morgan Lineberry, PK

Players All-Star Classic, *Little Rock, Arkansas*
- 2012   Aston Whiteside, DL; Daryl Richardson, RB

Medal of Honor Bowl, *Charlotte, North Carolina*
- 2014   Taylor Gabriel, WR; Charcandrick West, RB

ACU Wildcats in the Super Bowl

Super Bowl X (Pittsburgh 21, Dallas 17), *Miami, Florida*
- 1976   Clint Longley, QB, Dallas Cowboys

Super Bowl XV (Oakland 27, Philadelphia 10), *New Orleans, Louisiana*
- 1981   Wilbert Montgomery, RB, Philadelphia Eagles

Super Bowl XVIII (Oakland 38, Washington 9), *Tampa, Florida*
- 1984   Cle Montgomery, WR/KR, Oakland Raiders

Super Bowl XXI (New York Giants 39, Denver 20), *Pasadena, California.*
- 1987   Dan Remsberg, OL, Denver Broncos

Super Bowl XLI (Indianapolis 29, Chicago 17), *Miami, Florida*
- 2007   Danieal Manning, DB, Chicago Bears

Super Bowl LI (New England 34, Atlanta 28, OT), *Houston, Texas*
- 2017   Taylor Gabriel, WR, Atlanta Falcons

ACU Wildcats in the NFL

Atlanta Falcons
- OT Tom Humphrey (1975)
- OL Richard Van Druten (1989)
- WR Taylor Gabriel (2016–2017)

Baltimore/Indianapolis Colts
- OL Grant Feasel (1983)

Baltimore Ravens
- RB Bernard Scott (2013)

Chicago Bears
- RB Tipp Mooney (1942–1946)
- DB Danieal Manning (2006–2010)
- WR Johnny Knox (2009–2012)
- DE Aston Whiteside (2012)
- WR Raymond Radway (2012)
- WR Taylor Gabriel (2018)

Cincinnati Bengals
- LB Bernard Erickson (1969)

- LB Chip Bennett (1970–1971)
- WR Richard Williams (1974)
- WR Cleotha Montgomery (1980)
- RB Bernard Scott (2009–2012)

Cleveland Browns
- DT Bob Oliver (1969–1970)
- OT Tom Humphrey (1973)
- WR Taylor Gabriel (2014–2015)

Dallas Cowboys
- OT Byron Bradfute (1960–1961)
- QB Clint Longley (1974–1975)
- OT Keith Wagner (1994)
- WR Raymond Radway (2011–2012)

Denver Broncos
- DT Larry Cox (1966–1968)
- OT Tom Humphrey (1973)
- OL Dan Remsberg (1986–1987)

Detroit Lions
- C Moose Stovall (1947–1948)
- RB Wilbert Montgomery (1985)

Green Bay Packers
- OT Greg Feasel (1986–1987)
- DE Chris Reed (1999)

Houston Oilers
- TE Robert McLeod (1961–1966)

Houston Texans
- DB Danieal Manning (2011–2014)

Kansas City Chiefs
- OT Wayne Walton (1973–1974)
- OT Tom Humphrey (1974)
- OL Richard Van Druten (1988)
- RB Charcandrick West (2014–present)

Los Angeles Raiders
- WR Cleotha Montgomery (1981–1985)

Los Angeles/St. Louis Rams
- RB V. T. Smith Jr. (1949–1953)
- OT Mike Capshaw (1966)
- DB Justin Lucas (2004)
- RB Daryl Richardson (2012–2013)
- WR Raymond Radway (2012)

Miami Dolphins
- DL Steve Jacobson (1987)
- WR Clyde Gates (2011–2012)

Minnesota Vikings
- OL Grant Feasel (1984–1986)
- DE Chris Reed (1998)

New England Patriots
- WR Richard Williams (1975–1976)

New Orleans Saints
- OT Mike Capshaw (1967)
- WR Ronnie Vinson (1972)

New York Giants
- OT Wayne Walton (1971–1972)
- WR Johnny Perkins (1977–1983)
- WR Reggie McGowan (1987)

New York Jets
- WR Clyde Gates (2012–2014)
- RB Daryl Richardson (2014–present)

Philadelphia Eagles
- RB Wilbert Montgomery (1977–1984)
- PK Ove Johansson (1977)

Pittsburgh Steelers
- OL Trevis Turner (2010)
- RB Daryl Richardson (2016)

St. Louis/Arizona Cardinals
- DB Mark Jackson (1987)
- DB Justin Lucas (1999–2003)

San Diego Chargers
- LB Bernard Erickson (1967–1968)
- QB Clint Longley (1976)
- OL Dan Remsberg (1985)
- OT Greg Feasel (1988)

San Francisco 49ers
- WR Charles Smith (1956)
- FB Paul Goad (1956–1957)

Seattle Seahawks
- OL Grant Feasel (1987–1993)
- TE James Hill (1999–2001)

Washington Redskins
- OL Moose Stovall (1949)

• *indicates players were listed on an active or practice roster for a full season*

ACU Wildcats in the NFL Draft

Year	Player	Position	Round	Pick	Team
1951	Bailey Woods	Back	14	9	Chicago Bears
1951	Bill Ayre	Back	28	3	Green Bay Packers
1952	Les Wheeler	OL	21	4	Philadelphia Eagles
1952	E. J. "Tiny" Moore	OL	24	3	Chicago Cardinals
1954	Sonny Cleere	OL	21	5	Chicago Bears
1955	Von Morgan	WR	9	8	Philadelphia Eagles
1955	Jim Cobb	OT	19	2	Baltimore Colts
1956	Charley Smith	WR	8	3	San Francisco 49ers
1956	Gene Boyd	DB	15	3	San Francisco 49ers
1956	Paul Goad	DB	25	2	San Francisco 49ers

Year	Player	Position	Round	Pick	Team
1958	Mac Starnes	OL	17	1	Chicago Cardinals
1961	Robert McLeod	TE	13	5	Chicago Bears
1966	Mike Capshaw	OL	10	2	Los Angeles Rams
1967	Bernard Erickson	LB	5	14	San Diego Chargers
1967	Mike Love	RB	15	9	Pittsburgh Steelers
1969	Bob Oliver	DE	17	20	Cleveland Browns
1970	Chip Bennett	LB	3	8	Cincinnati Bengals
1971	Wayne Walton	OL	2	18	New York Giants
1972	Ronnie Vinson	WR	8	7	New Orleans Saints
1973	Tom Humphrey	OT	10	22	Cleveland Browns
1974	Richard Williams	WR	4	25	Cincinnati Bengals
1974	Clint Longley	QB	Supplemental		Cincinnati Bengals
1975	David Henson	WR	14	9	San Francisco 49ers
1976	Raymond Crosier	DE	14	9	St. Louis Cardinals
1977	Johnny Perkins	WR	2	4	New York Giants
1977	Wilbert Montgomery	RB	6	15	Philadelphia Eagles
1977	Ove Johansson	PK	12	9	Houston Oilers
1983	Grant Feasel	C	6	21	Baltimore Colts
1983	Steve Parker	WR	11	13	New England Patriots
1985	Dan Remsberg	OL	9	28	San Diego Chargers
2006	Danieal Manning	DB	2	10	Chicago Bears
2009	Johnny Knox	WR	5	4	Chicago Bears
2009	Bernard Scott	RB	6	36	Cincinnati Bengals
2011	Edmond Gates	WR	4	14	Miami Dolphins
2012	Daryl Richardson	RB	7	45	St. Louis Rams

ACU Wildcats in the American Football League (AFL) Draft

Year	Player	Position	Round	Pick	Team
1961	Robert McLeod	TE	12	96	Houston Oilers
1966	Larry Cox	DT	10	85	Denver Broncos

ACU Wildcats in the Canadian Football League (CFL)

British Columbia Lions
- Paul Goad, FB, 1957
- Tom Humphrey, OL, 1980

Calgary Stampeders
- Jim Lindsey, QB, 1971–1973
- Tom Humphrey, OL, 1978–1979
- Tony Washington, OL, 2011

Edmonton Eskimos
- Mark Jackson, CB, 1985–1986
- Tony Washington, OL, 2014–2015

Hamilton Tiger-Cats
- Mitchell Gale, QB, 2015

Ottawa RoughRiders/RedBlacks
- Mark Jackson, CB, 1989
- Aston Whiteside, DE, 2015–2016

Saskatchewan RoughRiders
- Mitchell Gale, QB, 2016

Toronto Argonauts
- Jim Lindsey, QB, 1974
- Clint Longley, QB, 1977
- Tony Washington, OL, 2012–2013
- Mitchell Gale, QB, 2013–2015

ACU Wildcats in the United States Football League (USFL)

Birmingham Stallions
- Dan Niederhofer, OL, 1984

Denver Gold
- Greg Feasel, OL, 1983–1985

Birmingham Stallions
- Dan Niederhofer, OL, 1984

ACU Wildcats in the World League of American Football (WLAF)

San Antonio Riders
- John Layfield, OL, 1991–1992

Amsterdam
- James Hill, TE, 2001

Scottish Claymores
- Keith Wagner, OL, 1996

Rhein Fire
- Keith Wagner, OL, 1997

All-America Teams

Since 1933, more than ninety ACU Wildcats have been named to All-America teams selected by the Associated Press, American Football Coaches Association, *Football News*, and other organizations.

First Team
1948	V. T. Smith Jr., HB
1951	Les Wheeler, T
1952	Wally Bullington, C
1953	Von Morgan, E
1954	Von Morgan, E
1959	Robert McLeod, E
1965	Larry Cox, T
1969	Chip Bennett, LB
1970	Jim Lindsey, QB
1973	Wilbert Montgomery, RB
	Clint Longley, QB
1974	Chip Martin, DT
1975	Johnny Perkins, WR
1976	Johnny Perkins, WR
1977	Chuck Sitton, DB
1979	Greg Feasel, OT
1980	Kenny Davidson, DT
1982	Grant Feasel, C
1983	Mark Wilson, DB
1984	Dan Remsberg, OT
1987	Richard Van Druten, OT
1989	John Layfield, OT
1990	Dennis Brown, PK
1991	Jay Jones, LB
1997	Victor Burke, DB
	Junior Filikitonga, DL
2002	Brad Raphelt, P
2003	Britt Lively, OT
2004	Danieal Manning, KR
2005	Danieal Manning, DB
	Clayton Farrell, DE
2006	Nathan Young, OL

2007	Bernard Scott, RB
	Nathan Young, OL
2008	Bernard Scott, RB
	Tony Washington, OL
	Sam Collins, C
2009	Tony Washington, OL
2010	Edmond Gates, WR
	Trevis Turner, OL
2011	Aston Whiteside, DL

Second Team
1940	Tugboat Jones, FB
1950	Alton Green, FB
1957	Jimmy Hirth, HB
1966	Mike Love, HB
1973	Clint Longley, QB
1975	Johnny Perkins, SE
1976	Ove Johansson, PK
1978	Kirby Jones, TE
	John Mayes, QB
1982	Richard Flores, DT
1983	Dan Remsberg, OT
1986	Arthur Culpepper, WR
1987	Bill Clayton, DT
1988	Bill Clayton, DT
	John Layfield, OT
1993	Chris Thomsen, TE
	Keith Wagner, OT
1994	Victor Randolph, DE
1995	Victor Randolph, DE
2004	Danieal Manning, KR
2005	Danieal Manning, DB / KR
2006	Travis Carpenter, DE

2007	Bernard Scott, RB
	Nathan Young, OL
	Sam Collins, C
	Johnny Knox, WR
	Cody Stutts, LB
2008	Billy Malone, QB
	Johnny Knox, WR
	Joseph Thompson, OT
	Tony Washington, OL
2009	Aston Whiteside, DE
2010	Edmond Gates, WR
	Matt Webber, OL
	Aston Whiteside, DE
2011	Matt Webber, C

Third Team
1939	Red Stromquist, E
1940	Tugboat Jones, FB
1950	Bailey Woods, HB
1952	Wally Bullington, C
1953	Von Morgan, E
1954	Von Morgan, E
1955	Paul Goad, FB
1957	Jimmy Hirth, HB
1960	Robert McLeod, E
1989	Bill Clayton, DT
1990	Jay Jones, LB
1993	Rex Lamberti, QB
	John Douglass, DE
1994	Angel Alvarez, WR
2003	Danieal Manning, DB
2004	Clayton Farrell, DE
2005	Danieal Manning, DB

2006	Nathan Young, OL
2007	Matt Adams, PK
2008	Matt Adams, PK
2009	Aston Whiteside, DE
2010	Trevis Turner, OL
	Aston Whiteside, DE

Honorable Mention

1933	Bill Maxwell, HB
1938	Red Stromquist, E
1948	Dub Orr, C
1950	E. J. "Tiny" Moore, G
	Alton Green, HB
	Pete Ragus, E
1951	Stanley Staples, E
	Ted Sitton, QB
1952	Jerry Mullins, HB
	Ray Hansen, E
	Stanley Staples, E
1954	Paul Goad, FB
1955	Paul Goad, FB
1956	Eddie Campbell, HB
	Leon Morgan, T
1957	Mac Starnes, C
	Don Harber, QB
1958	Robert McLeod, E
	Bill Lovelace, FB
1959	Robert McLeod, E
1960	Robert McLeod, E
	Thurman Neill, C
1961	Don Davis, QB
1962	Owen Morrison, TB
	A. M. Dycus, E
1963	Dennis Hagaman, TB
	Larry Parker, FB-LB

1968	Jim Lindsey, QB
	Bob Rash, OT
	Bill Lockey, E
1969	Jim Lindsey, QB
	Ronnie Vinson, SE
1970	Ronnie Vinson, SE
	Wayne Walton, OT
	David Smalley, G
	Jack Kiser, DT
	Phil Martin, LB
	Chip Marcum, DE
1973	Richard Williams, WR
	Jan Brown, DB
1974	Chip Martin, DT
1976	Wilbert Montgomery, RB
	Johnny Perkins, WR
	Jim Reese, QB
	Chuck Lawson, DE
	Ray Nunez, LB
	Chuck Sitton, DB
1977	Cleotha Montgomery, WR
	Harold Nutall, DB
	Kirby Jones, TE
1978	John Mayes, QB
	Greg Newman, OG
	Jim Flannery, C
1979	John Mayes, QB
	Steve Thomas, TE
1980	Kenny Davidson, DT
	Steve Thomas, TE
1981	Kris Hansen, OT
	Quinton Smith, SE
1982	Scott McCall, OG
	Mike Funderburg, LB
	Anthony Thomas, FB

1984	Anthony Thomas, FB
	Paul Frye, LB
1985	Reggie McGowan, WR
1986	Rex Lamberti, QB
	Rex Snell, C
	Steve Ates, LB
1987	Steve Ates, LB
	Jesse Bonner, DB
1988	Gerald Todd, FB
1989	Roderick Johnson, WR
1993	Jeff Milward, LB
	Keith Graham, DB
1994	Keith Graham, DB
	Victor Diaz, OG
1996	Junior Filikitonga, DE
1997	James Henderson, DE
2002	DaRay Sims, WR
2004	Danieal Manning, DB
	Clayton Farrell, DE
2007	Billy Malone, QB
	Johnny Knox, WR
	Cody Stutts, LB
	Jerale Badon, WR
	Nathan Young, OL
2008	Matt Adams, PK
	Emery Dudensing, FB
	Billy Malone, QB
2009	Aston Whiteside, DE
	Tony Harp, DB
	Royland Tubbs, OL
2010	Emery Dudensing, FB
	Ben Gibbs, TE
	Mitchell Gale, QB
2011	Mitchell Gale, QB
	Taylor Gabriel, WR
	Aston Whiteside, DL

All-Southland Conference

First Team

1964	Dennis Hagaman, TB
	Mike Love, FB
	Larry Cox, T
	Ron Anders, G
1965	Tommy Young, DB
	Larry Cox, DT
	Wade McLeod, OG
	Mike Love, FB
1966	Bernard Erickson, LB
1967	Dean Bagley, LB
	Bob Rash, OT

1968	Chip Bennett, LB
	Bob Rash, OT
	Jim Lindsey, QB
	Pat Holder, FL
	Bill Lockey, WR
1969	Ken Roberts, DE
	Jack Kiser, DT
	Chip Bennett, LB
	Jim Lindsey, QB
	Ronnie Vinson, SE
	Pat Holder, FL

1970	Jim Lindsey, QB
	Ronnie Vinson, SE
	Wayne Walton, OT
	David Smalley, OG
	Don Harr, TB
	Chip Marcum, DE
	Jack Kiser, DT
	Jack Stites, DT
	Phil Martin, LB
	Eddy Mendl, DB

1971	Stan Williams, TE
	Sonny Kennedy, C-PK
	Phil Martin, LB
	Eddy Mendl, DB
1972	Sonny Kennedy, C-PK
	Greg Stirman, TE
2014	Noah Cheshier, TE / FB
	Nick Richardson, DE
2015	Sam Denmark, LB
	Jabari Butler, CB
2016	Nik Grau, PK
	Sam Denmark, LB

Second Team

2014	De'Andre Brown, RB
	Cedric Gilbert, WR
	Codey Funk, OL
	Jonathan Epps, PR
2015	Codey Funk, OL
	Jonathan Epps, PR
2017	Sam Denmark, LB

Honorable Mention

2014	Parker McKenzie, QB
	Demarcus Thompson, WR
	Damon Williams, DL
	Justin Stephens, LB

	Justin Stewart, DB
	Nik Grau, PK
2015	De'Andre Brown, RB
	Cedric Gilbert, WR
	Josh Bloom, DL
	LaMarcus Allen, DL
	Byron Proctor, KR
2016	Riley Mayfield, OL
	Dakota Laws, OL
	Bryson Gates, LB
2017	Trevor Crain, TE
	Troy Grant, WR
	Brandon Richmond, S

NCAA Division II All-Region

First Team

1999	Ryan Boozer, LB
2001	Brad Raphelt, P
2002	DaRay Sims, KR
2003	Britt Lively, OT
	Danieal Manning, DB
2004	Danieal Manning, DB
	Clayton Farrell, DE
2005	Danieal Manning, DB
	Clayton Farrell, DE
2006	Billy Malone, QB
	Travis Carpenter, DE
2007	Johnny Knox, WR
	Jerale Badon, WR
	Matt Adams, PK
	Sam Collins, C
	Nathan Young, OG
	Bernard Scott, RB
	Cody Stutts, LB
2008	Billy Malone, QB
	Bernard Scott, RB
	Emery Dudensing, FB
	Johnny Knox, WR
	Sam Collins, C
	Tony Washington, OT
	Matt Adams, PK
	Joseph Thompson, OL
2009	Tony Washington, OT
	Justin Andrews, FB
	Aston Whiteside, DE

2010	Aston Whiteside, DE
	Edmond Gates, WR
	Emery Dudensing, FB
	Trevis Turner, OL
	Matt Webber, OL
	Kevin Washington, LB
2011	Aston Whiteside, DL
	Matt Webber, OL

Second Team

2000	Ryan Boozer, LB
2001	Ryan Boozer, LB
	Eric Polk, RB
2004	Danieal Manning, KR
2005	Marcus Brown, LB
2006	Chris Conklin, FB
	Nathan Young, OL
	Corey Jordan, DE
	Jerale Badon, WR
	Billy Malone, QB
2007	Billy Malone, QB
	Matt Adams, PK
	Emery Dudensing, FB
	Johnny Knox, WR
	Sam Collins, C
	Nathan Young, OG
	Cody Stutts, LB
2008	Edmond Gates, WR
	Joseph Thompson, OG
	Billy Malone, QB

	Aston Whiteside, DE
	Mike Kern, LB
2009	Royland Tubbs, OL
	Tony Harp, DB
	Kevin Washington, LB
2010	Matt Webber, OL
	Kevin Washington, LB
	Fred Thompson, DE
	Marvin Jones, DT
	Ben Gibbs, TE
	Mitchell Gale, QB
	Royland Tubbs, OL
	Morgan Lineberry, PK
	Courtney Lane, LB
2011	Neal Tivis, OL
	Matt Webber, OL

Third Team

2002	Barrett Allen, DT
	Eben Nelson, PK
2004	Clayton Farrell, DE
2006	Jerale Badon, WR
2007	Joseph Thompson, OT
2008	Aston Whiteside, DE
	Mike Kern, LB
2009	Kevin Washington, LB
	Tony Harp, DB
	Kendrick Johnson, RS

All-Texas Intercollegiate Conference

1926	Dalton Hill, C	1929	Price Sanders, G	1930	Brit Pippen, E
	Byron Rogers, T		Roy Bullock, T	1931	Brit Pippen, E
	Theo Powell, FB	1929	Goober Keyes, HB	1932	J. C. Gray, C

All-Texas Conference

1933 Bill Maxwell, HB
J. C. Gray, C
1935 Squib Carruthers, C
1936 Louis Parker, E
1937 Red Stromquist, E
1938 Red Stromquist, E
Tyson Cox, T
1940 Tugboat Jones, FB
Tyson Cox, T
Garvin Beauchamp, G
1941 Johnny Owens, HB
1946 Buster Dixon, FB
V. T. Smith Jr., HB
Dick Stovall, C
Charles Floyd, G
Willard Paine, T
1947 Billy Joe McKeever, E
Willard Paine, T
V. T. Smith Jr., HB

1948 V. T. Smith Jr., HB
Sonny Cleere, OG
Wally Bullington, C
Ray Hansen, E
Ted Sitton, QB
Jimmy Hirth, HB
James Cobb, DT
1949 Pete Ragus, E
Dub Orr, C
Alton Green, FB
1950 Harry House, DT
Stanley Staples, DE
Wally Bullington, LB
Pete Ragus, E
Les Wheeler, OT
Bob Bailey, OG
Alton Green, RB

1951 Ray Hansen, E
Les Wheeler, OT
Bob Bailey, OG
Rob Orr, C
Tommy Hinson, FB
Ted Sitton, QB
Stanley Staples, DE
Wally Bullington, LB
Don Smith, DB
1952 Stanley Staples, E
Bill Wilkinson, OT
Haskell Sinclair, DL
James Lyda, DE
Jerry Mullins, DB
1953 Bill Womack, C
Von Morgan, E

All-Gulf Coast Conference

1955 John Phillips, T
1956 Leon Morgan, T
Mac Starnes, C
Eddie Campbell, HB

All-Lone Star Conference

First Team
1973 Clint Longley, QB
Wilbert Montgomery, RB
Richard Williams, WR
Greg Stirman, TE
Jan Brown, DB
1974 Cleotha Montgomery, WR
Johnny Perkins, P
Chip Martin, DG
1975 Johnny Perkins, SE
1976 Wilbert Montgomery, RB
Johnny Perkins, SE
Ove Johansson, PK
Chuck Lawson, DE

Ray Nunez, LB
Chuck Sitton, DB
1977 Cleotha Montgomery, WR
Harold Nutall, DB
Kirby Jones, TE
1978 John Mayes, QB
Kirby Jones, TE
Greg Newman, OG
Jim Flannery, C
1979 Steve Thomas, TE
Greg Feasel, OT
Martin Perry, PK
1980 Steve Thomas, TE
Kenny Davidson, DT

1981 Richard Flores, DT
Kris Hansen, OT
Grant Feasel, C
Scott McCall, OG
Quinton Smith, SE
1982 Grant Feasel, C
Dan Remsberg, OT
Anthony Thomas, FB
Scott McCall, OG
Mike Funderburg, LB
Richard Flores, DT
1983 Mark Wilson, DB
Dan Remsberg, OT

1984	Dan Remsberg, OT			Richard Whitaker, RB		Marvin Jones, DT

1984 Dan Remsberg, OT
Paul Frye, LB
Anthony Thomas, FB
1986 Arthur Culpepper, WR
Rex Snell, C
Steven Ates, LB
1987 Richard Van Druten, OT
Roderick Johnson, WR
Bill Clayton, DT
Jesse Bonner, DB
1988 Bill Clayton, DT
John Layfield, OT
1989 Bill Clayton, DT
John Layfield, OT
1990 Jay Jones, LB
1993 Keith Wagner, OT
Chris Thomsen, TE
Rex Lamberti, QB
Angel Alvarez, WR
Barry Reese, PK
Jeff Milward, LB
John Douglass, DE
Shay Favors, DB
1994 Victor Randolph, DE
Angel Alvarez, WR
1995 Victor Randolph, DE
1996 Junior Filikitonga, DE
Shay Favors, LB
1997 Brandon Avants, OT
Junior Filikitonga, DT
James Henderson, DE
Victor Burke, DB
1998 James Henderson, DE
1999 Ricqui Blanco, OG
Michael Freeman, P
Steve Toto, DL
2000 Ryan Boozer, LB
Warring Vital, LB
Brad Raphelt, P
2001 Brad Raphelt, P
Ryan Boozer, LB
Eric Polk, RB
2002 Eric Polk, RB
Doug Ginapp, TE
Eben Nelson, PK
Barrett Allen, DT
2003 Brad Walton, DE
Devian Mims, DT
Cliff Compton, LB
Danieal Manning, DB

Richard Whitaker, RB
Britt Lively, OT
2004 Danieal Manning, DB
Clayton Farrell, DE
2005 Jerale Badon, WR
Clayton Farrell, DE
Marcus Brown, LB
Danieal Manning, DB
2006 Billy Malone, QB
Taber Minner, RB
Chris Conklin, FB
Jerale Badon, WR
Trey Simeone, TE
Nathan Young, OL
Travis Carpenter, DE
Marcus Brown, LB
Corey Jordan, CB
Mark Gaines, CB
Landon Kinchen, DB
2007 Bernard Scott, RB
Emery Dudensing, FB
Johnny Knox, WR
Jerale Badon, WR
Nathan Young, OG
Joseph Thompson, OT
Sam Collins, C
Matt Adams, PK
Jacob Passmore, DT
Cody Stutts, LB
2008 Billy Malone, QB
Bernard Scott, RB
Emery Dudensing, FB
Johnny Knox, WR
Edmund Gates, WR
Trey Simeone, TE
Kendrick Holloway, TE
Joseph Thompson, OG
Tony Washington, OT
Sam Collins, C
Matt Adams, PK
Aston Whiteside, DE
Vantrise Studivant, DE
Mike Kern, LB
Fred Thompson, LB
Tony Harp, DB
2009 Justin Andrews, FB
Edmund Gates, WR
Royland Tubbs, OL
Tony Washington, OL
Kendrick Johnson, RS

Marvin Jones, DT
Aston Whiteside, DE
Kevin Washington, LB
Courtney Lane, LB
Tony Harp, S
2010 Mitchell Gale, QB
Emery Dudensing, FB
Edmond Gates, WR
Ben Gibbs, TE
Royland Tubbs, OL
Trevis Turner, OL
Matt Webber, OL
Aston Whiteside, DE
Marvin Jones, DT
Fred Thompson, DE
Kevin Washington, LB
Courtney Lane, LB
2011 Justin Andrews, FB
Ben Gibbs, TE
Neal Tivis, OL
Morgan Lineberry, PK
Aston Whiteside, DL
Nathan Baggs, LB
Darien Williams, DB
Brent Schroeder, DS
2012 Taylor Gabriel, WR
Steven Ford, CB
L. B. Suggs, S
Spencer Covey, P

Second Team
1973 Charles Hinson, LB
Chip Martin, DG
Reggie Hunter, DB
1974 Greg Stirman, TE
Jay Reeves, PK
Reggie Hunter, DB
1975 Jim Reese, QB
Greg Stirman, TE
Raymond Crosier, DT
1976 Jim Reese, QB
Gary Stirman, TE
Cleotha Montgomery, WR
Johnny Perkins, P
Roy Carroll, OG
1977 John Mayes, QB
Mike Lively, DT
Ray Nunez, LB
John Usrey, LB
Chuck Sitton, DB

1978	Reuben Mason, LB	1992	Hurley Miller, TE		Chris Johnson, TE
	Kelly Kent, FB		Ethan Sheffield, WR		Cody Savage, OG
	Hal Wasson, P	1993	Bud Norris, DE		Matt Raesner, OT
	Martin Perry, PK		Keith Graham, DB		E. J. Whitley, CB
1979	Ken Hill, OT	1994	Victor Diaz, OG		Corey Jordan, CB
	John Mayes, QB		Selwyn Dews, DB	2008	Jonathan Ferguson, WR
	Kenny Davidson, DT		Keith Graham, DB		Royland Tubbs, OG
	Randy Morris, LB	1995	Shay Favors, LB		Trevis Turner, OT
1980	Travis Wells, OG	1996	Adrian Eaglin, OG		Bryson Lewis, LB
	Steve Freeman, LB		Matt Shane, DE		Alex Harbison, CB
	Bryan Bailey, P	1997	Clark Miller, OG		Craig Harris, CB
1981	Anthony Thomas, FB		Adrian Eaglin, OT		Nick Fellows, S
	Jim Tuttle, LB		Jody Brown, LB	2009	Reggie Brown, RB
	Mark Jackson, DB	1998	Jody Brown, LB		Daryl Richardson, RB
1982	Dan Niederhofer, DT		Casey Whittle, WR		Trey Simeone, TE
1983	Bob Shipley, FB	1999	Casey Whittle, WR		Matt Webber, C
	Paul Pinson, OT		Daniel Kelley, OT		Fred Thompson, LB
	Mark Jackson, DB		Ryan Boozer, LB		Mark Sprague, P
	Scott Reedy, LB		Brandon Bonds, DB		Cody Brown, DS
1984	Bill Lamkin, OG	2000	Aaron Birdwell, QB	2010	Kendrick Johnson, WR/RS
	Robert Fiore, DT		Adrian Rascon, RB		Neal Tivis, OL
	Mark McIntyre, DE		Rodney Vanduren, WR		Donald Moore, DE
	Monte Richburg, LB	2002	DaRay Sims, WR		James Williams, DB
	Paul Frye, LB		Don Hooks, WR		Darien Williams, DB
	Thomas Wilson, DB		Britt Lively, OT		Mark Sprague, P
	Richard Meister, LB		Shawn Taylor, LB	2011	Mitchell Gale, QB
	Terry Don Barrington, DB		Kendrick Walker, DB		Daryl Richardson, RB
1985	Eddie De Shong, OG		David Jones, DB		Taylor Gabriel, WR
	Greg Porter, OT	2003	Blake Lewis, C		Josh Perez, OL
	Reggie McGowan, WR		Joe Edwards, DT		Donald Moore, DL
	Theoplis Hickman, DB		Dawon Gentry, DB	2012	Darrell Cantu-Harkless, WR
1986	Rex Lamberti, QB	2004	Rashon Myles, RB		Elton Crochran, FB
	Reggie McGowan, WR		Jerale Badon, WR		Taylor Gabriel, RS
	Eddie DeShong, OG		Joe Edwards, DL		
	Mark McIntyre, DE		Greg Yeldell, LB		**Honorable Mention**
	Edward Bane, DB		Dawon Gentry, DB	1973	Hubert Pickett, RB
	Jasper Davis, DB	2005	Taber Minner, RB		Don Harrison, OT
1987	Lewis Myers, C		Robert Spells, WR		Garry Moore, OT
	Gerald Todd, RB		Alonzo Wines, DT		Clint Owens, C
	Dennis Brown, PK		Corey Jordan, DB		Mike Mayfield, OG
	Steve Ates, LB		Chase Fishback, P		Dub Stocker, DT
1988	Gerald Todd, FB	2006	Chancy Campbell, RB		Chuck Lawson, DT
	Darin Cook, OG		John Brock, WR		Richard Lepard, DB
1989	Roderick Johnson, WR		Cody Savage, OL		Ken Laminack, DE
	Brian Thompson, DB		Devorias Jackson, OL		David Henson, WR
1990	Dennis Brown, PK		Isaac Morales, OL		Monty Tuttle, DB
	Nils Almgren, C		Cody Stutts, LB	1974	Wilbert Montgomery, RB
1991	Jay Jones, LB		Brandon Henry, LB		Johnny Perkins, WR
	Hurley Miller, TE	2007	Billy Malone, QB		Don Harrison, OT
	Oscar Shorten, DE		Kendrick Holloway, TE		Garry Moore, OT

Clint Owens, C
Raymond Crosier, DE
Kevin McLeod, DE
Charles Hinson, LB
Monty Tuttle, DB
1975 Wilbert Montgomery, RB
Hubert Pickett, FB
Don Harrison, OT
Clint Owens, C
Kevin McLeod, DE
Chuck Lawson, DE
Ray Nunez, LB
Leroy Polnick, LB
Harold Nutall, DB
Chuck Sitton, DB
1976 Larry Norris, DG
Mike Belew, DB
Harold Nutall, DB
Mike Lively, DT
1977 Kelly Kent, FB
Jim Flannery, C
Bill Tydings, DG
Reuben Mason, LB
1978 Glenn Labhart, DB
James McCoy, DE
Harold Renninger, LB
1980 Lyle Long, WR
Richard Flores, DT
Kris Hansen, OT
Jim Tuttle, LB
Martin Perry, PK
1981 Loyal Proffitt, QB
Martin Perry, PK
Dan Niederhofer, DT
Mike Funderburg, LB
Mark Wilson, DB
1982 Steve Parker, SE
Paul Pinson, OT
Joe Hardin, OG
Mark Jackson, DB
Jim Tuttle, LB
Mark Wilson, DB
1983 Loyal Proffitt, QB-P
Boo Jones, PK
Lembia Kinsler, RB
Gary Fleet, C
Kirk Freytag, DE
1984 Craig Huff, OT
Loyal Proffitt, QB-P

Arthur Culpepper, WR
Steve Jacobson, DT
1985 Craig Huff, OT
Scooter Phillips, WR
Rex Lamberti, QB
Archie Green, DE
Mark McIntyre, DE
Steven Ates, LB
Scott Reedy, LB
Monte Richburg, LB
Edward Bane, DB
1986 Bill Clayton, DT
1987 Mark Davis, OG
Randy Arnold, WR
John Buesing, DE
Edward Bane, DB
Jason Watson, DB
1988 Sean Grady, WR
Richard Meister, LB
John Skoro, DB
1989 Stan Stephens, QB
Jim Gash, PK
Keith Lang, LB
Troy Solari, DB
1990 Sean Grady, WR
John Phillips, OT
Jon Bos, DL
David Wright, LB
Keith Gunn, DB
1991 Reggie Roland, DB
Ethan Sheffield, RB
1992 Oscar Shorten, DE
David Wright, LB
Reggie Roland, DB
1993 Keven Green, FB
Barry Reese, P
Lee Thompson, C
Victor Randolph, LB
1994 Richard Wooten, DT
Jeff Milward, LB
1995 Angel Alvarez, WR
Sammie Overton, RB
Stacy Brown, DB
Victor Burke, DB
Rickie Harris, DB
1996 Craig Cole, WR
Mike Breckenridge, WR
David Bennett, RB
Brandon Avants, OT
Derek Delk, OT

Trey Beeson, C
Brandon Baker, PK
Michael Freeman, P
James Henderson, DT
Jody Brown, LB
Stacy Brown, DB
Rashard Tinnon, DB
Victor Burke, DB
1997 Craig Cole, WR
David Bennett, RB
James Hill, TE
Richard Bogdon, C
Todd Fitzgerald, PK
Matt Shane, DE
Richard Wooten, DT
Robert Lewis, LB
Justin Lucas, DB
Ra'Shard Tinnon, DB
1998 John Frank, QB
James Hill, TE
Adrian Eaglin, OL
Brandon Avants, OL
Brandon Bonds, DB
Justin Lucas, DB
Carnell Green, DB
1999 Steve Brenan, QB
Adrian Rascon, RB
Brad Raphelt, P
Raylon Horn, DB
2000 Nick Gray, DL
Casey Hummel, DB
2001 John Stratton, OL
Britt Lively, OL
Brad Walton, DL
Jacob Pruitt, WR
2002 Colby Freeman, QB
Devian Mims, DT
Brad Walton, DE
2003 Colby Freeman, QB
Eben Nelson, PK
Clayton Farrell, DE
Kendrick Walker, CB
2004 Charles Mock, OL
Eben Nelson, PK
2005 Joseph Thompson, OL
Nathan Young, OL
Charles Mock, OL
Cody Stutts, LB
2006 Willis Hogan, DT

2007	Edmund Gates, WR		Josh Perez, OL		L. B. Suggs, DB
	Travis Carpenter, DE		Morgan Lineberry, PK		Nate Bailey, DB
	Julian Humble, DE		Spencer Covey, PK		Spencer Covey, P
	Tony Harp, S		Eric Edwards, LB	2012	Josh Perez, OL
2008	Eric Edwards, LB		Bryson Lewis, LB		Mitchell Gale, QB
	Drew Cuffee, CB		L. B. Suggs, DB		Darrell Cantu-Harkless, RS
2009	Levi Wolfe, OL		Richard Havins, DB		Melvin Shead, DT
	Trevis Turner, OL		Brent Schroeder, DS		Nick Richardson, DE
	Drew Cuffee, DB	2011	Blake Spears, OL		Thor Woerner, LB
	Major Culbert, DB		Jerrod Harrell, OL		Angel Lopez, S
2010	Daryl Richardson, RB		Charcandrick West, RB		Brent Schroeder, DS
	Darrell Cantu-Harkless, RB		Thor Woerner, ILB		

Academic All-America

First Team

1963	Jack Griggs, LB
1970	Jim Lindsey, QB
1974	Greg Stirman, TE
1976	Billy Curbo, OT
1977	Billy Curbo, OT
1987	Bill Clayton, DT
1988	Bill Clayton, DT
1989	Bill Clayton, DT

| 1990 | Sean Grady, WR |
| 2007 | Nathan Young, OL |

Second Team

1973	Greg Stirman, TE
	Don Harrison, OT
1974	Don Harrison, OT
1975	Greg Stirman, TE
	Don Harrison, OT

1978	Kelly Kent, FB
1982	Grant Feasel, C
1984	Dan Remsberg, OT
	Paul Wells, DT
1985	Paul Wells, DT
1989	Sean Grady, WR
2008	Matt Adams, PK

Academic All-Lone Star Conference

1973	Greg Stirman, TE
	Dub Stocker, DT
	Don Harrison, OT
1974	Greg Stirman, TE
	Dub Stocker, DT
	Don Harrison, OT
1975	Greg Stirman, TE
	Don Harrison, OT
	Jim Reese, QB
1976	Jim Reese, QB
	Billy Curbo, OT
1977	Billy Curbo, OT
	Kelly Kent, RB
1978	Kelly Kent, RB
	Kirby Jones, TE
1979	Scott Guyer, DB
	Bobb Scheihing, WR
1980	Bobby Scheihing, WR
	Grant Feasel, C
1981	Grant Feasel, C
	Scot Goen, DE
1982	Grant Feasel, C
	Dan Remsberg, OT

1983	Dan Remsberg, OT
	Roy Brumbaugh, LB
	Mike Funderburg, LB
	Paul Wells, OG
1984	Roy Brumbaugh, LB
	Robert Fiore, DT
	Craig Huff, OG
	Dan Remsberg, OT
	Paul Wells, OG
1985	Paul Wells, OG
	Jason Embry, OG
	Robert Fiore, DT
	Craig Huff, OG
	Mark McIntyre, DE
	Scott Reedy, LB
1986	Eddie DeShong, OG
	Jake Guarino, LB
	John Skoro, DB
1987	Bill Clayton, DT
	Mark McIntyre, DE
1988	Bill Clayton, DT
	Jim Gash, QB

	Sean Grady, WR
	Richard Bartel, DE
1989	Jon Bos, DT
	Bill Clayton, DT
	Jaf Fielder, OG
	Jim Gash, QB
	Sean Grady, WR
1990	Sean Grady, WR
	Craig Jones, OG
1991	Keith Gunn, DB
	John Phillips, OT
1992	Mike Fuller, QB
	John Phillips, OT
	Barry Reese, PK-P
	Ethan Sheffield, RB
1993	Bud Norris, DE
	Craig Jones, OG
1994	Travis Bass, LB
	Andy Newberry, QB
1996	Jody Brown, LB
	Brandon Avants, OT

1997	Richard Bogdon, C		Daniel Oppong, WR		Luke Luttrell, QB
	Jody Brown, LB		Jody Walker, LB		Hutton Lunsford, DB
	Cody Walton, FB	2007	Nathan Young, OL		Conner Moore, QB
1998	Jody Brown, DB		Mike Kern, LB		Aaron Bynum, TE
	Cody Walton, RB		Matt Adams, PK		Ryan Smith, DE
	Justin Lucas, DB		Travis Carpenter, DE		Austin Lindsey, QB
1999	Kyle Dempsey, DE		Cody Stutts, LB		Chris Summers, LB
2000	Kyle Dempsey, DE		Sam Collins, OL		Andrew Peters, WR
	Adrian Rascon, RB		Donovan Plummer, WR	2011	Thor Woerner, LB
2001	Alfredo Parra, DL		Travis Walding, DB		Samuel Ewalefo, WR
	Jody Clayton, DB		Cole Kiser, TE		Andrew Richards, WR
	David Jones, DB		Adam Myer, OL		Temi Ogunleye, WR
	John Stratton, OL		Jody Walker, LB		Andrew Peters, WR
	Kurt Poe, DB	2008	Matt Adams, PK		Blake Spears, OL
	Brad Walton, DL		Sam Collins, C		Ryan Owens, PK
2002	Shay Ratliff, WR		Emery Dudensing, FB		James Walker, WR
	Brad Walton, DL		Alan Copeland, FB		John David Baker, QB
2003	Greg Wiggins, QB		Adam Myer, OL		Max Priestley, OL
	Brad Walton, DL		Jody Walker, LB		Mike Wallace, DB
2004	Greg Wiggins, QB		Eric Edwards, LB	2012	John David Baker, QB
	David Jones, DB	2009	Eric Edwards, LB		Bryton Fernandez, OL
	Brett Unger, FB		Emery Dudensing, FB		Mitchell Gale, QB
	Craig Howard, FB		Derek Odelusi, LB		Lynn Grady, LB
2005	Travis Carpenter, LB		Adam Myer, OL		Darrell Cantu-Harkless, WR
	Craig Howard, FB	2010	Emery Dudensing, FB		Garrett Langthorp, OL
	Cody Stutts, LB		Samuel Ewalefo, WR		Morgan Lineberry, PK
	Nathan Young, OL		Christopher Rhoten, FB		Angelo Lopez, DB
	John Brock, WR		Hayden Nauert, QB		Derek Morrow, LB
	Marion Harris, LB		Alexander Muddiman, LB		Temi Ogunleye, WR
	Cade Ogilvie, WR		John David Baker, QB		Christian Rodriguez, OL
2006	John Brock, WR *		Eric Edwards, LB		Hayden Smiley, WR
	Nathan Young, OL		Thor Woerner, LB		Blake Spears, OL
	Sam Collins, OL		Josh Hall, LB		Justin Stewart, DB
	Travis Carpenter, DL		Blake Rudd, LB		Cade Stone, WR
	Cody Stutts, LB		Bryce Mueller, DE		Jamie Walker, TE
	Matt Adams, PK		Ben Gibbs, TE		Cy Wilson, LB
	Marion Harris, LB		Austin Harrison, OL		Thor Woerner, LB

indicates LSC Academic Player of the Year

ACU Coaching Honors

NAIA Division I Coach of the Year
| 1973 | Wally Bullington |
| 1977 | Dewitt Jones |

AFCA District VII Coach of the Year
1963	Les Wheeler
1973	Wally Bullington
1977	Dewitt Jones

AFCA Region IV Coach of the Year
| 2006 | Chris Thomsen |
| 2008 | Chris Thomsen |

Lone Star Conference Coach of the Year
1973	Wally Bullington
1981	Ted Sitton
1993	Dr. Bob Strader (south division)

2006	Chris Thomsen (south division)
2007	Chris Thomsen (south division)
2008	Chris Thomsen (south division)
2010	Chris Thomsen (south division)

FootballScoop.com Division II Coordinator of the Year
| 2010 | Ken Collums (offensive coordinator) |

ACU Division II Award Winners

Harlon Hill Trophy (top overall player)

2008   Bernard Scott, RB

Gene Upshaw Award (top lineman)

2008   Sam Collins, C

Dave Rimington Award (top center)

2008   Sam Collins, C
2011   Matt Webber, C

ACU Team Award Winners

Most Valuable Players

1972	Phil Martin, LB	
1973	Clint Longley, QB	
	Wilbert Montgomery, RB	
1974	Chip Martin, DG	
1975	Johnny Perkins, SE	
1976	Jim Reese, QB	
1977	Ray Nunez, LB	
	Kelly Kent, FB	
1978	John Mayes, QB	
	Glenn Labhart, DB	
1979	John Mayes, QB	
1980	Steve Freeman, LB	
	Steve Thomas, TE	
1981	Richard Flores, DT	
	Quinton Smith, SE	
1982	Grant Feasel, C	
	Richard Flores, DT	
1983	Mark Wilson, DB	
	Dan Remsberg, OT	
1984	Anthony Thomas, FB	
	Paul Frye, LB	
1985	Eddie DeShong, OG	
	Scott Reedy, LB	
1986	Rex Lamberti, QB	
	Jasper Davis, DB	
1987	Gerald Todd, FB	
	John Buesing, DE	
1988	Gerald Todd, FB	
	Richard Meister, LB	
1989	Stan Stephens, QB	
	Bill Clayton, DT	

1990	Jay Jones, LB	
	Sean Grady, WR	
1991	Jay Jones, LB	
	Hurley Miller, TE	
1992	John Phillips, OT	
	Oscar Shorten, DE	
1993	Rex Lamberti, QB	
	John Douglass, DE	
1994	Victor Randolph, DE	
	Angel Alvarez, WR	
	Pat Nichols, WR	
1995	Victor Randolph, DE	
	Sammie Overton, RB	
1996	Shay Favors, LB	
	David Bennett, RB	
1997	Junior Filikitonga, DL	
	Victor Burke, DB	
	Craig Cole, WR	
	James Hill, TE	
1998	John Frank, QB	
	Jody Brown, LB	
1999	Adrian Rascon, RB	
	Ryan Boozer, LB	
2000	Adrian Rascon, RB	
	Ryan Boozer, LB	
2001	Eric Polk, RB	
	Ryan Boozer, LB	
2002	Eric Polk, RB	
	Barrett Allen, DT	
2003	Richard Whitaker, RB	
	Brad Walton, DE	

2004	Rashon Myles, RB	
	Danieal Manning, DB	
2005	Jerale Badon, WR	
	Clayton Farrell, DE	
2006	Billy Malone, QB	
	Travis Carpenter, DE	
	Cody Stutts, MLB	
2007	Bernard Scott, RB	
	Cody Stutts, LB	
2008	Bernard Scott, RB	
	Johnny Knox, WR	
	Fred Thompson, LB	
	Aston Whiteside, DE	
2009	Reggie Brown, RB	
	Aston Whiteside, DE	
2010	Mitchell Gale, QB	
	Aston Whiteside, DE	
2011	Mitchell Gale, QB	
	Aston Whiteside, DE	
2012	Mitchell Gale, QB	
	L. B. Suggs, DB	
2013	John David Baker, QB	
	Nick Richardson, DE	
2014	De'Andre Brown, RB	
	Nick Richardson, DE	
2015	De'Andre Brown, RB	
	Sam Denmark, LB	
2016	Dallas Sealey, QB	
	Sam Denmark, LB	
2017	Troy Grant, WR	
	Sam Denmark, LB	

Coaches' Purple and White Awards

Spirit-Leadership

1968	Pat Holder, WB	
1969	Kenny Roberts, DE	
1970	Pat Holder, WB	
	Jerry Wilson, LB	
1971	Nicky Pruitt, WB	
1972	Sonny Moyers, DT	

1973	David Haynes, FB	
	Ken Laminack, LB	
1974	Leroy Polnick, LB	
	Clint Owens, C	
1975	Leroy Polnick, LB	
1976	John Usrey, LB	
	Hubert Pickett, FB	

1977	John Usrey, LB	
1978	Kirby Jones, TE	
1979	Randy Morris, LB	
1980	Bobby Scheihing, WB	
1981	Scot Goen, DE	
1982	Dan Niederhofer, DT	
1983	Bob Shipley, FB	

1984	Loyal Proffitt, QB
1985	Archie Green, DT
1986	Monte Richburg, LB
1987	Theoplis Hickman, DB
1988	Darin Cook, OG
1989	Joey Nanus, OT
1990	David Wright, LB
1991	Hurley Miller, TE
1992	David Wright, LB
1993	Chris Thomsen, TE
	Keith Graham, DB
1994	Richard Wooten, DT
1995	Bud Norris, DE
1996	Mike Breckenridge, WR
1997	Jody Brown, LB
1998	Ryan Benn, RB
1999	Marcus Jackson, RB
2000	Marcus Jackson, RB
2001	Marcus Jackson, RB
2002	Cameron Rosser, OL
2003	Blake Lewis, C
2004	Craig Howard, RB
2005	Clinton Farrell, TE
	Nick Anthony, TE
2006	Sam Collins, C
	Landon Kinchen, S
	John Brock, WR
2007	Sam Collins, OL
	Travis Carpenter, DL
2008	Sam Collins, C
	Billy Malone, QB
	Mike Kern, LB
	Eric Edwards, LB
2009	Tony Harp, DB
	Trey Simeone, TE
2010	Bryson Lewis, LB
	Eric Edwards, LB
2011	Matt Webber, C
2012	Reid Ware, C
2013	John David Baker, QB
2014	Justin Stephens, LB
2015	Adrian Duncan, RB
2016	Adrian Duncan, RB
2017	Sam Denmark, LB

Best Blocker

1968	Bob Rash, T
1969	Bob Keyes, C
1970	David Smalley, G
1971	Sonny Kennedy, C
1972	Sonny Kennedy, C
1973	Don Harrison, T
1974	Don Harrison, T
1975	Clint Owens, C
1976	Mark McCurley, T
1977	Jim Flannery, C
1978	Jim Flannery, C
	Greg Newman, G
1979	Ken Hill, T
1980	Travis Wells, G
1981	Kris Hansen, T
1982	Scott McCall, G
1983	Dan Remsberg, T
1984	Dan Remsberg, T
1985	Craig Huff, T
1986	Eddie DeShong, G
1987	Richard Van Druten, T
1988	John Layfield, G
1989	John Layfield, T
1990	John Phillips, T
1991	Lee Thompson, C
1992	Hurley Miller, TE
1993	Keith Wagner, T
1994	Victor Diaz, G
1995	Brandon Avants, G
	Adrian Eaglin, T
1996	Brandon Avants, T
	Adrian Eaglin, G
1997	Brandon Avants, T
1998	Brandon Avants, T
1999	Ricqui Blanco, G
2000	Clark Miller, C
2001	Britt Lively, T
2002	Britt Lively, T
2003	Britt Lively, T
2004	Charles Mock, OT
2005	Nathan Young, OG
2006	Nathan Young, OG
2007	Nathan Young, OG
2008	Joseph Thompson, OG
2009	Matt Webber, C
2010	Royland Tubbs, OG
2011	Neal Tivis, OT
2012	Josh Perez, OG
2013	Josh Perez, OG
2014	Codey Funk, OT
2015	Codey Funk, OT
2016	Riley Mayfield, OT
2017	Trevor Crain, TE

Best Tackler

1968	Chip Bennett, LB
1969	Chip Bennett, LB
1970	Phil Martin, LB
1971	Phil Martin, LB
1972	Phil Martin, LB
1973	Charles Hinson, LB
1974	Chip Martin, G
1975	Ray Nunez, LB
1976	Ray Nunez, LB
1977	Ray Nunez, LB
1978	Harold Renninger, LB
1979	Kenny Davidson, E
1980	Kenny Davidson, T
1981	Mike Funderburg, LB
1982	Mike Funderburg, LB
1983	Mark Wilson, DB
1984	Jasper Davis, DB
1985	Scott Reedy, LB
1986	Bill Clayton, DT
1987	Bill Clayton, DT
1988	Richard Meister, LB
1989	Bill Clayton, DT
1990	Keith Gunn, DB
1991	Jay Jones, LB
1992	David Wright, LB
1993	Jeff Milward, LB
1994	Keith Graham, DB
1995	Jody Brown, LB
1996	Jody Brown, LB
1997	Jody Brown, LB
1998	Justin Lucas, DB
1999	Ryan Boozer, LB
2000	Ryan Boozer, LB
2001	Ryan Boozer, LB
2002	Shawn Taylor, LB
2003	Cliff Compton, LB
2004	Clayton Farrell, DL
2005	Danieal Manning, DB
2006	Brandon Henry, LB
2007	Jacob Passmore, DL
2008	Tony Harp, DB
2009	Kevin Washington, LB
2010	Fred Thompson, DE
2011	Richard Havins, DB
2012	Thor Woerner, LB
2013	Angel Lopez, DB
2014	Justin Stewart, DB
2015	Sam Denmark, LB
2016	Sam Denmark, LB

2017	Sam Denmark, LB

Team Captains

1919	Ogle Jones, HB
1920	Vic Payne, HB
1921	Eldon Sanders, C
1922	Will Scott, G
1923	Matt Dillingham, HB
1924	George Brown, T
1925	Bennie Beall, HB
1926	Dalton Hill, C
1927	Byron Roger, T
1928	Roy Bullock, T
1929	C. B. Hendrick, E
1930	Frank Wortham, C
1931	Brit Pippen, E
1932	Lee Powell, T
1933	Jack Gray, C
1934	R. V. Hardegree, E
1935	Hayden Pyeatt, T
1936	Robert Carruthers, C
1937	Forrest Orr, C
1938	Earl Dunham, T
	Earl McCaleb, HB
1939	Graham Orr, C
	Wesley Cox, G
1940	Garvin Beauchamp, G
1946	Gladstone McLennan, OL
	Buster Dixon, FB
1947	Bill McClure, QB
	Willard Paine, T
1948	V. T. Smith Jr., HB
1949	Dub Orr, C
1950	Pete Ragus, E
	Alton Green, FB
1951	Les Wheeler, T
	Jerry Mullins, HB
1952	Wally Bullington, C
	Don Smith, FB
1953	Sonny Cleere, G
	Bobby Campbell, QB
1954	Joe Powell, QB
	Bill Womack, C
	Fuzzy Lunsford, E
1955	Paul Goad, FB
	Lanny Henninger, C
1956	Eddie Campbell, HB
	Leon Morgan, E
1957	Mac Starnes, C
	Pete Dean, T

1958	Standley Scott, T
	Bill Lovelace, HB
1959	Veon Scott, HB
	Robert Nickerson, E
1960	Thurman Neill, C
	Henry Colwell, HB
	Herman Phillips, T
1961	Denson Moody, HB
	Bill Bryant, HB
1962	Eddie Anderson, C
	Jerry Turner, T
1963	Martin Burgess, T
	Duane Hale, FB
1964	Owen Morrison, TB
	Dewitt Jones, E
1965	Ron Anders, G
	Joe Paty, HB
	Charles Reynolds, QB
1966	Mike Love, FB
	Jacky Roland, QB
1967	Courtney King, LB
	Joel Foster, DG
1968	Trent Lancaster, TB
	Courtney King, LB
1969	Jim Lindsey, QB
	Bob Keyes, C
	Chip Bennett, LB
1970	Jim Lindsey, QB
	Jack Kiser, DT
	Ronnie Tiner, OG
1971	Ronnie Vinson, WR
	Ron Lauterbach, QB
	Phil Martin, LB
	Travis Horne, DB
1972	Phil Martin, LB
	Sonny Kennedy, C-PK
1973	Mike Layfield, OG
	Steve Ricks, DT
	Clint Longley, QB
1974	Greg Stirman, TE
	Charles Hinson, LB
	Dub Stocker, DT
1975	Jim Reese, QB
	John Isom, LB
	Clint Owens, C
	Leroy Polnick, LB
1976	Wilbert Montgomery, RB
	Jim Reese, QB
	Ray Nunez, LB
	John Usrey, LB

1977	Cle Montgomery, WR
	John Mayes, QB
	Ray Nunez, LB
	John Usrey, LB
	Chuck Sitton, DB
1978	John Mayes, QB
	Reuben Mason, LB
	Kirby Jones, TE
	James McCoy, DT
1979	John Mayes, QB
	Greg Feasel, OT
	Randy Morris, LB
	Jimmy Harmon, DB
1980	Steve Freeman, LB
	Steve Thomas, TE
	Travis Wells, OG
	Kenny Davidson, DT
	Bobby Scheihing, WR
1981	Kris Hansen, OT
	Scot Goen, DT
1982	Scott McCall, OG
	Grant Feasel, C
	Jim Tuttle, LB
	Dan Niederhofer, DT
1983	Mark Wilson, DB
	Lembia Kinsler, TB
	Gary Fleet, C
	Mark Jackson, DB
	Mike Funderburg, LB
	Bob Shipley, FB
	Dan Remsberg, OT
1984	Dan Remsberg, OT
	Loyal Proffitt, QB
	Archie Green, DE
	Steve Jacobson, DT
1985	Scott Reedy, LB
	Craig Huff, OT
	Thomas Wilson, DB
1986	Jasper Wilson, DB
	Eddie DeShong, OG
	John Skoro, DB
1987	Gerald Todd, FB
	John Buesing, DE
	Theoplis Hickman, DB
1988	Gerald Todd, FB
	John Skoro, DB
	Richard Meister, LB
1989	Bill Clayton, DT
	Russell Moore, WR
	Stan Stephens, QB

1990	Sean Grady, WR	2000	Ryan Boozer, LB	2009	Eric Edwards, LB
	Jimmie Hays, FB-DE		Warring Vital, LB		Tony Harp, DB
	Todd Johnson, DB		Clark Miller, C		Kevin Washington, LB
	Brian Thompson, DB		George Fisher, RB		Trey Simeone, TE
1991	Jay Jones, LB	2001	Ryan Boozer, LB	2010	Eric Edwards, LB
	Hurley Miller, TE		Jody Clayton, DB		Kevin Washington, LB
	Keith Gunn, DB		Eric Polk, RB		Emery Dudensing, FB
	John Phillips, OT		Dallas Howard, OL		Mitchell Gale, QB
1992	David Wright, LB	2002	Cameron Rosser, OL	2011	Mitchell Gale, QB
	John Phillips, OT		Colby Freeman, QB		Matt Webber, C
	Oscar Shorten, DE		Steven Riddley, DB		Aston Whiteside, DE
	Hurley Miller, TE		Chad Crady, OL		Neal Tivis, OL
1993	Rex Lamberti, QB		Eric Polk, RB		Ben Gibbs, TE
	Keith Graham, DB		Barrett Allen, DL	2012	Mitchell Gale, QB
	Bud Norris, DE	2003	Colby Freeman, QB		Darrell Cantu-Harkless, WR/RB
	Jeff Milward, LB		Blake Lewis, C		Thor Woerner, LB
	Keith Wagner, OT		Danieal Manning, DB		L. B. Suggs, DB
1994	Keith Graham, DB		Cliff Compton, LB	2013	John David Baker, QB
	Selwyn Dews, DB		Brad Walton, LB		Darrell Cantu-Harkless, WR
	Victor Randolph, DE	2004	Rashon Myles, RB		Thor Woerner, LB
	Rodney Gober, C		Danieal Manning, DB		Josh Perez, OG
1995	Rickie Harris, DB		Charles Mock, OL	2014	Jonathan Parker, TE
	Victor Diaz, OG		Greg Yeldell, LB		Angel Lopez, DB
	Victor Randolph, DE		Clayton Farrell, DL		Justin Stephens, LB
	Angel Alvarez, WR	2005	Clayton Farrell, DE		Nick Richardson, DE
1996	Shay Favors, LB		Danieal Manning, DB	2015	Cade Stone, WR
	Misael Alvarado, QB	2006	Landon Kinchen, S		William Moore, DE
1997	Richard Bogdon, C		Jerale Badon, WR		Travis Tarver II, LB
	Jody Brown, LB		Billy Malone, QB		Lynn Grady, LB
	Victor Burke, DB		John Brock, WR	2016	None selected
	Rodney Lauderdale, TB	2007	Jerale Badon, WR	2017	De'Andre Brown, RB
1998	James Henderson, DE		Billy Malone, QB		Trevor Crain, TE
	Cody Walton, RB		Bernard Scott, RB		Kade Munden, QB
	Jody Brown, LB		Nathan Young, OL		Carl Whitley, WR
	Brandon Avants, OL		Cody Stutts, LB		Sam Denmark, LB
	Adrian Eaglin, OL	2008	Sam Collins, C		Dylan Douglass, DE
1999	John Frank, QB		Billy Malone, QB		Dante Hibbert, DT
	Casey Whittle, WR		Bernard Scott, RB		Royce Moore, LB
	Jose Nonalaya, DE		Tony Harp, DB		Carl Whiley, WR
	Brandon Bonds, DB		Mike Kern, LB		

Wildcat All-Century Team

Special Awards
Co-head Coaches—Garvin Beauchamp and Wally Bullington
Defensive MVP—Chip Bennett, LB
Offensive MVP—Wilbert Montgomery, RB

First Team
Jim Lindsey, QB
Wilbert Montgomery, RB
V. T. Smith Jr., RB
Johnny Perkins, WR
Cle Montgomery, WR

Ronnie Vinson, WR
Robert McLeod, TE
Dan Remsberg, OL
Grant Feasel, OL
Greg Feasel, OL
Wayne Walton, OL

Wally Bullington, OL
John Layfield, OL
James Henderson, DE
Junior Filikitonga, DT
Bill Clayton, DT
Larry Cox, DE
Chip Bennett, LB
Bernard Erickson, LB
Ray Nunez, LB
Chuck Sitton, DB
Mark Wilson, DB
Danieal Manning, DB
Mark Jackson, DB
Eben Nelson, PK
Leondus Fry, P
Danieal Manning, Return Specialist

Theo Powell, Utility
Clint Longley, Utility

Second Team
Ted Sitton, QB
Kelly Kent, RB
Mike Love, RB
Dennis Hagaman, RB
Arthur Culpepper, WR
Pat Holder, WR
Greg Stirman, TE
Keith Wagner, OL
Don Harrison, OL
Bob Keyes, OL
Les Wheeler, OL
Robert "Squib" Carruthers, OL

Victor Randolph, DE
Kenny Davidson, DT
Chip Martin, DT
Mike Capshaw, DE
Ryan Boozer, LB
Jay Jones, LB
Mike Funderburg, LB
Victor Burke, DB
Justin Lucas, DB
Glenn Labhart, DB
Travis Horne, DB
Ove Johansson, PK
Johnny Perkins, P
V. T. Smith Jr., Return Specialist
Alton Green, Utility
E. J. "Tiny" Moore, Utility

Wildcat All-Decade Teams

2000s
Billy Malone, QB
Bernard Scott, RB
Eric Polk, RB
Johnny Knox, WR
Jerale Badon, WR
Edmond Gates, WR
Kendrick Holloway, TE
Tony Washington, OL
Nathan Young, OL
Sam Collins, OL
Britt Lively, OL
Joseph Thompson, OL
Trevis Turner, OL
Royland Tubbs, OL
Matt Adams, PK
Clayton Farrell, DE
Devian Mims, DT
Barrett Allen, DT
Aston Whiteside, DE
Ryan Boozer, LB
Cody Stutts, LB
Fred Thompson, LB
Danieal Manning, DB
Dawon Gentry, DB
Kendrick Walker, DB
Tony Harp, DB
Brad Raphelt, P

1990s
John Frank, QB
David Bennett, RB
Cody Walton, RB
Angel Alvarez, WR
Sean Grady, WR
Chris Thomsen, TE
Keith Wagner, OL
Adrian Eaglin, OL
Brandon Avants, OL
Victor Diaz, OL
Ricqui Blanco, OL
Michael Freeman, PK
James Henderson, DE
Junior Filikitonga, DT
Richard Wooten, DT
Victor Randolph, DE
Ryan Boozer, LB
Jody Brown, LB
Jay Jones, LB
Victor Burke, DB
Keith Graham, DB
Justin Lucas, DB
Selwyn Dews, DB

1980s
Loyal Proffitt, QB
Anthony Thomas, TB
Gerald Todd, FB
Arthur Culpepper, WR

Quinton Smith, WR
Steve Thomas, TE
Grant Feasel, C
Scott McCall, OG
Travis Wells, OG
Eddie DeShong, OG
Dan Remsberg, OT
John Layfield, OT
Martin Perry, PK
Bill Clayton, DL
Mark McIntyre, DL
Kenny Davidson, DL
Richard Flores, DL
Dan Niederhofer, DL
Mike Funderburg, LB
Steve Freeman, LB
Jim Tuttle, LB
Jesse Bonner, DB
Mark Wilson, DB
Jasper Davis, DB
Loyal Proffitt, P

1970s
Clint Longley, QB
John Mayes, QB
Wilbert Montgomery, TB
Kelly Kent, FB
Johnny Perkins, WR
Cle Montgomery, WR
Greg Stirman, TE

Jim Flannery, OL
Mike Layfield, OL
Bob Harmon, OL
Don Harrison, OL
Greg Feasel, OL
Mike Lively, DL
Chip Martin, DL
Raymond Crosier, DL
Chuck Lawson, DL
Ray Nunez, LB
Phil Martin, LB
Reuben Mason, LB
Chuck Sitton, DB
Glenn Labhart, DB
Travis Horn, DB
Mike Belew, DB

1960s
Jim Lindsey, QB
Dennis Hagaman, RB
Pat Holder, WB
Mike Love, FB
Ronnie Vinson, WR
Bill Lockey, WR
Bob Rash, OL
Wayne Walton, OL
Larry Curtis, OL
Wade McLeod, OL
Bob Keyes, OL
Larry Cox, DL
Ron Anders, DL
Jerry Turner, DL

Mike Capshaw, DL
Jack Kiser, DL
Larry Parker, LB
Bernard Erickson, LB
Chip Bennett, LB
Tommy Young, DB
Buddy Rawls, DB
Eddy Mendl, DB

1950s
Ted Sitton, QB
Paul Goad, FB
Jerry Mullins, RB
Jimmy Hirth, RB
Wally Bullington, C
Bob Bailey, G
Sonny Cleere, G
Les Wheeler, T
Johnny Phillips, T
Ray Hansen, E
Stanley Staples, E
Von Morgan, E
Robert McLeod, E

1940s
Buster Dixon, QB
Alton Green, FB
V. T. Smith Jr., RB
Bert Brewer, RB
Milford Mason, RB
Dick Stovall, C
Charles Floyd, G

E. J. "Tiny" Moore, G
Willard Paine, T
Harry House, T
Pete Ragus, E
L. G. Wilson, E

1930s
Garland "Goober" Keyes, QB
Thurmon "Tugboat" Jones, RB
Bill Maxwell, HB
Johnny Owens, HB
Robert "Squib" Carruthers, C
Garvin Beauchamp, G
Wesley Cox, G
Tyson Cox, T
George Bech, T
Hulen "Red" Stromquist, E
Gene Sosebee, E

1920s
Ogle Jones, QB
Leslie Cranfill, FB
Victor Payne, RB
Theo Powell, RB
Dalton Hill, C
Price "Sad" Sanders, G
George Brown, G
Buck Bailey, T
Alfred Collins, T
Virgil Smith, E
Brit Pippen, E

Game-Deciding Field Goals

Eck Curtis v. Daniel Baker, field goal,
3–0, 1929
Bert Ezzell v. McMurry, field goal,
3–0, 1933
Elgin Conner v. Arlington State, field
goal with :18 left, 17–15, 1961
Elgin Conner v. Howard Payne, 15-yard
field goal with :07 left, 29–28, 1962

Brandon Baker v. Midwestern State,
field goal, 17–14, 1962
Brandon Baker v. Angelo State
University, 22-yard field goal, 17–14,
1996
Eben Nelson v. Eastern New Mexico,
49-yard field goal with :04 left,
20–19, 2002

Eben Nelson v. Central Oklahoma,
36-yard field goal with 2:33 left,
22–20, 2002
Matt Adams v. Texas A&M-Kingsville,
field goal on final play of game,
41–38, 2006
Nik Grau v. Stephen F. Austin, 31-yard
field goal with 5:48 left, 37-35, 2014

Game-Deciding Touchdowns

Theo Powell v. North Texas State, fourth down, fourth quarter, 13–10, 1926

Carroll Roland v. Daniel Baker, run, 6–3, 1927

Garland Keyes v. Texas Tech, 74-yard pass from Irvin Cheves, 7–3, 1929

Ted Sitton v. Texas Western, 5-yard run after fake, 20–13, 1951

Keith Davis v. Midwestern, fourth quarter pass from Leondous Fry, 13–7, 1956

Owen Morrison v. McMurry, 53-yard run, 14–12, 1962

John Mayes v. Northern Colorado, 1-yard quarterback sneak, 21–18, 1979

John Mayes v. Southwest Texas State, 1-yard quarterback sneak with :42 left, 28–24, 1979

Arthur Culpepper v. Northwestern Louisiana, fourth quarter pass from Loyal Proffitt, 20–17, 1983

Lembia Kinsler, v. Texas A&I, fourth quarter pass from Loyal Proffitt, 38–34, 1983

Rickie Harris v. Central Oklahoma, 7-yard run with 8:09 left, 35–31, 1992

John Hooper v. West Texas A&M, 12-yard pass from Andy Newberry with 1:09 left, 21–14, 1995

Danieal Manning v. Angelo State, 44-yard strip and fumble return, 29–25, 2004

Rashon Myles v. Northeastern State, 13-yard run in OT, 20-14, 2005

Bernard Scott v. Tarleton State, 10-yard run with 1:00 left, 70-63, 2007

Bernard Scott v. Midwestern State, 5-yard run with :43 left , 42-41, 2007

Drew Cuffee v. Texas A&M-Commerce, 85-yard interception return on first play of OT, 20-14, 2009

Daryl Richardson v. Midwestern State, 10-yard pass from Mitchell Gale with 2:40 left, 31-28, 2010

Daryl Richardson v. West Texas A&M, 23-yard run with 1:00 left, 41-34, 2010

Daryl Richardson v. Tarleton State, 23-yard pass from Mitchell Gale with 1:09 left, 27-24, 2011

Darian Hogg v. Texas A&M-Commerce, 85-yard pass from Mitchell Gale with 1:20 left, 24-17, 2012

Darrell Cantu-Harkless v. West Alabama, 14-yard pass from Mitchell Gale in OT, 22-16, 2012

Adrian Duncan v. Troy, 9-yard run with 1:17 left, 38-35, 2014

Jamie Walker v. Southeastern Louisiana, 1-yard pass from Parker McKenzie with :22 left, 21-17, 2015